SIX SECRETS

OF SUCCESSFUL BETTORS

SIX SECRETS
OF SUCCESSFUL BETTORS

Winning Insights into
Playing the Horses

FRANK R. SCATONI
and
PETER THOMAS FORNATALE

Published by
Daily Racing Form Press
100 Broadway, 7th Floor
New York, NY 10005

ISBN: 1-9329109-6-4
Library of Congress Control Number: 2004118360

Cover and jacket designed by Chris Donofry
Text design by India Amos, Neuwirth and Associates, Inc.

Printed in the United States of America

"Camus identified the love of winning at games as one of the prerequisites of happiness in the modern world."

—Michael Lewis, *Losers*

"In a weird way, being a gambler teaches you to deal with misfortune in life."

—Cary Fotias

To William Murray:
a great writer, a great handicapper,
a great mentor, and a great friend.

CONTENTS

ACKNOWLEDGMENTS

We would first like to thank everyone who participated in our interviews for this book. We are grateful that they took time out of their busy schedules to talk to us and share their insights into this great game. You will see all of their names on the following pages, and without them this book would not have been possible. We learned more from them in one year than we ever could have learned from a lifetime spent at the track. Many thanks to: Andrew Beyer, Kevin Blackwood, Paul Braseth, Dave Cuscuna, Paul Cornman, Steven Crist, Ernie Dahlman, Steve Davidowitz, Cary Fotias, Brad Free, Len Friedman, Randy Gallo, Clonie Gowen, Dave Gutfreund, Howard Lederer, Jim Mazur, Barry Meadow, Richard Munchkin, Gerry Okuneff, "Amarillo Slim" Preston, James Quinn, Roxy Roxborough, Andy Serling, David Sklansky, Alan Woods, our Maryland Player, our Kentucky Player, our Las Vegas Player, and our Baseball Bettor.

Mandy Minger at *Daily Racing Form* deserves a hearty thanks for putting us in touch with a lot of these pros. Mandy's reputation in the industry guaranteed that these guys would return our phone calls. Without her help, this book might have never gotten off the ground. Dean Keppler, the director of DRF Press, also happens to be a great handicapper, so we couldn't have been in better hands throughout this process. Dean's advice and encouragement made our jobs more enjoyable and made this a better book. Thanks are also due to Robin Foster for her keen-eyed copyedit, Chris Donofry for his excellent jacket design, and Sarah Feldman for all of her help along the way. And not only was Steven Crist a great interview subject for this book, but he was also a necessary sounding board and editorial advisor throughout every step of the process.

We'd also like to thank a few Del Mar regulars who deserve mention, partly because they make the Del Mar meet such a great experience, but also because they've got terrific insight into handicapping and horse racing: Felix Taverna, the "Duke of Del Mar," of *Race and Sports Radio*; Tom Quigley, publisher of *The Horseplayer Magazine*; Frank Tate, renowned handicapper; Jason Levin of *Inside Racing*; Bob Ike of the *San Diego Union-Tribune*; Bruno de Julio of *Today's Racing Digest*; Larry Weinbaum, public handicapper; Margaret Ransom of *The Blood-Horse*; Jay Hovdey, Jay Privman, and Steve Andersen of *Daily Racing Form*; and Steve Goldberg and Phil Berkovitz of the famed Pacific Coast Grill and Belly Up Tavern in beautiful Solana Beach, just a stone's throw from Del Mar racetrack.

Dan Smith, the director of media at Del Mar, allowed us to work and play for the last several years at what we think is the best track on earth so that we could continue our research and actually put into practice much of what our pros shared with us in this book. We couldn't have dreamed of a better "office" to go to work at every day, and Dan was responsible for that. The same goes to Joe Harper, president and general manager of the Del Mar Thoroughbred Club, and Josh Rubinstein, director of marketing, for the outstanding jobs they do in making the Del Mar meet one of the best racing experiences on the planet. It's virtually impossible to have a bad day at Del Mar (regardless of what the ledger might say), and Joe and his team are the ones who make it all possible. Thanks also to Alan Marzelli and Bob Curran of The Jockey Club, William Grimes, Joe Drape, Mark Cramer, Kim Isaac Eisler, David Halpern, Geoffrey Norman, Greg Hamlin, Jon Tannen, and Larry Loonin, and Dan Illman and Brian Pochman at *Daily Racing Form*.

On the East Coast, we'd like to thank Sean and Joe Clancy. Working with them these last few years on *The Saratoga Special* has given us entry into the sport and definitely taught us a lot about the racing game.

The patience award goes to Susan Van Metre and Jennifer Thornton, who somehow put up with our daily excursions to the racetrack every summer, year in and year out, and to Greg Dinkin, who miraculously allows his business partner at Venture Literary to spend all 42 days of the Del Mar meet working from the press box.

Last, William Murray was a constant source of inspiration for this book, and a lot of the insight we were able to share came from talking to and playing with Bill for the last few years. Hitting the pick six with Bill on the second day of the 2004 Del Mar meet, and celebrating with him and his wonderful wife, Alice, made all of the hard work we put into this book well worth it.

INTRODUCTION

Becoming a Serious Horseplayer, or:
Why You Need to Read This Book

Here's something racetrack managers don't want you to know: Only a tiny percentage of horseplayers consistently win at the track—as little as 1 percent, in our estimation. But it *is* possible to win consistently at the track, and our goal in writing this book is to help you do that by answering two simple questions: What is it that this 1 percent of players do that the other 99 percent don't? And how can we learn from the best players the betting world has to offer?

We're both what you might call casual-serious horseplayers. For most of the year, that means reading *Daily Racing Form* online every day and betting seriously on weekends. During the summer, we'll play Saratoga and Del Mar regularly. Throw in a January trip to the Fair Grounds or a spring trip to Keeneland and maybe a fall trip to the Breeders' Cup, and you get the idea—we follow the sport closely and are serious when we play, but racing takes a backseat to our professional lives. To most of the world, we're "degenerate horseplayers." To professional players, we're absolute minnows. Our combined handle for a year is less than what many pros bet on a single race. We've had winning years but we've had more losing years. Notably, we both had our best year ever after completing the research for this book.

Like everybody else, we want to do better—much better. Thoroughbred racing is an incredibly difficult game to beat, especially when you consider how tough it is to overcome the burden of a 20 percent takeout, a far greater bite than any other gambling game. If there's one thing a good horseplayer must know, it's this: Constant improvement is essential to long-term success. What better way to improve than to learn the tricks of the trade from some of the best bettors in the world?

So we decided that the best way to learn these secrets of winning players—the "whales" that we minnows have heard so much about—was to sit down and talk to them, to find out the things that they do that make them big winners over the long run. We began our research by relying on everyone we knew in racing for contacts. The responses we received were very encouraging. Not only did most of the players allow us to ask a few questions, but they were also incredibly generous with their time, and the insights they provided were invaluable. As a group, our players included many of the most interesting, intelligent, and articulate people we've ever met—not terribly surprising when you consider how quixotic and difficult their profession is. Best of all, we got great referrals from our initial group of players, and soon the group grew beyond our expectations—and they were all willing to share their views on handicapping, betting, the ever-changing game of horse racing, and, most important, winning at the racetrack over a long period of time (since most of our pros have been betting large sums of money for many years).

From the time we hatched this idea of interviewing the top players, we encountered many doubters—skeptics who wondered why these successful bettors would want to talk to us, let alone be on the record about their betting strategies and just how successful they are at the track. Why would they risk giving away any of their advantage by having their words and ideas printed in a book?

Fortunately for us (and for you), our subjects were all happy to speak openly about the game and their methods. Not only did they provide winning advice and expert analysis, but they also stressed the fact that there's a long apprenticeship associated with becoming a winning bettor—and that it was important to have a teacher or mentor to show a younger player the ropes. These players received advice when they were young from older bettors, and they were quite happy to return the favor. Some of them requested anonymity for various reasons. Our Kentucky Gambler gave the best explanation of why he didn't want us to use his name: "My dad always said that the lower you fly, the harder it is for them to shoot at you. I've tried to live by that." And who's to argue?

Throughout the interviewing process, it certainly helped that we were students of the game. Our players aren't interested in attracting attention to themselves—but they are interested in sharing their experiences. Being a winning player is a way of life, and there's no single way to live that life, as you'll read throughout the book. So what we have termed "secrets" of these successful gamblers weren't really secrets to these guys at all—they were a way of playing the game they loved that combined business acumen with handicapping methods, value analysis, money management, and betting strategy, and doing it all with mental fortitude.

3

In racing, there are no easy answers, no simple formulas or systems that can be copied or cribbed and used as consistent models for winning. The success of these men is much more complicated than that, and it lends itself to discussion. Every one of the players we spoke with was once where we—and you—are now: enthralled with a great game and wondering what it would take to win at it. Their hard work and dedication paved the way to financial success, and even if horse racing didn't exist, these men would have excelled at anything else they wanted to do. In fact, a lot of our players were quite successful in other professions—most notably the financial markets—before embarking on careers as professional bettors.

So how did we know that the players we spoke with really were winning players? Well, it's not like we looked at their tax returns. But we made every effort through referrals and by asking the right questions to ensure that the players in this book are in fact the real deal—and they are. Many of our professionals bet millions of dollars a year and make a very good living doing it—and have done so for the last several years. In a few cases, however, our interviewees weren't necessarily "professional" players today, though nearly all have been at some point in their lives. What unites them is that they've all made their livelihoods off their ability to give insights into betting and handicapping. We've also interviewed gamblers from other walks of life—sports betting, blackjack, and poker—to see if the mind-set of a winning bettor is the same across all lines. It is.

From the start, we had the idea that we'd try and identify some of the secrets that all of the players shared. Is there a link between a guy like Ernie Dahlman, who bets tremendous amounts of money using, among other things, proprietary shoe information, and a guy like Roxy Roxborough, who once made his living as a Vegas oddsmaker? Or between our Kentucky Gambler, who makes his own pace and speed figures, and Andrew Beyer, whose numbers are available to anyone who buys a *Daily Racing Form?* Or between a pick-six expert like Steven Crist and a guy who bets less on parlays and more on intra-race wagers, like Barry Meadow? Or between a contest specialist like Dave Gutfreund and a trainer-oriented player like Jim Mazur?

We think there is.

Through our research, we found that there are certain secrets that all successful bettors share. Casual players might know some of these secrets intuitively, yet need to spend more time thinking about how to pragmatically implement them in their own games. Other secrets involve a fundamental mind-set adjustment that will be very difficult for most casual players—but these adjustments are absolutely necessary if they want to win.

The six secrets of successful bettors, as gleaned from our extensive interviews, are as follows:

1. They're not really gamblers; they're entrepreneurs whose business is betting.
2. They make the best use of available resources and process information in an elegant way.
3. They only bet when they have an edge.
4. They manage their money to maximize their advantage.
5. They know how to handicap themselves.
6. They know how to handle their emotions as well as their money.

The first trait is the most obvious *and* the most important: *They're not really gamblers; they're entrepreneurs whose business is betting.* It's also the most antithetical to the way the casual player operates. These men aren't gamblers, they're entrepreneurs. This means that successful players treat playing the horses like a job. Each one is basically running his own small business. And we're not talking about putting in 40 hours a week here. This is a 60- or 80- or 90-hour-a-week gig. If you're not that compulsive, that committed, you need not apply. Still, there is much the casual player can learn from this approach, and even if he can't put in the time commitment, understanding how these big players treat their profession is a critical step toward thinking and acting like a winning bettor.

Chapter 1 will explain many of the ways in which playing the horses is like running your own small business. In addition to working hard, you need to have a contrarian mind-set, and you need to learn the fundamentals. Recently, after a big winning day, someone asked us how we first learned to play the horses. It was an easy question to answer, having just written Chapter 1. You need to read about the game, you need to have a mentor to help show you the ropes, and you need the experience of having played—it's never the same when it's just theory and not your own money on the line. Chapter 1 will also talk about the importance of dedication, preparation, focus, and the key idea that being a winner isn't a goal to be achieved so much as a constant journey that has no end.

Horse racing has been correctly described as an information game. In Chapter 2, we're going to take a look at the most important pieces of information you deal with at the track, which comprise the basic tenets of handicapping. Successful players *make the best use of available resources and process information in an elegant way.* This means having a firm grasp on the elements of handicapping as well as a sense of which factors are important in which situations. When it comes to the X's and O's of handicapping, these players are experts. Chapter 2 will walk the reader through the basics of handicapping in a way that's never been done before—through the words and thoughts of the world's best players.

Of course, merely processing the information you see in *Daily Racing Form* is only part of the battle. A successful player will come up with an opinion based on that information. But just because you have an opinion, it doesn't mean you necessarily should bet. Like all successful speculators, our players aren't just looking to roll the dice and get lucky. The third secret that unites them is that *they only bet when they have an edge.* Successful players aren't gambling at all; they're calculated risk takers who are using their information edge to exploit any inefficiencies they see in the marketplace. In this way, they're exactly like traders.

Thus, in Chapter 3, we'll delve into the concept of value. We'll explain what a value line is and why players use them—or don't.

5

We'll also discuss the potentially vexing issue of what these players do when it comes to betting the seemingly always overplayed favorite.

The most common lament around the racetrack goes something like this: "I'm an excellent handicapper but I'm not a very good bettor." All of our players know how to *manage their money to maximize their advantage.* In Chapter 4, we'll explore how successful players bet, as well as discuss the great debate of handicapping versus betting, and which part of the game is more important. The answers will surprise you.

This section will also include a look at one of the most important and misunderstood terms in betting: money management. Money management consists of many different elements, but it's a crucial part of every successful player's game. In order to take advantage of your edge and to maximize your value, you need to know what to do with your money when it's time to go to the window. Furthermore, you need to manage your bankroll over the long haul so that you don't go broke. One of the biggest complaints the average bettor has is that he isn't sufficiently capitalized. By managing your money effectively and betting methodically, you will put yourself in the best possible position to grow your bankroll.

One of the most surprising things we discovered in doing our research was that successful players aren't only good at handicapping horses. They're also experts in another area: *They know how to handicap themselves.* All of our pros are brutally honest in their own self-analysis. They know what their strengths and weaknesses are, and they know what types of plays have made them successful. They also know which types of races they can crush and which types give them fits.

Every horseplayer has a nearly infinite number of choices every day—a dozen different wagers at hundreds of different tracks. You can play dollar exacta boxes in turf sprints at Del Mar or you can bet thousands to win on one-turn dirt routes at Belmont. A huge part of a horseplayer's success lies in finding the right level to bet, the right tracks to bet at, and the right wagers to make.

In Chapter 5, the players will explain their own preferences and offer advice about how you can find what works best for you. As Dave Gutfreund said, "Self-analysis is the key to success." If you can't be honest with yourself—if you can't enhance your strengths and isolate your weaknesses—you're not going to win at the races. Thus, it's important for a player learning the game to keep sound records and, perhaps more important, to review those records with an eye toward self-improvement. Or at the very least you must be sensitive to what you're good at and unflinching when it comes to your weaknesses.

We mentioned earlier that there is a fundamental mind-set adjustment that one must make to be successful. Chapter 6 stresses that all good players *know how to handle their emotions as well as their money.* In other words, it's important to develop the right mental attitude if you're going to be successful at the races. That means showing discipline, having confidence, taking calculated risks, weathering losing streaks, and not letting bad beats affect your psyche. Our players view playing the races as playing one long game, and they are not affected by short-term fluctuations.

They are also resilient when it comes to losing because they understand that winning at the races is all about making good decisions and not focusing on the outcomes of those decisions, particularly if those outcomes are bad. In other words, you can do everything right at the races and still lose. External factors are always going to come into play and oftentimes those factors are completely out of your control. But if you consistently make good decisions, your outcomes, over the long run, will be favorable, and thus you will become a consistent winning player. That's why it's so important to keep your mental state on an even keel, because if you start to let your emotions affect your decisions, your outcomes will be disastrous.

It's essential to reiterate that these six secrets are not some kind of easy answer that will allow you to win at the races. The point of isolating them was to give aspiring players six characteristics of winning bettors that they *need* to integrate into the way they play the game. Becoming a winning player is a lifestyle change that needs to be implemented, and these six secrets are the blueprint for doing that. By incorporating them into your play, you can become a winner. It won't be easy, but it can be done. The purpose of this book is to give an overview of what it takes to achieve that.

There are no magic potions or fail-safe systems here, and anyone who tells you otherwise is a liar and is probably trying to sell you something. But if you create the right mind-set, show discipline, understand value, manage your emotions, and analyze your play, you can become a winning bettor. Our pros did it and so can you. If you work hard and dedicate yourself to beating the races, and if you incorporate the practical elements espoused by these pros, you will put yourself in the best possible position to succeed.

8

The last thing we want to address here isn't one of the six secrets, but it is just as important as one—that is, the big issues facing horseplayers today? In Chapter 7, we'll take a look at some of the most recent developments in the game and how they have affected our pros and how they will affect you. The topics include takeout, rebates, the computer players, and betting exchanges.

All of these topics are at the forefront of the handicapping world, and merit discussion. Because our players devote much of their lives to beating this game, they all had very strong opinions on these somewhat controversial developments that are changing the way the game is played. The last chapter of this book will explore these topics and show what they mean for the aspiring player. If you're serious about becoming a winning player, you'll want to understand these emerging trends in the game.

So where does all this leave the casual horseplayer? After talking to our pros, we're more convinced than ever that if we choose to follow their paths, we can win at playing the races. The path isn't easy and it might take years, but it's possible—our subjects are living proof of that. Whether this is something you want to do, however, is a different story; it's an individual decision and it's not one we're going to discuss in these pages. But the ultimate goal, even at our level of play, is to win consistently at the racetrack. After speaking with this extraordinary group of people we're convinced it's possible to do that. And it all starts with the six secrets.

ABOUT OUR SUBJECTS

Since so much of this book is going to be told in the words of our subjects, we'd like to start off by introducing our cast of characters and offering a few quotes from them on how they got started or on why their profession is so alluring to them. While some of the names will be familiar, a lot of the players in this book have managed to be successful in relative anonymity, only known to those others who bet the same amounts of money they bet—and these folks bet an awful lot of money. Throughout the book, you will come to know these players intimately, and hearing about their methods of success will help you become a better player.

9

■ Andrew Beyer

Andrew Beyer revolutionized the world of Thoroughbred handicapping. His Beyer Speed Figures ushered in a new era, giving all players who used them a distinct advantage over those who didn't. Beyer's seminal handicapping book, *Picking Winners*, also opened the door for a whole new generation of horseplayers who were able to use Beyer's winning techniques as a way to be competitive in a very competitive game.

In addition to his handicapping books, Beyer still occasionally writes for *The Washington Post*, where he was a regular columnist for many years. His work also appears in the *Daily Racing Form*. Not only is Beyer a terrific and respected player, but he's also one of the most recognized figures in racing, and his thoughts and insights are forever changing the way the game is played. In *Picking Winners*, Beyer accurately summed up the difference between amateur horseplayers and serious horseplayers:

> "Some people who become addicted horseplayers remain dilettantes all their lives. They do not truly believe that the races can be beaten so they do not make a determined effort to learn. They live not for the day when they will be expert handicappers, but for the one big lucky hit that will change their lives.
>
> "Serious students of handicapping are driven by the desire to learn so that someday they will have the skills to win consistently."

■ Kevin Blackwood

For the last two decades, Kevin Blackwood has lived what many would consider the American dream: earning big bucks while working only part-time. He chose the profession of card counting for one reason—to make money. Easy money. And he succeeded, winning consistently at blackjack tables in every country he played.

Blackwood has been interviewed and featured in several publications, including the *Chicago Sun-Times, Maine Sunday Telegram,* and the *Las Vegas Advisor.* He has written for *Midwest Gaming and Travel* magazine, *Jackpot* magazine, *Rolling Good Times,* and *Blackjack Insider.* He is also the author of *Play Blackjack Like the Pros,* an instructional book that teaches aspiring professional blackjack players how to count cards and beat the casinos at their own game.

KEVIN BLACKWOOD: "I read about card counting in a *Sports Illustrated* article that profiled a new breed of gamblers: a blackjack player, poker player, and a sports bettor. I had a mathematical background and a light went on when I read about [famous blackjack player] Ken Uston, and thought that that was something that I could do—memory and quick decisions in cards.

"I taught myself from books and then taught myself on the kitchen table with a couple of decks of cards.

"I've been doing it more than 20 years."

■ Paul Braseth

Paul Braseth is an expert at trainer analysis and is now based in San Francisco after spending many years in the Pacific Northwest, where he had given seminars on handicapping. He is also the former publisher of *Northwest Track Review,* which was a newsletter chock-full of handicapping information. He currently plays full-time.

PAUL BRASETH: "I got interested in horse racing when I was a teacher in the Seattle public schools and I was at the local library one evening and I said, 'Let me see if there are any books on handicapping in here.' And I got ahold of Tom Ainslie's book, *Ainslie's Complete Guide to Thoroughbred Racing.* And I read it and said, 'This makes sense.'

"Before that I'd just been buying the *Form* and looking at it like I knew what I was doing, but I didn't. So then I started making a serious study of it and got more involved. And when Andrew Beyer's book came out, *Picking Winners,* in the early seventies, I bought that and I started doing track variants. Steve Davidowitz's book, *Betting Thoroughbreds,* came out a little bit later and that sort of influenced me in trying to understand trainers and key races and trips. So I started making my own speed figures, keeping my own records, and by 1980 I'd become good enough at it where I decided to stop teaching. So I embarked on my handicapping and betting career in 1980."

■ Dave Cuscuna

Dave Cuscuna is a very successful securities trader from Florida, who also knows how to crush the racetrack. He is respected throughout the Thoroughbred racing industry and has served on various horse-racing advisory boards.

He has a finance degree from New York University and was a market maker on the Chicago Board Options Exchange. He's been a professional handicapper since 1988 and is an industry expert on rebate policy, bet types, future pools, and online exotic probables.

DAVE CUSCUNA: "My dad, a total non-gambler, is a musician, and he played in the band that played at Aqueduct, and when I was a little kid he brought me to the track. As a kid I always liked numbers, and his seat partner in the band was a horseplayer and he taught me how to read *Daily Racing Form* when I was eight. And I started going to the track when I was 12—although my dad didn't know that!"

■ Paul Cornman

Paul Cornman has seen and done it all in the Thoroughbred-racing industry. He's worked as a clocker, a chart caller, and a TV commentator, and he was a part-owner of Win, the first New York-bred millionaire. He has appeared as an analyst on NBC and CBS and has served on the National Thoroughbred Racing Association's Players' Panel, a group of expert horseplayers whose job it was to analyze various aspects facing the racing industry. He is currently a full-time professional handicapper.

PAUL CORNMAN: "I went to college and I had an opportunity to find everything else I didn't want to do. Racing was the only passion I had going through college and I had an opportunity and said let's run with it. I learned the game by trial and error. The first time I ever went to a racetrack I was 18 years old and I went with some friends to a harness track. I didn't go to a Thoroughbred track until I was about 19 or 20, and little by little I started picking things up. After college was over, I worked with the horses for a little bit, then I worked for a rag called *Sports Eye*. I had an opportunity to learn from people I worked with and people who worked for other publications.

"The first time I went to the track I was hooked. I was 18 and I'm 51 now. Since about age 25 or 26 it's been a major source of income. I've had jobs, always in racing, but for one reason or another they haven't lasted."

■ Steven Crist

Steven Crist is the former CEO and the current chairman and publisher of *Daily Racing Form,* which he helped acquire for financial backers in August 1998. A 1978 graduate of Harvard, where he edited the *Lampoon,* he is a former *New York Times* journalist who parlayed his coverage of horse racing into a successful career as both a columnist and a handicapper. He also was the founding editor in chief of *The Racing Times,* the short-lived competitor to *Daily Racing Form* that revolutionized past performances.

Crist's exploits of hitting the pick six are legendary, and his recent book, *Betting on Myself: Adventures of a Horseplayer and Publisher,* is one of the best insider looks at the racing industry. Crist is also the author of *The Horse Traders* and *Offtrack* and was a contributing author of *Bet with the Best,* a compendium of handicapping analyses by some of *Daily Racing Form*'s top handicappers.

In *Betting on Myself,* Crist shared this observation about playing professionally:

"I had always imagined that there was a successful network of professional players who earned regular and handsome profits at the track year after year, but I came to believe that there is at best a handful. Most recreational players share my original misconception and believe that there is an all-knowing circle of such winners. This is why so many players study the tote boards and probable payoffs for signs of the 'inside dope' and the 'smart money' when in fact there is very little of either.

"As I got to know the regulars, it became clear that there were few who were actually supporting themselves this way. Even the braggarts who said they beat the game consistently often turned out to be living off an inheritance or a wealthy spouse or at least a recent insurance settlement. There's an almost infallible rule of thumb equating how a horseplayer says he's doing with how he's actually doing. Those who are losing claim they're breaking even. Those who are breaking even claim to be way ahead of the game. Those who really do win say very little—except that the game is humbling and that betting horses is a very tough way to make a living."

■ Ernie Dahlman

Ernie Dahlman may be the most well-known big bettor in racing. According to Joe Drape of *The New York Times*—in his November 2002 feature on Dahlman and the state of the racing industry—"Ernie Dahlman is among the largest and most influential investors in horse racing wagering, betting as much as $18 million a year from his office at the Suncoast Hotel and Casino in Las Vegas. A horseplayer for more than 40 years, he relies on computers for information and calls in his bets by phone. But in some ways, he said, he longs for the days when a winning bet meant a ticket in your hand and a trip to the cashier's window." As a mere 21-year old, Dahlman gained fame by hitting a twin double at Yonkers Raceway for more than $171,000.

Dahlman is a respected pro who not only knows how to win at the racetrack, but also has an idea on how to improve the state of the game—and that means discussing rebates, takeout, and the way computer teams are affecting the pools. It's no surprise, then, that Drape sought him out for his article.

> **ERNIE DAHLMAN:** "I went to college to be a ceramic engineer. I never learned anything about engineering but I figured out something about harness racing. The biggest thing I learned was the importance of change."

In a recent interview with author and handicapper Barry Meadow, Dahlman explained how he applied this idea to his handicapping:

> "All I do is add and subtract. If I'm looking at a horse whose numbers are four lengths behind those of another horse, I've got to figure out

a way to make up those four lengths. Maybe it's a trainer change or a jockey change, maybe the horse got into a speed duel last time but plots for a much easier trip today, maybe he's getting a shoe change, maybe he's changing surface or distance."

■ Steve Davidowitz

Steve Davidowitz's groundbreaking book *Betting Thoroughbreds*, which was recently updated and expanded to cover modern handicapping situations and a wide range of advanced exotic-wagering strategies, is highly regarded as one of the best primers for handicapping. A leading professional handicapper, reporter, editor, consultant, and racing columnist for three decades, Davidowitz also manages a successful pick-six betting syndicate. He is a former editor of *The American Racing Manual* and is a frequent contributor to *DRF Simulcast Weekly*, for which he writes about handicapping.

In *Betting Thoroughbreds*, he writes:

"It is my belief, however, that thousands, perhaps even tens of thousands, of racing fans could win at the races but are presently unable to do so because they do not know what skills are important, what sources of information are reliable, and what tools are most useful for the task. Thousands more, maybe millions, gain considerable pleasure in their initial outings to the track but for lack of good teachers and other aids find the experience too expensive to pursue. And there are others, too many in fact, who continue to play the game without knowing some of the strategies that could reduce the cost considerably."

■ Cary Fotias

Cary Fotias is the author of *Blinkers Off* and the founder and president of Equiform, a company that produces The Xtras, handicapping information that helps users evaluate form cycles. He has a BA from the University of Michigan and an MBA from Indiana University. He has been a professional handicapper for the past 12 years, after having served as a currency trader on Wall Street. In addition to being a serious player, Fotias has led the charge against lowered takeouts and has participated in several industry-sponsored panels that discussed the state of racing.

He writes in *Blinkers Off*:

"Over the years, it gradually dawned on me that while handicapping had a mathematical aspect, it was an art as well. There were too many variables to quantify with anything approaching scientific accuracy. Consequently, relying on a fixed methodology would always be limiting. Applying a more eclectic approach would offer the best chance for long-term success."

■ Brad Free

Brad Free is the Southern California handicapper for *Daily Racing Form* and the author of the recently published book *Handicapping 101*, a terrific overview of how to play today's game and a much-needed addition to the genre. It is widely regarded as one of the best handicapping books in the last decade. In addition to writing his daily analysis of races at Santa Anita, Hollywood Park, Del Mar, and Fairplex Park for *Daily Racing Form*, Free is also a regular contributor to *DRF Simulcast Weekly*.

From *Handicapping 101*:

"Logical, creative handicapping that dares to be different affords bettors a reasonable chance to win. Sometimes being different means nothing more than being prepared. And the potential gains? They are both huge and attainable, so long as one recognizes the chief handicapping principles."

■ Len Friedman

For the last 20 years, Len Friedman has assisted in making the variants for the production of the daily numbers for Len Ragozin's performance ratings, The Sheets. A renowned bettor and horse owner, Friedman is also the winner of the 2003 Suncoast Invitational Handicapping Challenge and the co-author with Ragozin of *The Odds Must Be Crazy: Betting the Races with the Man Who Revolutionized Handicapping*.

LEN FRIEDMAN: "To me, this is a game. I'm trying to make money but when I play poker I try to make money too. I enjoy games. It's partly the competition but it's partly the challenge of using your mind. It's a puzzle to be solved. I like doing puns and anagrams too and I certainly don't get paid for that. Nor am I that good at it. But I enjoy it a lot. It's a lot of fun. To some extent, the enjoyment of playing the horses is the game."

■ Randy Gallo

Randy Gallo is in the enviable position of being both the customer and the house. He's a handicapping veteran who also owns his own off-track betting shop in Sioux Falls, South Dakota. Because Gallo owns his own shop—and, admittedly, accounts for half the handle—he's a big advocate of using rebates as a way to lower the takeout and give a big player like himself a decided edge. Instead of playing at a usurious rate of 20 percent, Gallo can get it down to about 12 percent—not an inconsequential amount when you're dealing with someone as shrewd as he is. Gallo began playing horses at the Marshfield Fair in Massachusetts in the early 1960's before making a life out of it. And he's been quite successful. Early in 2004, he was one of two holders of a pick-six ticket at Aqueduct that paid $1,120,287—the largest payout in NYRA history.

RANDY GALLO: "I've been fishing jackpots since 1977. I used to hang around the Plymouth Country Club, which is a golf club in Plymouth, Massachusetts, and I used to caddy there when I was 12, 13 years old. And a lot of the guys I caddied for went to the track at night, and I got invited one time and I fell in love with it after that.

"When I first took up the game, I was broke. I had an ego. I thought I knew more than everybody else when actually I didn't. I dropped out of law school in 1970 and went to work at Raynham dog track in the seventies. And then went to Newport Jai Alai in '76, and basically I got involved with jackpots after that. Not so much race-to-race stuff, but carryover jackpots.

"I've read a lot of books about handicapping. I'm actually a trip handicapper. I watch videos of race replays and take notes on the trips. I've watched people use Thorograph and Ragozin sheets and different speed ratings. Everybody has their own handicapping method and some are better than others."

■ Clonie Gowen

Former Miss Teen McAlester (Oklahoma) Cycalona Gowen, better known as Clonie, started playing poker while living in Dallas and driving to Shreveport, Louisiana, on weekends and making a few hundred dollars each week. She burst onto the poker scene by following up her Top 10 finish at the *World Poker Tour* Costa Rica Classic with a win at the *World Poker Tour* Ladies' Night event in 2003. Her victory against world-class players Annie Duke and Jennifer Harman was watched by millions of viewers and was the highest-rated *World Poker Tour* show ever broadcast to that time.

17

Gowen is currently a team member of Full Tilt Poker (www.fulltiltpoker.com), along with poker greats Howard Lederer, Phil Gordon, Phil Ivey, and Chris Ferguson, to name a few. She's also the author of a forthcoming poker-strategy book for women.

CLONIE GOWEN: "When I was about 15 and in high school, I dated a boy whose parents played poker with him. So on the weekends, instead of going out like normal kids, we'd go over there and play poker. They introduced me to seven-card stud and Texas Hold 'em and that's where I learned a lot of key values that I still have today. I developed that passion for wanting to get in the mind-set of somebody else.

"I lost for many years and there was never anyone who came to me and said, 'Okay, Clonie, here's the secret of poker.' I learned the game from experience. I spent the equivalent of a Harvard education to learn the game. I'm probably one of the best because of that. Since then I've made that money back. It was an investment of time and money to learn the game, but it was worth it."

■ Dave Gutfreund

Dave Gutfreund is a longtime handicapping-tournament player and handicapping analyst who currently co-hosts *Horsin' Around TV,* a weekly horse-racing magazine show airing on Fox Sports Net Chicago. He won back-to-back tournaments in Las Vegas in 1995, and his most recent tournament victory was the $60,000 Belmont Summer Handicapping Challenge, which qualified him for the Daily Racing Form/NTRA National Handicapping Championship—an event he has qualified for the past four years. He is a former commodities trader who has been called upon by the NTRA to analyze issues such as takeout and the integrity of the pools.

18

DAVE GUTFREUND: "I grew up as a type-A personality in a Chicago suburb. In junior high, I was the one running the football pool. By my freshman year of high school I was bowling for money, golfing for money, playing bridge, playing hearts, all kinds of stuff. And I was a total sports fanatic. But I never had any knowledge of horse racing.

"When I was 16 I had a pretty bad car accident and I was stuck in traction for a month. The one part of the sports section I had never read was the horse-racing part. They had this stupid show on Channel 26 every day called *Today's Racing*. And basically because I was so bored from lying on my back for a month as a hyperactive 16-year-old, I had nothing else to do so I watched the races and read the picks in the paper and saw what happened with the races on TV that day.

"I really didn't think much about it for a few months and then I went out to Sportsman's Park for the first time later that year and it wasn't a bad experience. I was very rebellious at the time and a lot of people around me, my mom and my dad, told me how bad the track was, how you never should go, how no one but losers and derelicts hang out there. And probably that was the wrong thing for them to tell me at that point in time!"

■ Howard Lederer

According to his Web site, www.howardlederer.com, Howard Lederer has been a successful sports bettor and poker player for many years. He is a multiple winner of *World Poker Tour* events and is one of the founding partners of fulltiltpoker.com. He is also a mainstay at the World Series of Poker (WSOP).

HOWARD LEDERER: "I grew up in New Hampshire, where my father was an English teacher. My competitive juices were stoked at an early age. I can remember many knock-down, drag-out card games played on the family-room floor. Our family played all kinds of card games, including poker. I don't think my father ever lost at anything to me on purpose. You might find that a bit unusual, but I think it prepared me for the hypercompetitive world of high-stakes poker.

"I moved to New York City at the age of 18 to pursue my passion for chess. I deferred college for a year so I could see where my chess development might lead. I soon discovered a poker game in the back room of my favorite chess club. I was immediately hooked. I started playing about 70 hours a week. I soon found myself broke and running errands for the game to get my nightly stake. During my first two years of play, I would end up broke about nine out of 10 nights. But I loved the game so I kept coming back. Things started to turn for me when I realized that I didn't have to play all weekend long. I would play on a Friday night and go home. Then I would come back on Saturday and the same faces would still be in the game. I'd be fresh and they would be tired. Needless to say, my results started to improve.

"My next leap of improvement happened when I started to play at the Mayfair club in New York. The Mayfair was a legendary bridge and backgammon club. Some of the greatest games players in the world hung out there. In the mid-eighties, they started to play no-limit hold 'em. We would play from 4:00 P.M. to 2:00 A.M. every day and then retire to our favorite bar and talk about the day's play. We were new to the game, but we elevated our games by sharing our ideas.

"In the late eighties I started working with my sister Annie Duke on her game. She had moved to Montana and needed to generate some extra income. She would play during the day, and go over her tough decisions with me at night. Her questions quickly started becoming more and more difficult to answer.

"I moved to Las Vegas in 1993. If I wanted to take my poker game to the next level, I needed to compete against the best in the world. And Las Vegas is the place to do that. I concentrated on cash-game play until 2002. With the coming of World Poker Tour, tournaments started to really take off. We can now play in a $10,000 buy-in tournament almost every month. Back in the eighties there was only one per year. I have always loved to play all forms of poker, but for sheer excitement, nothing can beat big buy-in no-limit hold 'em tournaments. I look forward to playing against the best in the world for many years to come."

■ Jim Mazur

For years Jim Mazur has been educating handicappers with his list of annual products, including *The Saratoga Handicapper* and *Guide to the Graveyard*. His specialty has been trainer angles, and his historical analyses of big meets and big racing days have often sparked big winning days at the track for those who use his information.

It's fitting that Mazur is a writer as well as a horseplayer, as his major at Duke University was journalism.

JIM MAZUR: "The whole trainer-angle thing came about in two ways. In college, I was a journalism major at Duke and I decided not to go into journalism, I just went into business. About 15 years out of school, I felt maybe I wanted to go back to journalism but I felt I needed a resume piece. A fellow named John Angelo had written a book called *The Saratoga Scorecard*. He was the pioneer. He did it by hand, just keeping track of stats at Saratoga and then writing these little profiles that were absolutely hilarious. The guy was way ahead of his time and a major talent. I called him up and asked if I could do one of those for Gulfstream. I felt he deserved a call to see if he wanted to expand. He had no ambition to do that so he said, 'Knock yourself out.'

"The handicappers loved the information in it because it wasn't available anywhere else. My friends and I would ask questions about certain situations with certain horses. Take a first-time starter—there was very little information available, so we'd ask, 'How does the sire do with firsters? How does the trainer do with firsters?'

"This led to questions about how the trainer does with layoffs. I was always told (from the Larry Vogel school) never to play a horse with a layoff greater than 30 days, but what I found was that for some trainers it was a really positive move. So I decided to come up with as many categories as I could and input all the data into a crude database. It was just a hobby and we'd crank out a book every year and sell about 60 to 100 copies in Florida because there was no simulcasting back then. I got some help from local writers—they wrote about the book—and before I knew it we were selling 250 to 300 a year. I got a call from The Meadowlands and they wanted me to do a book for them; then Monmouth wanted one. And then simulcasting meant we could sell the Florida book all over. It just sort of mushroomed."

■ Barry Meadow

Barry Meadow, who heads TR Publishing, has spent more than 30 years in the gambling world. He is the author of several books and manuals, including his well-regarded *Money Secrets at the Racetrack*, which was chosen by *American Turf Monthly* as the nation's best handicapping product in 1998. In 1988, Meadow began offering his Master Win Ratings, a daily phone and E-mail service that rates every California horse and gives an updated power rating based on a number of handicapping factors. Meadow has served on various industry panels for the NTRA.

BARRY MEADOW: "There was a television show called *Racing from Yonkers*; it was a harness-racing show that I used to watch when I was 11 years old, and I was totally fascinated by it because it was totally unlike anything my family ever knew about. So I used to watch the races on TV and apparently other kids were watching too because in the fifth grade I remember betting nickels on who had the most winners.

"I read everything I could about harness racing, all the books I could find. I used to go to the track before I was legally allowed to be in the track. I was about 17 when I started going, and I really enjoyed it. And I started to figure out why horses won and why horses lost.

"I did the harness races for quite a while. When I moved out to California, I'd been doing harness racing out here—at the time Hollywood Park and Los Alamitos had harness races and I was going out there every night. And I noticed that the pools in Thoroughbred racing were huge. They started having the pick six, and especially with the pick-six carryovers there was a tremendous amount of money available, and I figured, well, I knew harness racing so it shouldn't be that much more difficult to learn Thoroughbred racing. Boy was I wrong.

"The first year I went to the Thoroughbreds every day and I read all the handicapping books. I used to listen to these phone seminars every day—you could listen for free. I wanted to learn why handicappers would pick one horse and not this other horse. I tried to learn everything I could. The first year I played, I lost and I thought, 'Boy, maybe I'll never learn this at all.' But I stuck with it, and then by the second year I was doing okay, and by the third year I won a lot of money.

"Racing became a major source of income for me when I moved to California and I wasn't really working or looking for work. That was around 20 years ago."

■ Gerry Okuneff

Gerry Okuneff has been a handicapping mainstay on the Southern California circuit, making his home base the satellite facility at Del Mar. He has been playing professionally for almost 50 years and was featured as an expert handicapper in an episode of *60 Minutes*. He regularly gives seminars and has a pick-six syndicate that has been very successful over the years. Before Okuneff got into racing, he made his living as an actor, having appeared numerous times on both *Murder, She Wrote* and *Columbo*.

GERRY OKUNEFF: "I was going to UCLA and after I finished playing football there I was a graduate assistant. In 1955, when I had a free afternoon, I'd play golf or go to the racetrack—and then I stopped playing golf. I've been at it for 48 years. The first 20 or so years I was a guaranteed loser—I just enjoyed the glamour of it and I wasn't going every day. I was coaching in college—then I got into showbiz when I got out of the navy. I got hooked on all gambling. I used to bet on everything. Then when I got money I'd bet whatever. It was guaranteed that I would never have any money.

"In 1980, I said to myself, 'You are not an unhappy person, but if you continue doing what you're doing, you will never have a pot to pee in. Get rid of the sure losers and concentrate on Thoroughbred racing and see if you can show profit. And if you can't play successfully, then you'll know and have peace.'

"Now I play daily, and I don't lose at the races—I'm cautious, which is a weakness, but I will take my shots. I'll never go hungry again and I'll be damned if I'll let the racetrack bust me."

■ "Amarillo Slim" Preston

"Amarillo Slim" Preston is a world-renowned gambler who is best known for his 1972 victory in the World Series of Poker, a tournament that put poker on the map and made an instant celebrity out of the tall, lanky Texan. A successful horse owner and breeder, Preston is also known for some of his proposition bets, which included hustling Bobby Riggs in a table-tennis match (using a frying pan), beating Minnesota Fats in pool (using a broomstick), and hoodwinking a respected basketball coach by shooting free throws . . . with a football. Preston has made a career out of gambling and his insights into the mental side of the game, available in detail in his memoir, *Amarillo Slim in a World Full of Fat People*, and his poker instructional, *Play Poker to Win*, are elucidating.

23

AMARILLO SLIM: "If there's anything worth arguing about, I'll either bet on it or shut up. And since it's not very becoming for a cowboy to be arguing, I've made a few wagers in my day. But, in my humble opinion, I'm no ordinary hustler. You see, neighbor, I never go looking for a sucker; I look for a champion and make a sucker out of him . . . I like to bet on anything—as long as the odds are in my favor."

■ James Quinn

James Quinn is a respected handicapping author and a trailblazer in the racetrack industry. He is the NTRA players' representative, a "recently created role intended to help bettors obtain information, feedback, and support on any parimutuel wagering problems and concerns they may experience." Quinn has also been a consultant to Santa Anita Park on player development for the last 10 years.

JAMES QUINN: "I was in grad school at UCLA and I wanted to buy tickets to a Boston Celtics game. A guy pointed to Hollywood Park and said he was a handicapper. I told the guy I was going to come to the track; so I met the guy and he gave me winners. I'd go out once a week and he'd tout me. Next Christmas, six months later, an RA gave me Ainslie's book. I read it and graduated in March 1970; I liked it, and thought skillful players could win. I had $1,500 and wanted to play the season at Hollywood; I won $6,600. Half was on a daily double I had 10 times. I followed Ainslie verbatim as far as selecting goes; I won and was so naïve that when this meet was coming to an end, I just said to myself, 'I'm sorry it's ending.' I didn't know about Del Mar!

"But I soon found out and I went to that meet. I really enjoyed it so I kept pursuing it. I had an aptitude right from the start; if I had lost, maybe I wouldn't have pursued it. I started to play more and more races and I evolved into a full-time player. A decade later I played full-time to earn most of my income from it. I've never regretted it. I like people at the track—all kinds from all fields."

24

■ Roxy Roxborough

Roxy Roxborough is a name that has long been associated with Vegas and gambling. That's because for years Roxborough was a Vegas oddsmaker, setting the lines for every sporting event in America. He's also a very successful horseplayer who specializes in proposition bets that give him a decided advantage. Roxborough is a legend in the gambling world and his thoughts and ideas helped revolutionize linemaking and setting odds.

ROXY ROXBOROUGH: "I started in 1968 when I went to Exhibition Park—now Hastings Park—in Vancouver with my dad. I was in high school. Instead of reading Faulkner, like I was supposed to, I was reading Joe Hirsch. After six months of going to the track, I realized that I needed to get serious and develop a method, otherwise I was going to start hemorrhaging money. So I got serious. My interests in gambling were shooting pool and horse racing. Horse racing because it was the only legal type of gambling in most places. And pool because most gamblers hung out at the pool halls when they weren't at the racetracks. I was interested in gambling, so I hung out, too. I used to think it was great. I spent my formative years in Vancouver chasing girls, gambling, and drinking booze. I look back and realize how little things have changed!"

■ Andy Serling

Andy Serling grew up in Saratoga Springs, New York, going to the races. He learned the game as a teenager by hanging around a group of high-level players, including Andrew Beyer. He got the nickname Little Andy both because of his youth and because he was a foot shorter than Beyer. He spent several years in the 1990's as a professional player and has bracketed that with successful stints as an options trader on Wall Street. He has also worked in racing both as a regular on *Talking Horses* (on New York Racing Association broadcasts) back in the nineties, and as a regular guest and sometime host of the *Daily Racing Form* seminars at Siro's in Saratoga Springs. These days Serling is an enthusiast rather than a pro. But his strong opinions and experience make him a sought-after voice in the handicapping world. We asked him to talk about his background and contrast being a pro with being a weekend player.

2▮

ANDY SERLING: "I went to the track when I was 12 and looked around and thought this was a place I could make money. I was a kid and I was stupid. And I read Beyer's book and that confirmed that this was a place you could make money. I just loved the track. I met a lot of people in racing. I met Harvey Pack when I was 13 or 14. I ended up with a lot of connections and I stayed in racing, and in '94 I took some time off from downtown and decided I'd like to see what it would be like to be a full-time player.

"Before that, I used to think, 'Oh, I'm no different from a guy who plays every day.' Then you start going full-time and you realize how it changes your life. You realize that it's completely consuming. Not only are you spending six hours at the track every day, but you're spending four hours away from the track doing your work. And you're with people all year playing the horses with you. You're in Florida for the winter, you're in Kentucky; you're in Saratoga. An enormous amount of your life becomes consumed by the racetrack, which is something that doesn't happen when you work during the week—even if you play, and watch and read the Form every day. It's completely different. It becomes a way of life."

■ Maryland Player

Our Maryland Player has been a professional horseplayer for more than two decades, or as he likes to say, "since dinosaurs roamed the earth." He has asked not to be named, but was happy to offer a bit of information regarding his early years, learning the game, and getting into racing:

"I guess like a lot of kids I was interested in gambling, poker games, that kind of thing. It was a natural interest. I've always been a game player; I played a lot of bridge. What was attractive about horse racing was that it was a game you could play and you could make money at it. Poker was also like that; bridge, the way I played it, wasn't like that. I went to the track and said, 'This is pretty darn interesting.'

"I actually started out with trotters when I was a kid, and I had all the usual experiences—got kicked out, that kind of stuff. It wasn't until college that I became interested in the flats.

"Harness racing has become much more nuanced with the mile tracks and the change of rules with the passing lane. It's not quite as unidimensional as it used to be. When I started going it was half-mile tracks and, what do you know, 1-2-3 did better than 6-7-8. But the Thoroughbred game with the different distances and much greater ease of conditioning horses is a more complicated game."

■ Kentucky Player

Our Kentucky Player shares an affinity for the races with his father, and when he isn't playing seriously for millions of dollars, he and his father share wagers on what he calls specific prime plays—"the kind of plays I would be making if I were betting on a very limited budget." In other words, all of the basic handicapping factors have to be in order for our Kentucky Player and his father to make the bet. No surprise they've been successful over the long haul.

Though our Kentucky Player has asked not to be named, he did offer this information about himself and his career as a bettor:

"I kind of gradually worked my way into it. I've been playing the horses seriously probably for 25 years, closer to 30 years. I was in the antiques business and gradually went through my ups and downs at the racetrack until there was a time when there wasn't pressure on me to strictly make money by playing the horses. It was only about seven years ago that I gave up my other business.

"There were a lot of ups and downs at the beginning. The last 15 years I've had a very good consistent record but the first 10 or 15 years were very much up and down."

■ Las Vegas Player

Like some of our other subjects, our Las Vegas Player was successful at other areas of gambling before embarking on a career in racing. Now happily retired, our Las Vegas Player offers an interesting perspective on what it was like to learn the game:

"I've been doing this a long time, since I was 13 years old. I enjoy games. I enjoy poker. It's an intellectual game. It's one huge puzzle and each puzzle is different than the next. To solve the first puzzle it might have nothing to do with the next.

"I wasn't successful in the beginning. The dog track in college was easier. I read some books, etc.

"I never really bet horses seriously until I got The Sheets. I always enjoyed having a good time and not particularly working. My father would take a bus to the Long Island Rail Road and then a subway to work an hour and a half each way and my mother would tell him what a tough day she had, so I knew working nine to five wasn't what I wanted to do.

"It wasn't racing so much as any game: poker, backgammon, the dog track. The dog track was very unsophisticated in those days. Whatever box the dog had was key. It wasn't the past performances. Dog racing was very beatable. I still wasn't betting that much. As soon as I finished college I went to law school for a semester; I was living with a girl, and I really didn't want to memorize three hours on real-estate property—that just wasn't my thing. Guys like Ernie Dahlman spend hours preparing—I wanted to be able to make quick decisions without that much scientific study. So I fell into backgammon, and it was with people who were very rich and just played socially. I traveled around Europe doing that. The next game was horse racing. Now I'm very much relaxed and retired. To play the game now would be too much work.

"The idea was to have a good time and do as little as possible. When I first got here, though, I was working nine hours a day, six days a week because I couldn't believe what was available. Now I might be a sucker."

■ **Baseball Bettor**

Our baseball bettor also asked that we not use his name, but explained how he got involved in his chosen profession and why he makes his living that way:

"I was an undergrad in psychology—originally a math major and astrophysics minor, but that was too much work. Then I got my law degree.

"Now I do sports betting exclusively. I did at one time play blackjack in the same vein as Kevin Blackwood, and I played poker professionally for 10 years. Within sports betting, I bet nearly exclusively on baseball. My sports betting developed after many years of experience with blackjack and poker. Ever since I graduated from college in 1980, I never had a regular job. I was a pro gambler. I got into baseball through baseball research—the field of sabremetrics, Bill James, and *The Hidden Game of Baseball*. I was interested in sabremetrics and I'd always been analytical—I accept nothing at face value. Anytime I read anything of any import, the first question I ask is: Is that true? I believe nothing I see or hear unless it's fairly obvious without having to do any research or checking sources. That's important because gambling is filled with lore and myth and it's easy to go off on the wrong track. So I started doing research having nothing to do with gambling, and then a light bulb went off and I thought it could be useful for handicapping baseball games.

"So I've seriously been doing baseball betting since 1989—the second half of the baseball season. I spent the first six months of '89 putting together a mathematical computer model for handicapping baseball. But I had been researching baseball and sabremetrics before then. Then I started betting along with partners."

A HARD WAY TO
MAKE AN EASY LIVING

SECRET

They're not really gamblers;
they're entrepreneurs whose business is betting.

Most horse-racing fans don't associate the racetrack with hard
work. In fact, most of us go to the track as an escape from
work. That attitude is fine as long as you treat the races as a form of
entertainment, like playing golf or going to a ballgame. As Dave Cuscuna told us, "You don't make any money when you go to the Yankee
game either. You spend $60 for a box seat, you spend on parking and
food, and you have a good time. You go to the track and some days
you're smart and some days you're not, but either way, it's an enjoyable process."

And that's certainly true. Here's another way to look at it, though:
The more you win, the more times a year you're going to be able to
go to the track. By putting in more work, you'll get to have more fun.
And if you want to be more successful, the first thing you need to do
is to start taking the game more seriously. In this chapter, we're going
to take a look at how the professional player operates. We believe that
it's incredibly important to understand what it is that we're up against
as we decide to get more serious about playing the horses. We're also
going to talk about some of the lessons that we've learned from these
players and how we've applied them to our own play.

In a later chapter, we're going to go in-depth about why the term
"gambler" is really inaccurate for these men. But for now we'd like to

present what we feel is a more appropriate label for our pros: "entrepreneur." An entrepreneur is a person who organizes, operates, and assumes the risk for a business venture. That definition encapsulates all of the elements that these men possess. They have the same adventurous spirit that allows them to operate outside the realm of traditional jobs. They are willing to work harder in exchange for that freedom. They are also willing to work without a net and incur all the risk themselves.

IF YOU DON'T WANT TO WORK HARD, YOU'RE IN THE WRONG GAME

One thing that unites all of the players we've talked to is that they are willing to work incredibly hard—often much harder than people with traditional nine-to-five jobs. At 40 hours, your average serious horseplayer's week is just getting started. For most of our players, betting horses is a way of life, and that means putting in long, hard hours in order to succeed.

> **KENTUCKY PLAYER:** "One point that you might want to make is that playing the horses is not very glamorous. My wife keeps pretty good tabs on me and she says I'm never less than 80 hours a week when I'm playing. Now I take a month off at least once a year and I take another span of two to three weeks off, so I have to break it up or I go insane. But I'm between 80 and 95 hours a week."

We're not saying that you need to quit your job to be a winning horseplayer, though if you want to be a professional, that certainly would help. In the time we've spent speaking with these players and analyzing their work habits, we've learned a lot of things that have helped us improve our game. But it all starts with working harder.

> **MARYLAND PLAYER:** "If all you're looking for is entertainment, that's fine as long as you accept that. But if you're looking for more than entertainment out of this, then you have to treat it like a business.
> "I don't think you or I are going to hang a stethoscope from our ears and put a shingle on the wall and expect to be in the doctor business.

And people shouldn't expect to pick up a *Daily Racing Form* at one o'clock on a Saturday afternoon and be in the horse-racing business. It'd be nice if the world worked that way but it doesn't."

CLONIE GOWEN: "You absolutely have to treat it like a job. It may be 31 a job you enjoy, but every time you sit down at that table, you have to remember that you're there to make a profit. I require eight hours of sleep. I require a balanced meal. I require a very normal lifestyle to just go in and be focused at the table. Other players are very different from me. There are players that play better drunk—not very many, but there are a few. And there are some that play better in the 36th hour of their game. But for me, I have to have a well-balanced life for me to be at the top of my game."

ANDY SERLING: "There's no such thing as working too hard. I don't care what anybody says, you have to be prepared. You have to do your work. You have to watch all the races carefully during the day. You have to reanalyze them at night to see what happened. You've got to look at every horse. I'm not saying I do it all the time anymore, but you've got to be focused and you've got to be alert and you have to work."

A CONTRAST OF THE BUSINESS
AND GAMBLING WORLDS

All of our players are incredibly business-savvy, and if they weren't making their living betting the horses, they'd probably be making millions of dollars doing something else. It just so happens that they love what they do and playing the horses provides them with the necessary excitement to make each day of their working life an adventure. In *The Poker MBA: Winning at Business No Matter What Cards You're Dealt,* Greg Dinkin, a columnist for *Card Player* magazine, writes:

If you took the time to list the characteristics of a world-champion poker player, you would create a list that is almost identical to those of a world-class businessperson. World Series of Poker champion Amarillo Slim can be described in much the same way as billionaire Bill Gates. Both men are:

- Strategic thinkers.
- Shrewd decision makers.
- Cool under pressure.
- Driven by a purpose with an incredible desire to win.
- Able to balance risk and reward.
- Adept at reading others and seeing things from another's perspective.
- Willing to risk their last dollar when they have conviction about an idea.
- Disciplined enough to handle adversity and recover from a loss.
- Good enough actors to "fake it" and win—they can bluff.

Successful horseplayers can be described in much the same way. In fact, several of our players seemed to learn as much about their profession in the business and finance world as they did at the racetrack. At the end of Jack Schwager's best-selling book *The New Market Wizards* there is a list of 42 observations the author made about all the traders he interviewed. If you change the word "trader" to "horseplayer," all the same observations hold true. From the importance of hard work and confidence to the ability to control risk and keep emotions in check, the skill sets are essentially the same. Dave Cuscuna, who has a finance degree and is a securities trader, echoed this notion.

DAVE CUSCUNA: "Just because you're betting and you're playing horses, it's no different than being an analyst for Paine Webber; it's a job. The guy who's a successful analyst is making contacts, gathering information, taking time to process and learn the information—read that extra book, find that extra source. It's no different betting horses."

Another player who started off as a trader agreed that the professions are essentially very similar and that you need to see things differently from everyone else in order to be successful.

DAVE GUTFREUND: "You don't want to be on the same side as the public. You want to have a contrarian point of view. You want to think outside the box. You don't want to see what everybody else sees.

"What's the difference between the stock market and horse racing? I'll blurt it out: respectability. That's the only difference. It's a huge difference. I know it firsthand as somebody who was, pre-fall 1995, thought of as a very, very good catch, and after 1995, when I became a full-time horseplayer, nope!"

This sentiment was reiterated by a few different players, one of whom points out that in today's world, working as an entrepreneur has more security than traditional employment.

MARYLAND PLAYER: "A contrarian streak is a good thing. It should go without saying that this isn't a business your family hopes you'll be in. Certainly my family in any case, this isn't what they hoped I would be. But that said, I have a lot more job security than some awfully bright people in all kinds of other businesses. I have a lot more job security than the poor guy working for Arthur Andersen or Enron or one of the telecoms that collapsed. You need a bit of a contrarian streak to say, 'I don't buy what the world says.' And at the racetrack that does you a lot of good too."

Of course, steeling yourself against what the world thinks isn't always easy. A lot of people outside the racing world just don't get it.

JIM MAZUR: "If you're going to play professionally, you also need to have a good foundation, a supportive family or whatever because there's a stigma that even I run into, an overall value system—should I be playing five days a week at Gulfstream? Shouldn't I be in my office working?"

Andy Serling, who is currently a trader, also contrasted the two worlds.

ANDY SERLING: "In trading you do trades because there's an edge and a lot of the trades are trades that are actually presented to you. Somebody comes in and they quote a spread, they quote an option, and they say, 'Where do you want to buy it? Where do you want to sell it?' You find the price and if the price works, you make a trade.

"In horse racing, you're looking for situations with edge. You *know* these options have edge because you understand the mathematics of it. So that's a major difference. In horse racing you're assuming you have an edge because you have an opinion and you think, 'Okay, I'm a successful horseplayer; I have a good opinion. Over time, it's going to bear out.' But it's not the same because it's not a purely mathematical concept like options. There are ways you can do trades where you can lock in a profit. You have to find a way to hedge an option. Horse racing isn't about hedging, it's about finding situations you think are good situations and betting."

■ The Importance of Being Contrarian

A few of the above quotes touch on one thing that really unites horseplayers and entrepreneurs: the importance of having a contrarian streak. If you're someone who's happy with the way things have always been done, who isn't interested in finding a new, improved way, then you're probably better off as somebody else's employee—and there's nothing wrong with that. But if you're the type who's always looking for some better way of doing things, who wants to avoid inefficiency at all costs, who's willing to risk everything for an idea you believe in, then being an entrepreneur—in this case, a professional horseplayer—might suit you.

Steve Davidowitz and Gerry Okuneff shared their thoughts about how being contrarian is a big asset to a winning horseplayer.

STEVE DAVIDOWITZ: "Sure, some races you can't play anymore because there's no longer any advantage, but there are so many more people now who think they know the game because of speed figures or who think there's a track bias because three horses went wire to wire in a row. But there's so much money in the pool that there are opportunities. A lot of people just look religiously at the number a horse ran last week and think, 'He's too fast for these.' Well, sir, he was too fast for them last week . . .

"If a football team has everyone on the line to stop the run, you throw a pass. And if they play a three-man line and have all defensive backs, you run through the line—you take what they give you. What they are giving you now is a lot of people robotically going in the same direction. They are very often right, but the prices are out of whack with the contenders that have other credentials.

"Consider the 2003 Hopeful, a race I missed. Silver Wagon got a low figure breaking his maiden, but he had already won at seven furlongs, running his last furlong in 12, and he paid a big price because he was running against horses with big numbers. Sure they were good horses, but the prices didn't reflect their actual odds of winning."

GERRY OKUNEFF: "I have a Ten Commandments of racing, and one of them is, if most people do it at a racetrack, then it's wrong! If you do the opposite, you have a better chance. Most people bet less if the odds go up, and when they go down they bet more. *Wrong!* Most players who get ahead tend to wrap up, and most players who are losing press. *Wrong!* Every natural instinct you have, regardless of your IQ, is wrong at the racetrack."

Of course, even if you generally have a contrarian attitude, there are still going to be times when your opinion falls in line with the crowd's. As we'll discuss later, the crowd is too good a handicapper for that not to happen at some point. In these instances, caution is advised.

JIM MAZUR: "I take my best shots when I'm being contrarian. But even after all these years, I can get caught in a trap where instead of being a contrarian, I find myself perhaps going with the crowd. I found that out Breeders' Cup Day 2003. In the *Form*, they have that big grid with everybody's picks. I like it when most of them aren't on my horses because that means I'm going to get a decent price. When I saw that one of the guys in there had maybe five of the same horses I had, I said, 'I think I might be in trouble here. But I'm not going to go off my horses.' I wasn't successful in this Breeders' Cup and we were pretty successful in our analysis, but I wasn't able to make some adjustments during the day and it didn't work out."

LEARNING THE FUNDAMENTALS

Being a contrarian is one thing. But every entrepreneur needs to learn the rules of business before he can go out on his own. This holds true in particular for the horseplayer. The importance of learning the fundamentals can't be overstated—and our pros had very strong opinions about this.

JIM MAZUR: "In any endeavor, it pays to learn the fundamentals. Learn to read *Daily Racing Form*. Get as many handicapping books as possible and read them. You don't have to kill yourself with all the details but you need a general knowledge about the basic fundamentals of handicapping—what's worked over time and what hasn't worked over time. Then it's important to handicap as many races as you can. A lot of people say to play on paper but that's boring, not many people are going to do that.

"Mentally you've got to make notes about your mistakes. Don't knock yourself out about it but try and learn from those mistakes, so the next time you don't make that mistake. Even me, I don't make the same mistakes too often but they do recycle. It's a great game though. I find that the gambling end aside, I got into it for the cerebral challenge. To me there is no better thrill than picking a $30 or $40 horse because that means that most people don't have it."

ANDREW BEYER: "Just being as studious as possible is crucial to being successful. Every good horseplayer is constantly looking for ideas, for insights, for little observations in races, for anything that's going to give him an edge. It's hard work. You never hear a successful player say this is an easy game, except with heavy irony. We all know that it takes a tremendous amount of work and you have to constantly invest the energy and time and take it seriously as an intellectual discipline. That's something everybody does."

Another way to continue to reinforce the fundamentals of handicapping is to step outside your own circuit once in a while. We were impressed that Brad Free, *Daily Racing Form*'s Southern California handicapper, was able to win the handicapping contest at the DRF Expo in Las Vegas in 2004, because the contest covered two Eastern tracks, Aqueduct and Gulfstream. We asked him about handicapping races at unfamiliar tracks.

BRAD FREE: "I like it because you handicap without all those built-in prejudices that you may have accrued over the last few weeks, months, or years looking at the same jockeys, trainers, and horses. You can look at things with no preconceived notions about whether the horse exceeded or failed to reach expectations last time. All you're looking at is today. And there's no sentimentality at all attached to your decision-making when you're not looking at horses that you were wagering on three weeks ago and you're not going to be wagering on three weeks from now. It's all about today, black-and-white, nuts-and-bolts handicapping. It reemphasizes the basics of handicapping. And that's a good lesson for anybody.

"At the Expo, I was able to win that contest handicapping Gulfstream Park and Aqueduct. What do I know about those tracks? I sat down the night before and identified 10 races with large fields and used nuts-and-bolts handicapping and got lucky. I had no ideas about how trainers do in certain situations or whether a certain horse ran against the bias last time. And I'm not discounting that information. That's stuff you do need to know. But when you step outside your own circuit once in a while, it reemphasizes the fundamentals of handicapping."

When you're learning the game, if you're not playing, you should be reading about playing.

BASEBALL BETTOR: "Most successful gamblers are information hogs—they share information and support; emotional, moral, and intellectual support. Also, read everything you can in your field. Most successful gamblers have read everything in their field. It's difficult to be successful without doing that."

For most players, reading about the game is an essential part of the process of learning the fundamentals. Decades after it was published, Tom Ainslie's *Ainslie's Complete Guide to Thoroughbred Racing* remains a great (if very dated) source for this. Speaking of dated but useful, Edward Cole's *Racing Maxims of Pittsburgh Phil,* originally published in 1908, is also a book that should be in every handicapper's library. Steve Davidowitz's *Betting Thoroughbreds* is a terrific overview that was cited as influential by many of our players. Any of Andrew Beyer's books will introduce you to the ways that many of today's pros learned the game. And the most recent addition to the handicapping genre is Brad

Free's *Handicapping 101,* which serves as a great guide for beginners as well as a refresher course for experienced players by one of today's leading public handicappers.

38

> **MARYLAND PLAYER:** "The first thing I did was get Ainslie's book. I've known Andy Beyer for a long time. Like any college kid, you read books, you talk to people, that's pretty much the way it started. That's what I did and that's pretty much the learning process for anything in life."

Book learning is obviously only part of the process. There are lots of opportunities to expose yourself to good handicapping advice, day in and day out. The *Daily Racing Form* handicappers who write detailed analyses of each card are a great source. Many of the writers who do the "Closer Looks" in the *Form* also have something to offer. Some tracks also provide useful handicapping seminars, like the one at Siro's before the races in Saratoga. We'd never advocate blindly following anyone else's opinion, but when you're learning the game, listening to others who write or speak about the process of handicapping is of paramount importance. Obviously, there will be a wide range of divergence in quality among these handicappers. Don't worry: The folks who know what they're doing will become apparent rather quickly. As you learn more about the game and more about your own style, you'll learn which ones you want to pay attention to. And if you still don't believe the value of good information, check out what one of the country's biggest bettors has to say on the subject.

> **ERNIE DAHLMAN:** "I would recommend looking at the *Daily Racing Form* handicappers, reading their stuff, seeing what they say, seeing if it makes sense to you—anything you can do to try and pick up an edge. And then after the race, look back and try to figure out why things happened."

■ It Really Pays to Have a Mentor

There are no shortcuts to becoming successful, in business or at the track. But one of the things that can give you the advantage that can make all the difference in either endeavor is to have a person or group of people who are willing to show you the ropes. Reading is a great first step, but it's not enough. Richard Munchkin, gambling expert and author of a collection of interviews with successful gamblers called *Gambling Wizards*, explains:

39

RICHARD MUNCHKIN: "Another thing that I think is really important, not just in gambling, but in life in general, is that you need to always be learning. I started out as a professional backgammon player and my approach to the game was to go out and read every book I could find on the subject. But then I went out and found really good players and played with really good players to learn what I could from them. When it comes to gambling, I think that is a great strategy. You want to get yourself hooked up with people who are already successful, who already know things, who are willing to teach you."

DAVE GUTFREUND: "In the summer of 1977, I read *Picking Winners* by Andy Beyer and *Betting Thoroughbreds* by Steve Davidowitz. I read them both and I had no idea at the time how groundbreaking and relevant they were. You could make an argument that for 15 or 20 years there wasn't a horse-racing book as good as either of those two books. That summer I hit a $1,000 trifecta and I was hooked.

"I ended up my first year of college in New York City at Hunter College. And a really good friend's father was an awesome horseplayer in New York. And I mentored under him that summer in New York. I had some really good experiences early on in my developmental stages that other people didn't have. I didn't know until 15 or 20 years after the fact how lucky I was to have read those two books and studied under Maurice that summer, learning about turf races and how the game is really played."

RANDY GALLO: "When I first started handicapping I was 14 years old at the Marshfield Fair, which was a horse track, a small fair that is no longer in existence in Marshfield, Massachusetts. They ran for something like 10 days a year. And I got my first look at a *Daily Racing Form* then. There was an old gentleman there who worked behind the windows, he was a teller there and he pointed things out to me, what to look for, how to pick horses. And I've been doing it ever since."

We asked Gallo to elaborate about the importance of having someone to learn from:

RANDY GALLO: "I would tell you to try and get on an even keel with
some of the bigger players in terms of what they're doing, and you
might want to observe before you start jumping in and watch the
methods they use. You're going to have to be pretty astute at what
you're doing; you're going to have to be looking at replays; you're
going to have to have all the information at your fingertips. I don't
know if you want to use Thorograph sheets or Ragozin Sheets or
whatever. But you have to have a library at your fingertips, and once
you have it there you're going to have to learn how to apply it to the
racing and the odds—that's about all I can tell you.

"The key is to observe and find somebody that as you go along will
answer your questions. Basically, lead you through."

Andy Serling pointed out that you can have more than just one
mentor.

ANDY SERLING: "I don't think it's important to have a mentor so
much as it's important to know many smart people—as many as you
can—and listen to what they all have to say. If you've decided that
they're smart and knowledgeable, you listen to what they have to say
and then you sit down by yourself and think about what they told you
and apply it to racing to see if it works for you. Some of these theories
aren't going to be things you're going to agree with. But you want to
be able to say 'I don't agree with this because I've thought it through.'
I think it's important to try and glean as much information from as
many different smart people as you can."

Our Kentucky Player was very fortunate. His mentor lived right
under the same roof.

KENTUCKY PLAYER: "My dad, he played horses all his life. I've had
this conversation with a lot of people over the years and something I've
said before is that I think to be a really top-notch handicapper one of
two things is required. Number one is you have to have a father who

shows you the ropes like mine did—who keeps you from making a bunch of mistakes. Someone who has already made those mistakes and that clears those 10 or 20 years out for you. Or you have to have a mentor. You have to have someone who's done basically the same thing—someone who takes you in as a son, in the handicapping sense anyway, and is willing to share with you 100 percent from the heart what he's learned.

"I think it's almost a two-generational thing. I know from reading Beyer's books that he ran into a couple of guys like that, that pushed him ahead, that he learned a lot from. And more important than what you learn from them are the dead ends that they close off to you. They tell you, this doesn't mean anything, this is no good, don't listen to that. They close those paths off to you and explain why and you buy into that and they keep you focused on the right path to where you end up figuring a lot of it out for yourself but you stay on the road instead of going off on all these little tangents that lead nowhere."

What was it like growing up in a house like that?

KENTUCKY PLAYER: "My dad was a lifelong horseplayer and loved handicapping, and he was the guy at the track who people would come up to and want to learn about handicapping from. And he was tireless. I saw him sit at Turfway Park when you used to have to drive to the races, and he would sit up there until the cleaning people would run us out, and I had to go to school the next day. And he's talking to some guy he's never met before. But the guy is enthusiastic about handicapping, has heard that my dad is a good handicapper and wants to ask him some similar questions to maybe like what we're talking about now. And my dad would sit there until they would close the place down and run him out. Not for any monetary benefit or for any benefit really other than to just try and help somebody and talk handicapping. So that's the atmosphere that I was brought up in.

"So I got kicked out of my history class as a junior in high school for reading the *Racing Form*. My punishment was I had to call my dad. He picked me up and took me to Keeneland—on a school day! I don't know if that's what the teacher had in mind.

"That's the way I grew up. He's a great guy and he taught me a whole lot and he keeps me in line still as a sounding board and as a voice of reason."

We asked our Kentucky Player if he has ever played the role of mentor to someone else.

KENTUCKY PLAYER: "I meet a lot of people, and in handicapping terms they're wandering through the wilderness. They think there's an answer. They don't really know where it is but they're interested in finding it, real interested in finding it.

"There's a kid in town here that heard about me some way and tracked me down, called me at home and talked to my wife. She said, 'I want you to talk to this kid because he's real nice.' She gave him my cell-phone number and he said, 'I want to be a professional gambler.' He just got out of college. And I said, 'You don't know what you're buying into.' And I went through two or three meetings with him telling him how hard you have to work and how you go to a cocktail party and you're going to get seated next to the drug dealer. There's no respect for this profession. You send your kids to school and it's not a good sign when it's show-and-tell time and you stand up and explain that Dad plays the horses for a living.

"I tried to explain all that to him but this kid has got it in his head that he wants to be a horseplayer and I think eventually he'll do it. I'm trying to mentor him some and it's brought it all back into focus for me just how much there is to learn and how long a path it is. I think I'm an excellent mentor and it's still going to take a long time; it's going to take years and years and years. He's a sharp kid but he's like most of us: He has his own ideas and he's got to experience both sides of it before he buys into certain things, and I don't know that there's a shortcut for that."

Our last question along these lines was if his own kids might be interested in playing the horses seriously.

KENTUCKY PLAYER: "I guess this will say a lot about what the life of a handicapper is: From day one I've tried to push them totally the other way. I know that there are things that they can do that are better for them that are easier. I think it's a great pastime. I think as a way to make a living it's nice when you get to the point where I am now, but the path that leads there is a very self-destructive path that if you can come out the other end of it successfully, then you're forged in steel, I think. But a lot of people don't come out the other end of that."

Or, as Amarillo Slim likes to say about being a professional gambler: "It's a tough way to make an easy living."

■ There Is No Substitute for Experience

Once you're armed with the theoretical knowledge that comes from books, and the observational knowledge of watching others, you still need the experiential knowledge that can only come by making the decisions for yourself. Paradoxically, it's your mistakes that will become your best teacher.

PAUL CORNMAN: "Learn from your mistakes. When the race is over, why did I lose and why did the horses that finished first, second, and third, finish first, second, and third?"

JAMES QUINN: "Experience—the more varied your experience the better you'll be at solving problems."

ERNIE DAHLMAN: "You should be always looking at what just happened. The best teacher is what you just saw happen and you can use that to make you a better player in the future. Always be reevaluating. It's a complicated game and if you can start ticking off one piece of the puzzle or another piece of the puzzle, pretty soon you know enough to be a winning player, and if you know enough of the puzzle it's like doing a jigsaw puzzle—when you get near the end it's easier to do the rest of it."

JIM MAZUR: "Experience will also give me an edge over younger players. Knowing the different trainer angles is part of it. Also, if it's a big race, knowing the historical background will help give me an edge. I've come to develop a little database of situations you need to move away from."

Of course, many of us don't have the disposable income to go out and actually play a lot in the early stages, when we're more likely to lose money than win. Is that a solvable problem? Our Kentucky Player says yes.

KENTUCKY PLAYER: "When I went off to school, when most of my buddies were off chasing women and so forth, I would get the *Racing Form* at the bus depot. Some days it would be a day or two late. I would take the *Racing Form* after the races had already been run, get one of my roommates and have him get the paper with the results charts in it. I'd go back to the earlier *Form* and ask him what the weather was and what the scratches were in the first at Beulah. He'd give them to me; I'd scratch those horses out of the race and I'd sit there while we drank some beer and watched a ballgame and handicap all day long.

"Play the horses on paper! I had several different roommates and they all loved calling the races, being in control of what I heard and when I heard it. I would usually lose but we had a hell of a time. I'd hit a trifecta or pick two winners in a row and it was big excitement. I did that when I couldn't go to the track. I worked my way through college and had a job and wasn't able to get away a lot of times, and that's how I kept my fire going for playing the horses. I played on paper and I've suggested that to people over the years as a way to improve.

"I think it's great and you focus in on playing the horses with none of the distractions of being at the track. It was a very valuable experience for me and it promotes good betting habits because you're more comfortable. It was like a tutorial and it was great practice."

Today, this idea can be implemented much more easily. Get an on-line subscription to the *Daily Racing Form*. Set your VCR, or better yet your DVR, to record the day's races from your local track. Before you look at the charts or watch the show, handicap the races, make a few theoretical wagers, and watch the results. Not only will you gain valuable practice, but the extra time you spend getting familiar with the horses, jockeys, and trainers on your local circuit will pay dividends in the long run.

THE DEDICATION IT TAKES TO WIN

GERRY OKUNEFF: "Dedication—you have to have passion; the two of mine have been football and the racetrack; my girlfriend excepted."

In putting this book together, our goal was to break the advice we got from all these great players into categories. In a lot of places, these categories overlap. That's definitely true when it comes to the issues of dedication and discipline. On one hand, dedication and discipline have everything to do with the mental side of the game, which we cover in Chapter 6. But they're also important assets that an entrepreneur must have. When you're the one assuming the risk for a business venture, if you don't have the dedication and discipline to do the work, you don't eat—there's no coasting through days or weeks at your job and collecting a paycheck. Plenty of people dream of getting paid for doing nothing, but that's just a pipe dream. As noted author William Murray quipped, "If you want to write a best-selling book, all you need to do is title it: *How to Become a Concert Pianist without Ever Having to Practice.*" We all want something for nothing, and we all look for shortcuts. But nothing comes free at the racetrack, and shortcuts will only lead to the poorhouse.

In the previous section we went into detail about the ways in which our players learned the game. Those options are available to everyone but only if you have the dedication and discipline to follow through.

KEVIN BLACKWOOD: "You need to be dedicated—you can't dabble in what you're doing; you need to learn the correct strategies on how to do it."

CLONIE GOWEN: "The dedication to learn the game and to continue learning the game are just so important. If you go even a few weeks without thinking about poker and you go and try and sit in a game, I think that you've lost something—especially, in cash games. You need to play on a regular basis."

MARYLAND PLAYER: "Discipline is another important factor to any successful player. You need to have the mental discipline to do the work.

To do the work when things are going badly. To do the work when things are going well. If you're the kind of person who goes on a hot streak and starts carousing in bars until three o'clock in the morning, it's a pretty good bet that your hot streak is going to end in a hurry."

DAVE CUSCUNA: "Hard work for me means trying to incorporate as much information as possible into your job and processing that information and learning from that information. It is being able to factor all those things into play and think it through and process and reevaluate for next time. It's one thing to learn from your mistakes, it's another thing to properly apply what you've learned the next time it comes up. You have to have dedication. You can't just go to the track and buy the *Form* and have a couple of beers. It's a job and it's a job that you work at real hard."

Most often, the amount of dedication needed comes from within.

HOWARD LEDERER: "I would say the number-one, most important characteristic of a successful gambler would be a love of what you're doing. I just don't know any successful poker players or sports bettors or horseplayers who don't just love it. Horseplayers just love going to the track and looking at horses and talking about horses. Poker players who really get good, you just have to do it a lot. Larry Bird probably played more basketball than just about anybody when he was a kid, and that's what made him good. And Wayne Gretzky, I heard legendary details about how much hockey he played when he was young. I think it's well-focused practice at what you do, which can only come through love; I think that's what makes you really successful at something."

Is there any such thing as being too dedicated to doing the work?

HOWARD LEDERER: "It is a balancing act. Having a crazy personal life is a bad thing but not having a personal life is a bad thing professionally too. If you have no personal life you're not out there spending money on friends or girlfriends or wives or whatever. There's no incentive. You just lose their drive."

■ Time Management

BASEBALL BETTOR: "It's not how hard you work; it's how smart you work."

The equation is not as simple as just punching a clock and putting in the hours. You could read the *Racing Form* every day and watch 50 races, but if you're just going through the motions, it won't make a difference. While a time commitment is essential, you must also use your time efficiently.

LAS VEGAS PLAYER: "I think that having a good work ethic is the most important thing you can have in this business. A good work ethic will help you know which opportunities to go after—more quality than quantity. It's not how much time you put in, it's knowing what to identify as a good bet. It's also knowing what you're good at and what you're not good at and trying to capitalize on what you're good at."

And sometimes the equation is even more complicated:

DAVE CUSCUNA: "If you could do a 98 percent job in 30 minutes or a 100 percent job in three hours, what would you do? It's situational. It depends. If I'm an astronaut and I have to fix the space shuttle to get back to Earth, I'll do the 100 percent job. But if that same astronaut has 30 minutes of oxygen left, you go for the 98 percent job and hope you do it right. You have to find that balance in your own life between when you have to do the 100 percent and when you need to do the 98 percent. Often, if you can do a 98 percent job on six races, it's better than doing 100 percent on one race—because the opportunities you're going to find in those six races exceed the extra 2 percent information you'll have on the one race. But there will also be times when that extra 2 percent information is the difference between winning and losing. And you have to determine that, and you need to do it before the event, rather than after.

"When I talk about hard work, hard work is being able to factor all those things into play and think it through and process and reevaluate for next time—to know I did the 98 percent job in this situation when I needed to do the 100 percent job, and if I encounter this situation again, I'm going to do the 100 percent job."

■ Preparation and Focus

48

Dave Cuscuna alluded to the importance of preparation. How many people do you know who just show up at the track and the only handicapping they've done beforehand is for 20 minutes on the train ride out?

This is another thing that separates the great players. Not only do they do their work beforehand, of course, but they go in with an idea of where their opportunities might lie.

PAUL CORNMAN: "You have to go in with a game plan. I'm a nut for preparing. I go in there and I'm ready if the situation should happen. I'm referring to handicapping but also to thinking about what betting strategies I might be ready for when the day begins—pick-three situations, or this may be a good trifecta situation."

ANDY SERLING: "I know going into the day what races in all likelihood I'm going to be interested in. I might know that there are two races where no matter what happens I'm not betting because I don't like them. I can't figure them out or I have no edge. I'll watch those races but I won't bet them. Other races, I'll say, if a horse is a certain price I'll look at that. Most of the time I have a reasonable idea of where I'm going before the day starts."

Another thing the average player can do is try to minimize distractions.

ERNIE DAHLMAN: "You have to do your work; you have to be prepared. There was a guy who used to bet next to me. He could show up at any time. Someone could call him and he'd go out to lunch and miss like three straight races, and I'd grind my teeth and say, 'What the hell is this guy doing? He's losing, he can't make money, and he's leaving it up to chance what races he's here for?' I would see this guy quit in the middle of the day and I'd go down and he'd be playing blackjack or something."

And getting back to our earlier thought about mistakes being the best teacher—most players move so quickly on to the next race that there's no opportunity to learn from their mistakes.

KENTUCKY PLAYER: "I sit around the track and I see people when the simulcast is done and they're betting three or four tracks at the same time, they don't have time to watch a replay. They're up betting the next race. Half the time, they don't know who won the race if their horse didn't win. They couldn't tell you if the horse was running in the four path or the one path. You could ask them five races into the card, how's speed holding, and nobody there knows. If you're going for pure entertainment, if you just want the juice of gambling, the rush, that's one thing and that's fine. But if you're going to be serious and you're going to aspire to doing better at the windows, then that's different and you have to focus yourself that way and you have to start doing the things that are not so much fun in order to head in the right direction.

"It's pretty simple. After the race, don't just head for the bar. Look back at the *Racing Form* and see if you missed anything. Watching replays can give you even more of an edge. Was there a horse with hidden trouble that you might want to bet next time? Throughout the course of a day, was there a bias that you noticed that will help you evaluate these horses' form better in the future?"

While we could all benefit a lot from doing these little things when we're playing, most of us have too many other demands on our time, namely our day jobs, to be able to devote the kind of attention that the pros do to racing year-round. One option, though, is to do your own version of what Andrew Beyer does: Rather than trying to constantly follow the game at the highest level throughout the year, focus on just one or two sections of the racing calendar.

ANDREW BEYER: "When I do it right, I want to watch the races every day, two or three times, and I make notes and put them in the computer and that alone is so time consuming that it's not something I could maintain year-round. For most of my gambling life, I've taken a couple of segments of the year that are really intensely focused on gambling and I'm a little more casual the other times."

The importance of focusing was echoed by our Kentucky Player:

KENTUCKY PLAYER: "My main advice in that vein would be to pick out your circuit, or maybe two circuits, and to throw yourself into those. To know as much as you can about the horses, the trainers, the owners, the jockeys. To really know your circuit—I think that is the single best thing that people could do."

50

EVOLVE OR DIE

"It's what you learn after you know it all that counts."

—Earl Weaver

CARY FOTIAS: "Always look to improve, don't get discouraged. And be open to new ideas. What works today may not work tomorrow."

It's common for entrepreneurs to start several different businesses during their careers. Sometimes this is because one business simply doesn't work out, but sometimes it's because a change is necessitated by the marketplace. Businesses grow and change. Better ideas come along. For those with an entrepreneurial spirit, if there are too many other people doing what you are doing, it's time to do something else. So it is with betting the horses—only this example is even more extreme. Because of the nature of markets, what works today is actually unlikely to work tomorrow. In the parimutuel system, the more a certain type of horse is bet, the smaller the price on the board will be. Any value there once was betting that type of horse will be diluted. So you have to stay nimble and be willing to change. Like sharks, players have to keep moving for survival. If they don't evolve, they'll die.

ANDY SERLING: "There's an enormous amount you have to continue to learn at all times. About handicapping. About playing to win. And someone who is closed-minded and doesn't listen to things that other smart people say and who isn't willing to adapt and figure out why something they might be doing is wrong is in trouble. I may seem like I'm a know-it-all and I may think I'm a know-it-all but I know enough to know when to change."

ANDREW BEYER: "Two things happen in horse racing. The markets self-correct. One of the great illustrations of that fact today is with the trainer factor. When certain trainers become invested with mystical powers, the public is just right on top of them and all of their horses are bet down. That may be the best example of the market self-correcting very quickly.

"And the other thing that happens is that the game subtly changes. And nobody puts up a road sign saying, 'Hey, the game has changed,' because it happens slowly and imperceptibly. I'll give you an example in my racing lifetime where it's changed 180 degrees. When I started playing the horses there was a huge emphasis on horses getting conditioned from racing that would give them an edge in fitness. You loved horses coming back in seven days. You loved horses with a race over the track or turning back in distance. There was an old-time handicapper in New York when I was first coming around by the name of Manny Kalish, who was a professional, and when the Saratoga meet opened he loved horses who had a race over the track, maybe coming back in five days and turning back from 1⅛ miles to seven furlongs because the track was tiring and it gave them an edge in fitness. Now, people are looking for horses who've been freshened up for two months. Lots of people almost automatically go against a horse with a tough recent race."

As the game changes—as different types of horses start winning or losing more often—the whole process of handicapping obviously must change as well.

DAVE GUTFREUND: "Handicapping is an evolving process, it changes all the time. The fundamentals now are different than the fundamentals 10 years ago in a lot of cases. The most important difference is the Beyer numbers being in the *Racing Form*. It's amazing how bad most of the morning lines are given the fact that the Beyer numbers are in the *Racing Form*. You can basically figure out what the final odds are going to be based on the Beyer numbers, especially in older claiming races with horses with established form."

In a later chapter, we talk to the players about the process of how they handicap a race. Our Kentucky Player explained that one of the things he looks for is different things at different tracks and distances that might give him an edge—maybe a dead rail at seven furlongs at one track or a wide post that really hurts horses going two turns at another track. We asked how he goes about discovering these.

52

KENTUCKY PLAYER: "It's not so much the discovery of something peculiar at a certain distance at a certain track. All that can change from time to time too. You think you have an angle on a certain track and then it can disappear. Everything can change."

STEVE DAVIDOWITZ: "What I do now when I handicap a race isn't something I was capable of doing years ago when I first started playing. There are always new angles coming into the game. You can't be a static handicapper because the game is always evolving, like a living organism, and you have to be aware of the early shifts before the rest of the crowd catches on."

DAVE CUSCUNA: "As a horseplayer you have to be able to redefine and reinvent yourself. If one group of players is all over something, then you have to find a different niche."

CARY FOTIAS: "Get on to the trends before everyone else, pay attention to first-year sires like Elusive Quality a few years ago when so many of his first crop won first out."

So what can one do to keep up? As Buddy Jacobson used to say, "It pays to pay attention." Always be looking for new information that can give you an edge. Some of the best opportunities will come when you can find a short-term trend that contradicts a long-term trend. Maybe for a week in the fall the historically dead Belmont rail will become golden. Most players assume that Keeneland is always favoring speed. But handicappers like the *Daily Racing Form*'s Steve Klein have done intriguing work showing that this isn't always the case. You have to stay ahead of the curve. As we will see later on, this means different things to different people, depending on where your strengths lie. Are you breeding oriented? Then do what Cary Fotias suggests above and look at the first- and second-year sires and how their offspring are performing. Do you like to bet maiden races and have access to good clockers' information? Read it and incorporate it into your handicapping. No one is going to find success switching willy-nilly from one handicapping methodology to another, but you also can't be afraid to change.

BARRY MEADOW: "The game keeps changing and there's more and different information available, and as you can get more and different information, you're going to change what you're doing. For example, even five years ago I wasn't getting any kind of workout service and now there are a couple of workout services I subscribe to where clockers will rate horses in the mornings and then I'll try and integrate that into my handicapping. Trainer data is a lot more easily available, and as more stuff becomes available, I try to use it and see where it's going to help me so I don't do exactly what I did years ago, although it's basically the same—you either have to find horses that have proven they have the ability to win against this group or look like they have the potential to win against this group and then work your way from there."

STEVE DAVIDOWITZ: "Look at Nick Zito with his first-time starters. He never used to win with them—for years he was about 5 percent in that category. Well, he won with one early in the meet at Saratoga in 2003 and in an interview after he explained how he's changed the way he trained and he was asking more of these horses early on, and sure enough he won with other firsters at the meet. The statistics still said he was only 5 percent but there was no excuse for not playing those horses, and they paid better than they should have. [In 2004, Zito won again with multiple firsters at Saratoga.]

"Laz Barrera used to be terrible statistically with horses going from sprint to route, but then he wins the Derby and Belmont with a sprint-oriented horse, Bold Forbes. I asked him about it and he said he'd changed what he was doing. He realized he was training them to go too fast too early in the American style so he went back to what he did in Cuba, when he was successful stretching out sprinters. I made a lot of money betting him stretching out sprinters after that."

And the changes in handicapping are only half the battle. Betting is another area where a player is likely to change.

ERNIE DAHLMAN: "Maybe I do a little more hedging now than I used to do. It used to be easier to pick cold numbers, especially at the trotters. I occasionally have cold numbers on the Thoroughbreds but not nearly as much as I did at the trotters. Thoroughbreds seem to have more suspicious drops, more layoffs. It's what makes the game great, though, that it is tough, that you have to be prepared for a horse that hasn't run in six months and has two slow works and you have to figure out if he'll be able to run his A race or if his A race is even good enough. A lot depends on who the trainer is, who the connections are, if they've done that kind of thing before. The *Daily Racing Form* is doing a great job of giving information on stuff like that—stuff that before you really had to keep your own good records to know."

PAUL CORNMAN: "Over time, my play has changed dramatically. When I started out I was trying to bet to win or bet win and place. Then you know enough where you want to bet exactas, daily doubles, trifectas, then the pick three came around. And now, because the players are fewer and the players that are left are smarter, it just really comes down to playing the right race."

JAMES QUINN: "It has changed from a game where you grind it out in the win pool to one where you try and look for value in the exotic pools and look for bigger scores. That's a major change. In the contemporary game it seems to be much harder to win straight betting and grinding it out, which I was always able to do—the fields are smaller, more information is available, and the customer base isn't growing. The shift into exotics has been universal—trying to make generous value in the exotic pools. That's been a big change in the game. You can be successful over a short period of time and unsuccessful over a long period of time—so put a cap on your losses . . . don't play out of pocket in your exotics. You could win big even after five years of losses. You should look at exotic bets as a long-term capital investment over a long period of time."

As the wagering menu continues to evolve, players will need to adapt to find the new opportunities there as well.

JAMES QUINN: "With any new wager, there's a learning curve for the betting public—a two- to three-year learning curve for the public and then the edge is no longer available. In '94 the average Southern California pick three was $1,500. It's nowhere near that now. Bettors adapted to that wager and the edge went away."

When we attended the DRF Handicapping Expo in February 2004, one of the seminars, hosted by some of the brightest minds in the business, concerned exotic wagering. When the panel asked the floor for questions, one attendee asked them specifically about strategies for superfecta wagering. None of the three panelists claimed enough expertise to answer the question. A light bulb went on for us. If these guys don't know how to bet supers, who would? There must be an opportunity for an enterprising handicapper willing to do the research and hard work to try and crack the correct strategies for the bet. This idea was echoed in our talk with James Quinn:

> **JAMES QUINN:** "Right now, superfecta strategies could make you a lot of money. I had two winners on Breeders' Cup Day [2003]. Islington paid $7.80 on track; the superfecta was $18K. Six Perfections won at 5-1; the super was $39K. Exotic pools are very inefficient. There is a pattern here where even when favorites win, the super can pay astronomically. If you like something strongly to win and it's a full field, go ahead and gamble and guess that the two-three-four holes are going to be double-digit horses."

■ The Only Rule Is That There Are No Rules

An important corollary to the idea that the game is always evolving is that while the game is filled with guidelines, there are no rigid rules—as we learned above in Andrew Beyer's example about Manny Kalish's success in betting horses that were raced into condition and in Steve Davidowitz's examples about Laz Barerra and Nick Zito. The answer to many of the biggest questions in handicapping is simply, "It depends."

> **ROXY ROXBOROUGH:** "I think things always depend on the situation. I was a poker player for a while and every hand is different; ever player is different; odds are different. There are so many variables in horse racing that I look at every race as an independent event. In poker, I

could have two aces and throw them away in one situation; or I could go all-in in another. Every race is different, and that's the challenge of handicapping."

STEVEN CRIST: "Different factors have different importance in different races. You need to use the whole toolbox; you can't just go after everything with the same screwdriver. Speed figures are the most significant data points for me and frame the contemplation of any race: What's it going to take to win this race, and who's capable of running that fast today? But that's just a start. Sometimes other factors—distance, pace scenario, etc.—are so strong that you end up making a play on a horse with seemingly weak figures."

ERNIE DAHLMAN: "A lot of times players say, 'I love this guy off a claim'—and they don't even think about who the horse was claimed from. There are two sides to the equation: The guy who claimed the horse and the guy he claimed it from. I would rather bet a horse Richard Dutrow claims from somebody I consider very weak than to bet a horse that Dutrow claims from Scott Lake or someone. A lot of times you'll see on a guy's selection sheet, this guy's 30 percent off the claim. Yeah, but he's not 30 percent off the claim from Scott Lake. Maybe he's 2 percent off the claim from Scott Lake."

As we've discussed in this chapter, a lot of hard work goes into winning at the races and playing the game at the professional level. It's not for the faint of heart. It requires all the dedication, preparation, and willingness to adapt that go into running any small business. The question that remains: Is it worth the 80 hours a week some of these guys put into it?

KENTUCKY PLAYER: "Absolutely. I had a very profitable business that I closed six or seven years ago. I would never allow myself to do that until I had three years consistent profit, three years where I was making more money gambling than I was in my business. Once I did that I thought, 'Well, it's safe enough to try it now,' and I haven't had to go back, so that's good."

2

THE INFORMATION EDGE

SECRET

They make the best use of available resources and process information in an elegant way.

Horse racing is an information game at its heart. It doesn't matter what your specific approach to handicapping is, if you want to win, you've got to use the available information better than the crowd. In the next chapter, we're going to be talking all about edge and how great players view and use their edge to make money. But in this chapter we want to examine the very building blocks of that edge—the factors of handicapping. We're going to take a look at the major tenets of handicapping—speed, condition, pace, and class—and how the pros use them. We'll also look a little bit deeper into some of the other aspects of handicapping, like track bias and trips, that many players use to get an information edge. Lastly, we're going to take a look at the process of handicapping—how do our players go about breaking down a race in the first place?

SPEED FIGURES

One of the most important things that a new player needs to realize is a point we touched on in Chapter 1: Information edges are change-able because as information and knowledge become more recognized by the public, the betting markets self-correct and the prices become smaller. Historically, there is no better example of this than with speed figures. There was a time when Andrew Beyer had such a big edge over the crowd that he was able to play his "figure" horses with only minimal regard for the other factors of handicapping. But times have changed, and Beyer Speed Figures are available to anyone who buys a *Daily Racing Form.* Of course, even though the figures are no longer proprietary information, that's not to say they're not still an important factor in the game. They most certainly are.

ANDREW BEYER: "Obviously for most of my life, my speed figures have been my number-one focus. Years ago, before the world had figures, they were my overwhelming number-one factor. That was it, I bet the figures. Obviously, that approach isn't going to work today but nevertheless, the figures are always a frame of reference for me, they're rarely out of the equation."

It is amazing how much figures have changed the way that people play. Now, it's an everyday event to see a horse step up in class against a field with established form and still go off as a heavy favorite—if he has an advantage speed-figure wise. In the old days, these situations provided great betting opportunities. Now, many shrewd players try to plan their days around betting *against* these very same horses, which they would have been betting on 20 years ago.

DAVE GUTFREUND: "The best bets that you can make these days are when you have a horse with a lower Beyer number than another horse in the race but you think the horse is going to run better than the one with the higher number. Anybody can see that a horse that runs 90's is faster than one that runs 80's, and that gets taken into account in the betting."

We asked Beyer if he ever regretted his decision to sell his figures, thus making them available to the public.

ANDREW BEYER: "Not really. It was going to happen. If I hadn't done it, somebody else was going to. So at least I'm getting a nice check from *Daily Racing Form* as a compensation for the lower prices. The tool was just too potent. If I didn't do it, somebody else would have."

So why is it that the public has taken to speed figures like so many ducks to water? Are they *that* potent a tool? Yes and no. Yes, in the sense that nearly every player we talked to uses them in one form or another. But no in that, as Gutfreund implies above, their primary attraction to most of the crowd has more to do with ease of use than efficacy.

BARRY MEADOW: "When something is readily available, it's going to be utilized. For example, the Beyer figures are now available in the *Racing Form* so people are going to look at those figures and use those accordingly. People will do what's easier rather than what's more difficult. If there's a number sitting up there, people are going to rely on that number rather than delve into the race a little more deeply. That's just human nature."

The classic next step, as outlined by Beyer in his books, is to ask the question, how was the figure earned?

DAVE CUSCUNA: "You need to know, what were the conditions of the last race? If you run around the reservoir in Central Park, it's going to make a difference on your time whether you're doing it in February with snow on the ground or on a nice cool spring morning with low humidity and 60 degrees and no wind. If you start in a sprint, running as fast as you can, that's going to affect your final time versus an optimal steady-paced jog. If you lock yourself into looking at a horse's speed figure, you can get trapped if you don't consider what's behind that speed figure, and how is that speed figure going to be relevant as to what's going to happen in today's race."

BARRY MEADOW: "Many people just look at speed numbers. I always try to look at the context rather than just the figures. And you have to find discrepancies between what you think is going to happen and the tote board. Every race unfolds differently."

We asked Meadow to go into more detail and his response mirrored a lot of what Dave Cuscuna said above:

60

BARRY MEADOW: "Final times are always a product of what happened during the race. For example, if there was a fast pace and the horse was able to sit tight behind three duelers, then he's going to be able to run faster than he ordinarily would. Final time is only one factor and it's just one thing I look at; it's more important how the horse did the time and what he's capable of. If a horse usually runs Beyers in the 70's and then suddenly runs a 90, where did that 90 come from? Is he going to go back and run a 70 again or is he actually getting better? Maybe he had first-time Lasix or a big trainer change; maybe he suddenly stretched out when he was always sprinting. It's not just looking at figures and saying this one has a high figure so therefore he wins."

So what does he think of just betting the horse who runs the fastest figures?

BARRY MEADOW: "It's much more complex than that, everything is in context. A horse will run a good figure when he gets everything his own way. You can't base your handicapping on the fact that a horse had every miracle going his way on a particular day. You have to look at what that horse is basically capable of, the same way that if you're watching a basketball game and a guy who normally scores 10 points a game suddenly scores 24 points—is he suddenly going to score 24 points every game the rest of his career? Probably not, he'll probably end up scoring 10 points again."

Most of our players agreed that in today's game the most important use for speed figures is using them to separate the hopeless horses from the true contenders.

PAUL CORNMAN: "Speed figures play an important role in determining who is too slow. Plain and simple, if a horse has a high-percentage trainer (unless it's first time with that trainer) and it's coming off races where it didn't have good setups or whatever, if it's too slow, it's just too slow. But, in this day and age of many horses being over-raced, they're not going to run the same race all the time, you just have to be in the ballpark and get the right setup."

Brad Free offers up another way to use speed figures: by looking at pars. Pars are the average winning figure for a certain class level at a certain track. They can be obtained, at the time of this writing, through *DRF Simulcast Weekly*, or can be compiled by doing a little legwork with *Daily Racing Form*'s Formulator 4.0 software.

BRAD FREE: "The Beyer pars appear now in *Simulcast Weekly* and at some point in time they'll become part of the past performances. Beyer pars are crucial. Particularly so when you're handicapping a circuit that you don't know. And that's another reason why I like to step out of my own comfort zone sometimes and handicap other circuits. I have all the Beyer pars and it makes handicapping a claiming race at Laurel so easy for me. Even without knowing these horses, I know what it takes to win at that level, and I can eliminate horses easily who have never competed at that level if there's no reason to believe that they will today. So you're left with a handful of horses who can meet par.

"If you're going to use speed figures, you need to use the pars. Let's say there's a race where the par is 90 and none of the horses have ever exceeded 80, then the mistake that many players make who are using speed figures is to just take the horse who's been earning the highest numbers. If nobody can reach par, the speed-figure analysis is completely moot. If nobody can reach par, there's no standard of measure. None of them are fast enough. None of them qualify on speed figures. So don't use them. But many people will gravitate to the horse who's been earning 80's over the horse running a 74. And invariably that higher-figure horse who hasn't met par will be overbet and find a way to lose.

"The same thing happens in pace-figure analysis. If a horse cannot match the pace-figure par for the level, he almost always becomes a throw-out. And you see it all the time."

Andy Serling doesn't look at pars, but the way he uses speed figures is similar.

ANDY SERLING: "I look at speed figures as a guide. I believe in speed figures. Patterns and tops don't interest me. I'm not saying they're useless; they just don't interest me. I want to know that somewhere in a horse's form, he ran a race good enough to win this race—at least once. Because in at least one of his 12 races he must have gotten an ideal setup. And if his best possible race is good enough to beat any horse in this race, maybe I'll take a chance. Sometimes I'll find a wise-guy horse though and then I'll say, 'He's just too slow.'"

It was Steven Crist who first widely disseminated the Beyer Speed Figures when he put them in *The Racing Times*. Yet even he remains cautionary about accepting them at face value.

STEVEN CRIST: "Even though I think the Beyer Speed Figures are by leaps and bounds the best figs out there, I have continued to make my own during those periods of my life when I was handicapping and playing very seriously. It isn't that there are mistakes in the Beyers, but you learn so much more by rolling up your sleeves and analyzing the times yourself. And the truth is that there are races that just don't fit with the rest of a card or that come up suspiciously fast or slow, and even the Beyer crew is only making the best possible very-educated guess that they can, pending future verification. Knowing which races those are, and which figures are open to question, gives you a huge edge. The only way to put yourself in that position is to learn how to do it yourself."

■ Sheets

Unlike Beyer Speed Figures, which appear in each past-performance line, Len Ragozin's The Sheets and Jerry Brown's Thorograph numbers are printed on graphs, and modify basic speed figures by taking into account additional factors including ground lost and weight carried. The lower the number, the faster the race.

As with the Beyers, there was a time when the advantage from using the numbers alone was so strong that many players simply relied on them with little or no regard for other factors. None of our players, however, approaches the game this way. Still, a few of them, most notably Ernie Dahlman, do use these figures in their handicapping.

We asked Len Friedman, a professional player and also a partner at The Sheets, to describe them:

LEN FRIEDMAN: "Basically, the big advantage of The Sheets is that they give an accurate picture of the history of each horse—an accurate evaluation of each effort the horse has put out. And by graphing them on a piece of paper the way we do it, it gives you a visual picture that can enable you to read the direction that horses are going. It isn't just a question of which is the fastest horse in the race, which is of course an important thing, but it's also a matter of reading The Sheets and determining which way horses are going. To do that, you need very accurate numbers."

The Sheets and Thorograph have vociferous critics as well:

STEVEN CRIST: "Len Ragozin and Jerry Brown are extremely smart guys and they take their work very seriously and are true believers in their methodology. I just personally don't agree with them that you can arithmetically quantify the impact of things like ground and weight. So to my mind they're distorting speed figures and then drawing conclusions about patterns emanating from those distorted figures."

ANDREW BEYER: "Obviously a lot of high-end players use sheets, but I've always been kind of dubious about the idea that by looking for patterns of numbers, they are going to be able to foretell who is going to bounce and who is going to improve. I think that's even less so in this age of miracle-working trainers. To think that you can foretell horses without any reference to who is training them I think is a little delusional."

Friedman agrees 100 percent that the trainer angle is something that must be considered.

LEN FRIEDMAN: "The thing that I look at the most other than The Sheets is trainers. Trainers have a very big impact on the game now and there are trainers who you can expect different results from than other trainers. Certain trainers who if their horses just ran big, you can't be assuming that their horses are going to react from those efforts the way you would assume it for other trainers. Also, I look a lot at how a horse is being maneuvered. If I like a pattern on a horse and the trainer is moving it up even though he doesn't have to—let's say he didn't win last time and the trainer is still moving him up—I'm going to have a very positive opinion of that horse. I'm going to take that as a very positive sign."

We asked Friedman his opinion on the Beyer figures.

LEN FRIEDMAN: "The Beyers are a mechanical way of evaluating how fast the track is by averaging the various races and comparing them to pars for those races. You're going to get a figure that's in the ballpark that way. You're not going to get the kind of precise accuracy that we feel that we're getting. I don't think Beyer's an idiot. He's a very smart guy, a very good handicapper. What he's doing with his numbers isn't crazy, but it has its limits."

Some of our other players were critical of the idea that The Sheets and Thorograph are more "accurate" than the Beyers. One player, who wished to remain anonymous, said of sheets customers: "They're using what they perceive to be more advanced speed figures than the Beyer figures. In a lot of ways, and Len and Jerry wouldn't be too thrilled about my saying this, all they are selling is confidence. People who use sheets have this mind-set that they're getting better numbers than anybody else, and that confidence helps them as much as the numbers do."

In the end, it all comes down to context and one's ability to interpret the data in a unique way. There's no better example of a player using The Sheets in a unique way than Ernie Dahlman. As we'll get into a bit more in the next section on condition, a lot of players who look at sheets are looking for horses who might "bounce" and run poorly after a taxing effort or ones who have a nice "line" in their form, suggesting that they might improve significantly in today's race. Not so Dahlman.

ERNIE DAHLMAN: "No. I don't pay too much attention to the line on The Sheets. I don't believe in horses bouncing. I'm probably the only sheets player who doesn't believe in the bounce. I think there are usually other reasons why horses run well and run badly other than peak performance. When horses run their best races usually it's when things go well for them—a front-runner who gets a soft pace and goes off and runs a huge number, and I don't think it takes that much out of a horse. Or when a closer gets a fast pace and then goes running by everybody. It takes more out of a horse to get involved in a speed duel. And horses will run better numbers when they get a soft pace. To me, it's counterintuitive to think a horse running a big number in a race takes a lot out of them; to me they run a big number because they don't get as tired as the other horses."

65

CONDITION/FORM

CARY FOTIAS: "Len Ragozin did something very smart with The Sheets. Traditionally, a handicapper would ask of a certain horse, how does he stack up against this field? Instead, he was asking, how does he stack up against himself?"

That quote gets to the heart of what's known as condition analysis. One of the most important aspects of the game, and one that is still underrated by a good section of players—especially casual players—condition analysis is basically a fancy way of asking a simple question: Based on his current form, how is a certain horse going to run today? Will he improve? Can we expect him to do worse? Does it seem more likely that he'll give his usual effort (assuming he has one)? We asked Len Friedman to define condition analysis.

LEN FRIEDMAN: "Condition analysis is basically looking at the lifetime history of a horse to read whether it's in improving condition or declining condition. Mostly, it's looking for horses in improving condition but it's also looking for horses who have done something to indicate that they're going backwards. That's all that it really means. There are a lot of different aspects to it. On young horses it's generally a question of whether their peak performances are improving but it's also useful on older horses who are what we call recovery horses—horses who are moving back to prior peak efforts—to read their patterns to see if they're showing some indication that they are running back to those good numbers."

Condition analysis certainly wasn't invented by sheets players. Current form has always been an essential factor handicappers have used.

CARY FOTIAS: "Condition analysis is probably as old as the game itself, going back to Pittsburgh Phil and beyond. A lot of it before was probably more visual analysis. What's changed is that it's become more quantitative versus qualitative. But it's been there since the dawn of handicapping really, that's what it's all about."

Traditionally, the question asked was more along the lines of whether a horse would run a race good enough to be competitive.

BRAD FREE: "You have to be confident that your horse is going to fire. When I make a bet on a horse, I have to be relatively sure that he is going to fire, that he's going to put forth an effort. I want to be confident that it's a go. And that sounds a bit conspiratorial but let's face it, for various reasons, it's not always a go. I want to know that everybody's trying today."

In this traditional sense, form can often be sussed out simply by looking at a horse's last race. Did he run well? A good running line can also be less obvious: Was he in contention at the pace call or in the stretch? And form can be hidden much farther back in the running lines as well; for example, a horse who's been fading in grass routes now cuts back to seven furlongs on the dirt, where he's been successful before.

The concept of form has evolved over time into something more complicated. We asked Friedman about this.

LEN FRIEDMAN: "I'm not saying that we're doing something that nobody else ever thought of or that other people don't do in other forms. I'm sure that they do. We're looking to play horses whose recent form is strong and indicates that it's about to go forward. Everybody else is trying to do the same thing. The question is, how do you come to that conclusion? What's your methodology in deciding which horse fits and which horse doesn't fit? Small differences in what the pattern looks like have a very big impact on how we read the condition of the horse."

Joe Cardello demonstrated in his excellent book, *Speed to Spare*, that many of the same principles and patterns traditionally used by sheets players can be used with the Beyer numbers in the *Form* as well. "What's important is not just the speed figure a horse earned in his *last* race," Cardello wrote, "but how his recent Beyers led up to that figure. How does that figure fit into the overall pattern of Beyers for that horse? Can that pattern tell us anything valuable about what we can anticipate in that horse's next race?"

Cardello's book is full of interesting ideas about how to use the Beyer figures effectively in this day when the horses with the most recent top figures are nearly always overbet. In fact, he tackles this problem head-on by giving advice about which high-figure horses should be targets to bet *against*. He doesn't use the word "condition" to describe the kind of analysis he's doing, but to us, that's what it looks like, and it's the type of analysis that all horseplayers should try to do.

Cary Fotias also talked about the benefits of trying to view a race in terms of a horses' condition.

CARY FOTIAS: "My game is based on finding horses that are ready to make a move. The public thinks in a linear way, not a cyclical way. Most handicapping methods try to predict what's going to happen based on the past but the real goal is what's going to happen *today*."

This is where the real edge comes in for condition-oriented players. But the applications of form can be a lot simpler as well. Perhaps there's a horse in an allowance race. When last seen on the track in the afternoon six months ago, he was running in stakes races. You notice in the *Racing Form* that his trainer has a very low percentage in races returning off a long layoff. Will he win the race? That's unknowable, and it's dependent on a number of other factors. But from a condition standpoint, you can certainly expect that horse to run a race that's significantly less than his peak effort. In turn, regardless of whether he wins or loses in his comebacker, you can generally expect him to improve in his second start back, and quite possibly in his third start back.

This makes several assumptions—that he had enough time between his second and third starts, that he didn't produce an aberrant figure for another reason (he was lone speed in the comebacker, for example). This simplistic example makes an important point: You need to be able to look at a horse's past performance for clues as to how he's going to do in this race, today, based on his form, as much as you need to decide where he fits with the others in the race.

> **BRAD FREE:** "I'm not good enough to tell you which horses are about to make a big move up or down. Honestly, I'm not that clever. I can see a horse who's improving or a horse whose recent lines don't really paint the full picture, but I don't think I'm good enough to say, this horse is going to go through the roof today. And I don't have to be that good either. With the types of bets that I make, I can afford to be wrong an awful lot of the time. Do I expect every longshot I bet will make a giant forward move? Absolutely not. I just thought that the horse had a chance to win the race, maybe a 1-out-of-10 chance, and when I made the bet she was 20-1."

We asked Free for some examples of where looking at form has helped him:

> **BRAD FREE:** "There are many instances, though, where you can see just by looking at a horse's form that impending improvement just makes sense. Second-start maidens. Those are huge. They can jump up 30 points in one race. Sometimes it's obvious. I love horses moving into Grade 1 stakes races off of a series of losses. I love those horses, as long as they're trained by a guy who knows what he's doing and isn't just shooting for the moon. I typically assume that the Grade 1 race is the one they've been trying to knock down, that's been the goal all along and these losses do nothing more than cloud the form. People look and see, well, this horse isn't good enough. He's been losing Grade 2's and Grade 3's and he's not good enough. We see it every single year in the Kentucky Derby. How many times have we seen

horses who've been battling, coming off a loss into the Derby? Funny Cide, Monarchos, Unbridled, Ferdinand. Go for Gin. Thunder Gulch. The list goes on and on. That's why I love to bet the Derby, it's my favorite wagering event of the year. I think maybe the tide is turning with the types of horses that win but I'm not sure about that."

On the front lines of 21st-century condition analysis is Cary Fotias.

CARY FOTIAS: "As I've said, the most important factor for me is condition. My figures are based on speed and pace."

Like The Sheets and Thorograph, Fotias's commercially available product, The Xtras, provides final-time numbers in a graph format. They also include a pace number that helps the user understand at a glance something about how the race was actually run. Fotias believes that looking at the pace number in conjunction with the final-time number is more beneficial in determining the horse's current condition—that is, in figuring out what is likely to happen in a horse's next start.

CARY FOTIAS: "The whole idea is that by looking at the interrelationship between the pace and final numbers, you develop a truer model of the horse's current condition than you can by just looking at a final number. A final number doesn't tell you how that number was earned. But when you look at it with a pace number, you see how it was earned, which helps you understand better the overall development of the horse."

PACE

Fotias's pace ratings in The Xtras are based on sophisticated concepts developed by handicappers such as Howard Sartin and Tom Brohamer. Simply put, pace analysis is concerned with the way a race is run. On dirt, the main question is usually: How fast did they run early? On turf, more of an emphasis is placed on how quickly they came home. A few of the professional players we spoke with create and use similar ratings in their own handicapping. One thing they all share is that they try to envision the way a race is likely to set up.

PAUL CORNMAN: "I try and paint the picture of how the race is going to develop. That may be the most important thing to me, painting the picture of how the race is going to develop, put the contenders in certain spots and think how they may fire coming home. I'm a portrait guy. Say it's a six-furlong race, one of the things that I do that not many do, instead of looking at speed to see who's going to be there at a quarter of a mile, I'm pretty good at noticing quickness out of the gate. If there are three horses who appear to want to be on the lead, one of them will be quicker and that guy is going to establish the running order. I'm trying to paint the picture and set up where the contenders will be. Will the horse on the lead or the horse stalking have enough kick to be there at the end? Or do I think the race is going to collapse and on come the closers."

We don't plan on getting into a lengthy discussion about pace concepts here, as there is a ton of good stuff written about that in other books, most notably Brohamer's *Modern Pace Handicapping*, but we do want to take a look at how our players use pace in their calculations.

ANDREW BEYER: "For the main track or tracks that I'm following I do a pace rating that more-sophisticated handicappers would call pretty half-assed, but I want to be able to see at a glance if the pace of a horse's last race was fast, slow, or neutral. I'm not so much trying to see who's going to be one length in front after a quarter mile because I don't think realistically, given the nature of jockeys, that you can do that. I want to be aware if a horse is coming out of a super-fast or super-slow pace in his last race."

ANDY SERLING: "Obviously you want to see if it's going to be a fast pace or a slow pace and see how that's going to effect the participants. And you can also use it to judge a horse's previous races by saying, 'Wow, this is a speed horse and he's been caught in two vicious speed duels the last two races.' Maybe today he's in a better situation so it doesn't matter that he finished eighth the last two times. This is obvious stuff."

Brad Free talks about the impact of pace analysis on his handicapping:

BRAD FREE: "Pace analysis has been the biggest influence on my handicapping over the last six or eight years. When I moved back to Southern California a few years ago and took up my old position as a handicapper here, one of the things I knew I had to learn, because I knew it was a weakness, was the whole pace-analysis/pace-figure methodology. So I sat down and I learned it. I read all of Tom Brohamer's stuff and I subscribed to his service. I started making my own rudimentary pace figures and started incorporating them into my handicapping. I cannot handicap a race without using pace figures.

"Pace is huge to me because it clarifies everything. It's the old saying, 'It's not how fast the horse runs, but how a horse runs fast.' That's a cute little cliché saying but it doesn't mean anything if you can't quantify that. And what pace figures do is paint the picture in black and white. It tells you exactly how a horse earned that final figure by giving a number to the pace call. It has opened my eyes so much.

"The unfortunate thing is that I see it on the tote board because it's opened a lot of people's eyes. But I still use them and I can't come to a complete understanding of a race without looking at the pace figures that all the horses have earned."

There are many players who believe that early speed—sometimes called the universal track bias of American dirt racing—may be the single most important factor in handicapping. Gerry Okuneff explains one reason why this is.

GERRY OKUNEFF: "The first thing I look for is a horse with a turn of speed—if a horse has speed, he's rarely going to break poorly and he'll be able to avoid trouble during the course of the race. The only way a horse who fits that description isn't going to be a contender is if he's in over his head in class terms or off form or if there's too much other speed in the race. Speed and pace of the race are incredibly important."

What questions does he ask himself specifically when looking at the positional pace matchups in a given race?

GERRY OKUNEFF: "I can narrow it down to: Does this race have a pace that will help speed? Do I have a fit speed horse who was cooked previously, and who quit, setting it up for a closer? Did the other speed horse from the previous race come back and run well?"

For serious players like Okuneff, this is still just a starting point. It's not like you can just look at early pace in isolation; it needs to be used in conjunction with all the other factors.

STEVEN CRIST: "I've met people who say they are 'speed handicappers,' and it turns out they like to bet on horses with early speed. I don't even know what that means. It's like someone saying he's an investor and likes to buy stocks that begin with the letter 'B.' I resist those labels. I don't think you can win without an understanding of speed *and* pace *and* class *and* a bunch of other things."

As you've already seen by now, in the ever-evolving game that is horse racing, the crowd catches up. Take the classic pace player's example of the lone front-runner:

ROXY ROXBOROUGH: "In my opinion, the strongest factor is the lone front-runner. But now everyone knows it and pays attention to it; so I'll take it a step further. I'll look for a horse that can go to the front even though its form shows that it typically doesn't. I'll typically bet one horse who's going to get an easy lead—but I'll also watch that it's not overbet."

DAVE GUTFREUND: "When there's only one front-runner in the race and he's definitely going to make the lead, that's a bad situation because everybody sees it. What you'd like to find is a hidden pace scenario in a situation like that. A simple example is a sprinter stretching out. If a horse has been fourth in sprints, he's more likely to be a leader in a route race."

An interesting contrarian point of view about pace comes from Len Friedman:

LEN FRIEDMAN: "I don't look at pace at all in races. The only exception to that is long-distance grass races, and I mostly handle that problem by not betting them. It's just that so many of them are ridiculously slow paces these days that I don't want to spend the time and effort if it's going to be that way."

So what does he think about pace analysis in general?

LEN FRIEDMAN: "I think that the influence of pace is grossly overstated. I think there are some isolated incidents where what the horse does early does have an impact on what it can do late. I've often had the temptation to try and work that out myself and we've done a little work on that and someday we may even finish it. But the little work that we did suggested that it was a rare occurrence, not a regular occurrence. That is, what these horses are doing is only a result of what they did early under extreme circumstances. There are numbers that we give out of horses that we call quit numbers—numbers of what they did in an earlier part of the race than the finish line. And I would say that one of the reasons that horses get quit numbers is that they ran unrealistically fast early. But it doesn't happen all that often."

But surely he agrees that pace has *some* influence. Friedman explains:

LEN FRIEDMAN: "I think a very careful pace analysis could be useful to other people. Maybe it could allow somebody to avoid a situation—which doesn't happen often but does happen occasionally— where you have a front-runner and it's up against some other horse who runs so fast early that your horse is going to get killed by that horse, because the people who manage that horse think he has to have the lead. I think that it's almost always the case where if the people were willing to take the front-runner and just sit three lengths off the other horse, then they could run their number. But since they won't do that and they will go to the lead, then they're going to get killed by that other horse."

What about a situation where a closer is compromised because there isn't enough pace in the race?

LEN FRIEDMAN: "I don't think it's nearly as common as other people think that a closer can't win because there's no pace. The only time I think that happens is on the grass. On the dirt I don't think that happens hardly at all. And if you look at dirt races you can see why it doesn't make sense that that would happen because the truth is that they're all slowing down at the end anyway in all dirt races. Even in the races where there isn't any speed early, the horses are all running faster at the beginning than they were at the end. But that's not true on the grass. You can have a grass race where they're running much faster at the end than at the beginning. The funny part of it is that on the grass, you can get caught by having a closer who doesn't have as much of a chance because the pace is too slow and on the dirt you can get caught by having a closer when the pace is too fast early. The risks are exactly opposite in dirt and turf racing."

Another player, who wanted to remain anonymous, saw things differently. He said, "It is certainly the case that turf racing and dirt racing are two fundamentally different animals. The fractions tell you everything. You don't see increasingly fast fractions on the dirt. I've always had the feeling that some closers do better in paceless races on the grass—because the fields are bunched, and in those kinds of races it can turn into a European type of race. In European races, they walk early and closers win all the time. The ability to accelerate is more valuable in turf racing because of the way the races are run. But if he wants to bet closers in 24, 48 on the dirt, God bless him."

The next question is: How can the average player endeavor to incorporate a deeper pace analysis into his or her handicapping?

MARYLAND PLAYER: "Just off the top of my head here are arguably three ways. One is to just look to play races where the speed looks like it's going to win. That's not as profitable now as it once was but that's the easiest way.

"The second way would be to use Formulator 4.0. It's really changed the tools at your disposal. You no longer need to be one of these guys who saves charts and all that. It's there for you. [Using Formulator, with a few clicks you can look at a horse's individual incremental splits and the fractions of all the races run that day.] The only excuse you have now is laziness. And the third way is kind of a reverse of the first way. To bet races where there are nothing but speeds and wait for the race to fall apart. It's never as easy as it sounds but you do see races where the speed just has to fall apart."

ANDY SERLING: "Always remember that time is relative. I don't make my own pace figures but you better have the notes in front of you or look up the charts for a given day before you decide whether a pace was fast or not because there are times when 22⅘ will be faster than 21⅗. Faster is relative in horse racing.

"Also, you could make a diagram for yourself. Set the horses up where they're going to be after the first quarter-mile of the race. I've done that for big races like the Breeders' Cup races. You teach yourself. Where are they going to be at the quarter, the half, the top of the stretch. Give yourself an idea. It teaches you to look at the races logically and there's no substitution for good, sound logic in handicapping."

BRAD FREE: "I wish there was an easy answer but it requires an awful lot of work. Even now, six years later, I'm still learning about what I'm doing in terms of using pace. I don't think there are any shortcuts in any area of handicapping, particularly not in pace. You probably have to sit down and get through Brohamer's book, *Modern Pace Handicapping*. Understand the Sartin methodology. *Pace Makes the Race*, the book by Tom Hambleton. Read Quinn's *Figure Handicapping*. Those were the big influences for me. You also need to get the pace figures somehow. There are some that are available commercially."

STEVEN CRIST: "I taught myself to make pace figures in 1991 just as I had done with speed figures 10 years earlier, by inputting thousands of times and creating my own parallel-time charts and pars. It's tricky but when you get it right the light goes on and there's a Eureka moment. Final time is often a function of pace, and knowing which final-time figures were either enhanced or compromised by the pace gives you insights that 999 of every 1,000 horseplayers won't have."

CLASS

CARY FOTIAS: "I think class is overrated and is only really a factor for me at the highest levels."

Traditionally, class has been considered a handicapping factor on par with the others we've been discussing in this chapter. The term "class" refers to the level at which a horse is able to compete. Class, however, has its critics, notably Len Ragozin, who has written that very often, what people call class is really speed in disguise.

Others think of "class" as being synonymous with "form," and it often is. When you hear people talk about the form of a given race, they are discussing the class of the horses who competed in it. As far as we're concerned, the difference between form and class was recently summed up by a soccer announcer on the BBC during the Euro 2004 championship tournament: "Form is fickle; class is permanent." In other words, sometimes what a horse needs to do to find his form is to run at the level he was born capable of competing at. And some horses are born with the ability to compete at a higher level than others.

We think that the debate over class is largely one of semantics. The fact is that you need to at least understand the basics of numerous class angles if you want to improve your game—whether you ultimately decide that you believe class is on par with the other fundamental factors or not.

None of the players we interviewed considers class on a par with the other fundamental factors, though the great majority agree that it's a concept you must at the very least understand if you want to improve.

MARYLAND PLAYER: "I look at class. The classic example would be a horse who's shown speed in a maiden special weight dropping into a maiden $35K or something. Horses off that kind of drop are just light years ahead. But in terms of a horse who was running for $25K and now he's running for $20K, who cares?

"I wouldn't say that I'm dismissive of class because I'm not. It matters, but not as much as it did in handicapping 20 or 25 years ago. I just think that now there are so many other methodologies out there."

BRAD FREE: "All I typically insist on is for a horse to have shown that he or she has been competitive at that level. And for me, competitive is a very broad guideline. Maybe they've hit the board, or maybe they were in contention at the pace call—even if they were just in the top half of the field at the pace call at a couple of levels higher. Class is not a specific measurement. I just want to show that he's in the hunt. If he's in the hunt at that level, then he fits. I'm not going to bet a horse that has 20 starts, one win, and eight seconds. But if a horse wins 15 or 20 percent of his starts and has established himself at that level, then I'm going to assume that he fits on class."

Are there instances where class takes on more importance?

BRAD FREE: "Class becomes paramount when you're dealing with grass routes. Everything else is extremely speed- and pace-figure oriented. Class just takes on so much more importance when you're going two turns on grass than it does at any dirt distance, with the possible exception of Grade 1 for older horses. On grass, class is a helluva lot more important to me than any figure or come-home time that you can possibly have. Grass racing to me is much simpler to handicap. That doesn't mean it's easier to win at, but it's simpler to handicap because it's all about class. It's who beats who. I do look at figures on the grass but I don't even really need to."

ANDY SERLING: "In grass racing I do look at which horses the horse has raced against, because speed figures are basically useless in turf racing so you better have a good understanding about relative horses' abilities. You better be smart enough to be intuitive about that."

KENTUCKY PLAYER: "I'm not a big believer in class. Probably the weakest part of my game is turf handicapping and that might be why."

Class provides a great example of how the basic factors of handicapping are intertwined. Brad Free, writing in *Handicapping 101*, commented: "The fundamentals of handicapping are codependent. Analysis of current form, class, speed, and pace cannot be done independently of one another. A horse in peak condition can only be

77

expected to run well if he is spotted at a realistic class level. A horse at the proper level can only compete, typically, if his speed figures are appropriate to the level and the competition. A horse will earn credible speed figures only if the pace is suitable. It's a circle."

TRAINERS

No individual has more of an impact on how a horse is going to perform than the trainer. Some seem to move up every horse they put a halter on. Others seemingly couldn't train a squirrel to run up a tree. Every one of the players we spoke with gives at least some consideration to the trainer in most instances. For some, it's more of a secondary factor. But several of our players use the trainer as their main frame of reference when looking at a race. Others go even farther than that—barely considering the basic building blocks of handicapping in favor of detailed trainer analysis—though none of our guys advocates such an extreme approach.

Trainer-angle handicapping has had some major developments in recent years. One is the supertrainer phenomenon. Another is the proliferation of information available in the *Daily Racing Form*, first with Steven Crist's introduction of race-specific trainer statistics into the past performances in 2002 and then the launch of Formulator 4.0 two years later. We'll delve deeper into an analysis of these things later in the chapter, but let's start off by taking a look at why trainers are important.

PAUL BRASETH: "I look at trainers because the trainers have such a huge influence over how a horse is going to perform. Not only do they train their horses well, but they put their horses in the right places and they put somebody on the horse that is going to give it a good chance to win. So the form is more likely to go in some sort of logical progression than it is with poorer trainers."

GERRY OKUNEFF: "I believe the trainer is infinitely more important than the jock overall. There's a different relationship. A jock listens to instructions, largely ignores them, and then gets on the next horse.

The trainer has a much larger job and they're not as visible as the jockeys. The good ones spend tremendous amounts of time around their horses and make decisions, read a condition book, spot horses. It seems so elementary, but some don't believe it. I've survived the racetrack knowing training patterns, those who can't train—I call them magicians. Their horses disappear at the head of the lane."

PAUL BRASETH: "Steve Davidowitz said it a long time ago: In the hands of one trainer a horse with improving form may continue to improve and go on to win again. If it's an incompetent trainer, the horse may collapse."

There is another school of thought that says while the importance of the trainer is undeniable, it can't be considered on a par with the fundamental handicapping factors.

JAMES QUINN: "Traditional handicapping factors are extremely important. Like any game worth playing, it's important to be fundamentally sound. I believe speed and pace are primary in claiming races. In non-claiming races, I'm looking more at class and form patterns.

"Situational factors—distance, trips, trainer, jockey, post—none of these factors are unimportant. These can become important and decisive, but they don't directly affect the abilities of the horses.

"I'm always amazed at players who are playing for a while and they have a hard time fundamentally handicapping the race. Most aren't sound—they really haven't come to terms with analyzing a horse's basic ability—class, form, speed, and pace."

BRAD FREE: "I do consider secondary factors. There are very few circumstances when they are more important than the fundamentals, but you do need to address them. It's not very often that you're going to have an advantage if you only consider those four basic things. In fact, the argument has been made that in this day and age, there should be five factors and the fifth should be the trainer. I disagree. I want to address the horse and the horse's ability. I don't want to address the guy who's pulling the strings over the animal. Is he in form, does he fit at the class, how fast is he? If I start with the trainer as a fundamental factor, I would have to trust in him or her too much. I want to make the assessment of the horse myself. I don't want another person doing it for me. I want to be right or wrong based on my own knowledge. That is not to say I don't consider the trainer—I do. Just not as one of the fundamentals."

While Jim Mazur is among those who consider the trainer more fundamentally, he also agrees that the trainer factor does not trump everything else.

JIM MAZUR: "You have to be a really sharp handicapper and a generalist. You can have a specialty but you can't just use speed sheets at the exclusion of everything else. That's a total fallacy. There are guys who do it but I don't think it's a healthy approach. I tell our readers you can't just use our trainer stats. Just because a guy hits with 50 percent on a certain angle, if the horse is a cripple, he's not going to win. You have to look at everything."

Mazur's meet-specific books are a terrific handicapping product. In addition to sharing the statistical data in a portable, convenient form, he and his partners write informative, entertaining essays detailing certain potent moves and intriguing tendencies from different trainers.

So how exactly does a guy like Jim Mazur go about incorporating his trainer data into his handicapping?

JIM MAZUR: "The first thing that I do is use our material and isolate the trainers in the race that have a high-percentage winning average in a certain category, if there are any, and I simply jot down next to the trainer's name a shorthand of what kind of category that would be: a stretchout, a drop in class, etc. Then I write the actual winning percentage of the trainer. I do the same with low percentages. If a trainer is 0 for 50 on the turf, I'll note that. Before I even look at the horses, I'm looking at which trainers I think can win the race and which trainers I don't think can win the race, and then at that point I start looking at the actual horses.

"Then I do basic handicapping like any other handicapper; I'll look at the pace scenario, the running styles of all the participants to see if there's likely to be a lone front-runner or a speed duel that benefits a horse that might sit back a little bit, and I'll also look for a few other items I think are very important, like horses for the course; I'll circle their record for the distance as well, and then I'll maybe take a look at some other intangibles like horses who were maybe bet heavily in their last race and are maybe forgotten today.

"Also horses who are getting a change of jockey or certain workouts that look enticing, just general handicapping after that and then I'll make my decision on what I'm going to do.

"The information I have usually enables me to move away from the pack."

Looking at the trainer factor first is an uncommon technique and leads to many contrarian plays. Another interesting thing that Mazur's numbers chart is how trainers do when their horses go off at different price ranges on the board. Importantly, this information isn't as readily available as many of the other trainer stats out there.

JIM MAZUR: "There are some amazing stats with trainers in the odds category. Enrique Alonzo is a guy who's 9 percent at Gulfstream Park, which is below average. But he is 3 for 4 when bet down to 5-2, and his other horse hit the board as well. If he's got something good, it's going to run. At greater than 20-1, he's 1 for 44. Because he's sort of an obscure trainer, he'll hit a few in the 5-2 to 10-1 range that'll slip by. He's 3 for 21 between 5-2 and 5-1, but he's 71 percent in the money. When his horses are bet, that's a good sign.

"Look at Eddie Broom at Gulfstream. He's 0 for 34 at 11-1 or higher. He's a 17 percent trainer overall. In your pick threes you don't want any part of his longshots.

"Mark Hennig? He's 0 for 71 at 11-1 and higher at Gulfstream. Todd Pletcher: 1 for 37 over 10-1 at Gulfstream."

There was a time when doing the legwork to keep your own trainer stats could give you a big edge on the crowd, but as more information becomes available, it gets a little trickier.

JAMES QUINN: "On training patterns: I do look but it's less profitable today because a lot of the training form patterns are in the

Form, plus there are other services that provide that kind of information—unless you have an angle that no one else has. One of the best players I ever met was Paul Braseth; he's great with trainer form and form patterns."

PAUL BRASETH: "When I started playing the races seriously I decided I wanted to know as much as I could about trainers, and in those days there wasn't much information available on trainers. So I started keeping records on their individual percentages in various categories and various trainer maneuvers—class drops, layoffs, first-time starters, second out after a layoff, you name it. I developed what I used to call my hierarchy of handicapping needs. James Quinn actually coined that phrase. But for me, the number-one priority in races was knowing as much as I could about the trainer—that became number one on my handicapping-hierarchy list.

"And number two, I felt I could get an edge on trips and track biases, incidental handicapping factors in the races.

"And number three was speed figures and pace figures. I still pretty much hold to that progression when it comes to what I think is most important."

■ If Everyone Has Trainer Data, Is It Still Important?

When trainer data first began appearing, it was in the form of macro statistics—how a trainer performed in certain categories over the past few years (e.g., first off a 30- to 60-day layoff, on turf, etc.). Now the *Daily Racing Form* offers a tool that is, in our eyes, far more powerful. With Formulator 4.0, you can access the past performances of every horse sent out by every trainer in the last five years. Best of all, there are filters so you can check a trainer's performance customized to specific categories. In other words, you can look at every layoff horse, or every turf horse, or every stretchout horse that a certain trainer ran at a specific meeting.

If you look at how a trainer operates in this micro way, it's easier to see the patterns emerge in a more meaningful way, as opposed to just trying to find significance in the cold data of the statistics. How important is it when a trainer puts a certain rider up? How often does a trainer really give a horse a race? How are his or her horses bet in certain situations? In the old days, these questions would have taken hours and hours of labor and clipping past performances to determine. Now they're available with the click of a few buttons.

STEVEN CRIST: "Formulator just completely turbocharges trainer analysis. I'm most interested in trainer info in very specific situations, like first-time starters and first-time back off long layoffs. It was helpful to be able to tell people that a certain guy is 12 percent with a certain move, but being able to go into a sortable database with every horse that he's run under those circumstances takes it to a whole other level. I can look at that guy's record and see where that 12 percent comes from—what class and distances of races, what riders he uses. I'm a multirace player and I'm frequently betting blind into races with firsters. Instead of saying, 'Gee, that guy's 12 percent, I guess I have to include him,' now I can get a much better fix on whether he's more like 4 percent or 20 percent in a situation like today's."

STEVE DAVIDOWITZ: "I found my edge originally by doing a lot of homework, and now a lot of that info is included in the *Racing Form*—training patterns, like which trainers give a horse a race, which ones point for which meets, etc.

"Now everyone has access to the info but few people know how to use it. When information becomes more available it's still important—but you have to use the information more precisely, whether it's speed figures or training patterns."

PAUL BRASETH: "Yeah, it does bother me that so much trainer info is now available. On the other side of that, though, the trainer angle is something that a lot of people aren't very comfortable with. They like numbers. They like figures. This is a little too esoteric for a lot of people, even big players, so there's still an edge there."

Ernie Dahlman is another player who uses trainer information to provide context to his handicapping. We asked him if he also minds how readily available trainer info has become.

ERNIE DAHLMAN: "I should say yes but the answer is no. Because I always just kind of remembered that stuff anyway, I didn't really keep the records. So the fact that the Racing Form keeps the records, I kind of like that, because I think a lot of people don't put enough meaning into trainer stats anyway."

In an interview he did with Barry Meadow in the newsletter *Meadow's Racing Monthly*, Dahlman mentioned an instance in which there was more to understanding the game than just looking at a statistic in a vacuum.

ERNIE DAHLMAN: "Mack Miller always used to fire with his grass horses in May off a layoff, because there were no grass races in the winter in New York, so he freshened them for the upcoming season. So Miller had good layoff numbers. But if he had a dirt sprinter in September who was laid off since May, that would be a negative—the horse was probably injured, rather than being rested. If you didn't understand the difference for those two types of layoff horses, you were in trouble."

In the previous chapter we talked about how betting opportunities can arise when the short-term trend differs from the long-term trend (or perceived trend). Paul Braseth and Dave Cuscuna both touched on this when it comes to trainers.

PAUL BRASETH: "I place a lot of emphasis also on what trainers are doing at the moment. I do that regularly. I don't know what causes trainers' hot and cold streaks but they certainly exist. I think their horses all just cycle up at the same time. Some trainers just point for various meets. A lot of it is just that when things are going well, the attitude around the barn is good, and maybe people who are working for the trainer do a better job. I hesitate to say that that feeling of optimism moves up the horse. But you know yourself, that whatever you do, if everyone around you is in a good state of mind, it does make a difference."

DAVE CUSCUNA: "I have a friend, a good handicapper, and what he'll do is find when a particular stable is about to win 9 out of 19 races—he'll figure it out when he's 2 for 4 and he'll ride those next seven wins at good prices a lot of the time. I guess the way he does it—I haven't asked him—but if he sees a horse who figures to run dead pop a big race, he'll file that away right away and say, 'Maybe this barn is heating up.' If a couple of horses outrun their odds for a particular stable that tells him that maybe the stable is getting hot. Of course sometimes it can also just be a fluctuation. If you flip a coin, sometimes it's going to come up heads eight times in a row. Heads didn't get hot, that's random chance. Or sometimes a guy who hits .212 is going to go 6 for 8 at some point during the season; he'll also go 1 for 26 and in the end it'll work out to .212."

PAUL CORNMAN: "As far as narrowing down the field and looking for winners or looking for a key, that changes all the time. Thoroughbred racing to me has turned into a trainer's game. It's almost like you're looking at the people more than the past performances some of the time.

"Look at the percentages. When I started out obviously the fields were bigger so it was harder to put up a high percentage, but there were hardly any 20 percent trainers and now you have 25 percent and up all over the place. Ah, the tricks of the trade!"

■ Supertrainers

Following trainers is one thing, but a recent trend has emerged—certain trainers who are almost certain to move up the horses who arrive in their care, as if controlled by some metaphysical force. These are what Andrew Beyer calls the supertrainers.

ANDREW BEYER: "I'm always going to pay attention to trainers. In my early days as a horseplayer, I kept index cards on all of the major trainers on the circuit, looking for patterns, etc. You have so much racing data that's in the Form now with trainers' percentages doing a hundred different things that I've kind of stopped doing that and this winter I've decided to go back to the basics. The trainer factor today is having a greater impact than it almost ever has.

"My seminar at the DRF Expo was about that. In the past you had trainers making conventional moves, guys who were good with first-time starters or stretching them out in distance. Now, the major concern is trainers whose horses' performances defy all logic. I just want to be attuned to who these people are. If Gulfstream opens and some trainer I've never focused on suddenly wakes up a couple of horses, I want to be immediately conscious of that. When a trainer does something interesting I'm going to put it in kind of a rudimentary spreadsheet and be more focused on trainers than I ever have been before."

Our own suspicions aside, we had to ask Beyer what he thought was at the root of the supertrainer phenomenon.

ANDREW BEYER: "We're only dealing with the effects. Even though we all suspect larceny, whether it is or not is almost irrelevant. Just knowing that a trainer one way or another has the power to transform horses, you just have to be aware of who is doing it and if they are so potent that the horse's previous form means nothing."

What has this done to the more traditional trainer analysis?

ANDREW BEYER: "Trainer analysis used to be full of subtleties. You'd pore over stacks of *Racing Forms* and find a guy who was good with first-time starters or good on the stretchout. Now, you look at the *Form* and say, 'Hey, Michael Pino is winning 40 percent at Delaware Park.' Unfortunately, the most important trainer angles are the unsubtle ones that most people see."

Len Friedman also spoke us to us about the supertrainers, though he used different terminology:

LEN FRIEDMAN: "You need to know who are what we call the 'move-up' trainers; you can't play a circuit without knowing that. You can't possibly play Oaklawn without knowing about Cole Norman. It's just silly. Or California without knowing about Jeff Mullins. There was a horse in California recently that ran five times and his line was something like 27-19-35-18-25. It hit a 19 and then an 18. You could even say it was a positive condition horse except that the in-between numbers were so terrible. Then it switched to Jeff Mullins and ran 5-11-5. Now you've taken a horse who can't win a maiden $35K claimer and now it's running numbers that could win a Grade 3 stakes. It just happened overnight. If you're trying to play and you don't know things like that, you're going to be at an awful big disadvantage."

So how do professional players deal with this phenomenon?

RANDY GALLO: "You know something, I try to stay out of those races, like with Michael Gill's horses last year (2003) at Gulfstream. I can't prove that anything was done wrong. But I can tell you when horses don't run over a 70 Beyer and then Michael Gill claimed this horse and he ran 6½ furlongs in 1:15 ⅗, won by eight, and ran a 108 Beyer or something like that; it can't happen, it just can't happen. I want to stay out of those races."

MARYLAND PLAYER: "You can duck them to some extent. Most of these trainers tend to not be very good on the grass. Michael Gill and Mark Shuman didn't win a grass race in the first two months of Gulfstream last winter (2003).

"From the Oscar Barrera days forward, these miracle workers have always seemed to be much more effective on the dirt than they have on the grass. And that's because grass training is a skill. You need fit horses. It seems to require more horsemanship than the dirt does. You look at the percentages of these guys—and that's a bad generalization because these guys certainly aren't all the same—but for a number of the trainers people put in that category, they tend to be a lot better on the dirt than the grass, so that's one place you can look to avoid them."

Many believe, however, that the problem is spreading rapidly, right up to the highest levels of the game, making it nearly impossible to avoid.

ANDREW BEYER: "In this era where we think that the drug problem is out of control, the lesser tracks seem to be the cleaner ones. This is a change from the way racing used to be but the new drugs that are making trainers into miracle workers are sufficiently expensive that they're really more apt to find them in Grade 1 stakes than in a $5K claimer at Tampa Bay."

It doesn't seem to us that there's any real solution to the super-trainers problem except trying to be aware of who they might be and avoiding them when we can. If you use Formulator 4.0, you can at least try to ascertain if there are any situations in which trainers who win races at a 30 percent clip suddenly become fallible.

OTHER EDGES

The five factors we examined in this chapter—speed, form, pace, class, and trainers—are the starting points for most of the players we talked to. It's important to note that an extremely patient non-professional player might be able to wait for opportunities when the crowd gets it wrong and only make plays based on the fundamental factors.

BRAD FREE: "I'm not a professional handicapper, though I play every day. But I don't have to make a bet every day. I can wait until I see something screwed up on the board. For example, Saturday, I went out to the track to get caught up on all my stuff because I'd been off for a week. I had no intention of betting on anything. I was interested in watching the Mother Goose, which was a nonbetting race for me. So it was like 15 minutes to the first post and I was sitting there going, 'Okay, this favorite is just a bad animal. I know this horse. She finishes second every time she runs.'

"So I look around and I find a horse that I kind of like and she's 20-1. I say, 'You know what, the public has made a mistake.' The horse I liked was a Doug O'Neill stretchout. The last time she routed on turf she was on the lead at the eighth pole and then propped and lost the rider. She had four lifetime starts and been beaten 13 or 20 lengths every single time. She wins by a nose and pays $91. But that's not the type of horse that I'm shopping for. It's just sometimes they're there and you just have to make the bet."

This is a model of play that we casual-serious players are able to emulate. For the pros, though, it's more complicated. If you're looking to make a living playing the horses, you need to make more bets, a lot more bets. A study of trips and track biases gives many of the professional players we spoke with a powerful tool to separate themselves from the crowd.

■ Trips

A horse's trip describes what happens to him during a given race. Was he inside or outside? Close up or far back? Did he break slowly? Did he have to check while he was gathering his momentum? Did he not have enough room to get through a hole in the stretch? The answers to all these questions can help us interpret a horse's form and put his speed and pace numbers in context.

When looking at trips, you're really looking for a reason a certain horse is going to run better or worse next time than would be expected just by looking at the *Daily Racing Form.*

ANDREW BEYER: "I put a great deal of emphasis nowadays on horses' trips. When I'm following a race meet seriously I'll watch the races, make notes on the horses, enter them in my computer so I'll have my own notes about how the horses ran. If I see any blockbuster trips they'll also go in the *Racing Form*'s Horse Watch so I'm absolutely sure I'm not going to miss them or overlook them."

RANDY GALLO: "I find my edge in what I see. I can only judge a race by what I see. I'm a trip handicapper and I'm trying to find an edge where the public might not see it or I think I see something that the public doesn't see.

"I watch every race. I can't see every race at every track but at the track that I'm dealing with, I try to stay on top of it. The public has so much more information now that they didn't have years ago as far as breeding goes and firsters and whatever—they're educated so there's hardly any margin for error. You've got to be pretty good."

Admittedly, Cary Fotias doesn't do a lot of trip work but he respects the guys who do it well.

89

90

CARY FOTIAS: "It takes a really trained eye to see what is a good trip and what isn't a good trip, especially in grass racing where you see horses get steadied all the time. It doesn't really mean anything unless a horse is really blocked late in the race because they're all storing up their energy anyway. I think the biggest edge there—and I don't have the time to do it—is with people who have the time to train themselves not to watch their horse, but to watch all the horses and, more important, to watch what's happening in the rear of the field. Most people see trouble in the top three or four but they don't see it so often with the trailers."

But don't just think you can watch a couple of replays and suddenly start reaping the benefits of a real trip player.

MARYLAND PLAYER: "I'm looking for what I call hidden tough trips, where a horse is making a move and I think they've got horse and then something happens and they don't continue to move. I'm looking for trips that give you prices. The obvious tough trips are the worst bets in the world. The horse that gets stopped at the sixteenth pole and then runs on and gets third when he would have won? Who cares? It's a much more subtle thing than that."

ANDY SERLING: "A lot of trip handicapping is legwork. Taking down extensive notes. Writing down where every horse was on the turn. And it's not so bad. Because one thing it does, especially if you're a newcomer, is it teaches you to watch races. And it teaches you things about race-watching that don't necessarily have to do with what many people would categorize as trips. A certain horse is on the rail but he maybe doesn't like running inside of horses and he got kind of trapped in there and maybe he saved all the ground but he didn't have a clear running path. And even though ground loss can be a factor on both turns, I think it's much worse to be wide on the first turn because you're jockeying for position and trying to save ground. On the second turn, you'd rather be on the outside, running unencumbered.

"And it's things like that, learning about winning trips and what kind of trips aren't winning trips. You have to learn to watch races and understand—did the flow of this race help or hinder this horse? Maybe the average guy is going to tell you, 'This horse saved all the ground and didn't run.' I'm going to tell you he could have had an easier trip outside. These are things you have to teach yourself. I can't defend them on a mathematical level. You have to hope you have a good eye for it and you're smart enough to be right."

CARY FOTIAS: "To really draw any firm conclusions from it you've really got to be an expert at it. Too many people that say they're trip handicappers don't really know what they're talking about. I respect people that are really good at it. That's what's so great about the game. There are so many ways to attack it and it just isn't humanly possible for someone to be an expert in all areas. There just aren't enough hours in the day."

Our Maryland Player talks about how trip handicapping has evolved over the years:

MARYLAND PLAYER: "Like anybody else when I started playing the flats I was totally clueless. I thought I knew what I was doing long before I knew what I was doing; that's kind of a normal human characteristic to think you're smarter than you are. I suppose in many ways the things that made the biggest difference to me were peculiar. Really for me, the availability of films of the races in bars and places like that was very important.

"In terms of a single event that made my handicapping better, it was the invention of the VCR. Because once you had tapes, you could see the races as often as you wanted to.

"The other thing that made a huge difference, and this is advancing up to the mid-eighties, when [Frank] De Francis bought Laurel, he put in the Sports Palace and put in the tapes at the track with the head-ons; that made a huge difference. It went from a binoculars game to a videotape game. I'm kind of sad to say, I don't even have a decent pair of binoculars anymore."

One of the most notable things about trip handicapping is how subjective it is. It cannot be quantified with a number the way that speed and pace can. In fact, what one person thinks is a bad trip, another can think was just fine. A perfect example has to do with being wide. Both the Ragozin and Thorograph sheets add extra credit for a horse who runs wide on the turns, and these horses do in fact end up running farther than horses that save ground around the turns. But there are other considerations as well.

> **CARY FOTIAS:** "Ground loss can be a factor, I'm not denying that. But to make a standard, up-front adjustment for it is courting inaccuracy. Sometimes the rail is bad and you're penalizing horses for running on the worst part of the track. Meanwhile, horses that are swinging four- or six-wide in the best footing, you're making their numbers better. And it's not just that. Anybody can figure out from geometry how much ground you lose from being out. A horse loses about a length per path. The fallacy with that is—and I've done studies with hundreds of thousands of horses—well over half of them run their best running when they're outside, free of horses. To me, you can't generalize. Do you think Forego would have run better numbers running on the rail? No. He would go four- or five-wide, eight-wide. He ran better on the outside. Plus, he was carrying a lot of weight and he didn't want to take a chance on getting stopped. To say he would have run better if he stayed on the rail is ridiculous.
>
> "That solves the geometry of it, but there's also physics. Depending on the degree of banking of the turn, the horses on the inside have to overcome more centrifugal force. When you drive a car into a turn, do you want to take the turn tight? No, you try to go out and ease down into the turn. And to suggest that going three- or four-wide at Belmont is the same as going three- or four-wide at Pimlico is a joke. You see horses going wide all the time at Belmont. If you try to go wide around two turns at Pimlico, you're dead. To treat all those situations with a straight geometrical adjustment doesn't work in my opinion. Yes, ground loss counts. If a horse going two turns breaks from the 12 post and gets hung out four-wide on the first turn, I'm going to give him a little extra credit next time he comes back."

Similarly, there is frequent debate about how much a horse's trouble really affects his performance.

MARYLAND PLAYER: "Everybody sees trip handicapping differently. It's completely subjective. I've got very close friends who do things the same way I do and we disagree about what is and what isn't a good trip. It's a difficult question to answer because it's in the eye of the beholder. Some people think getting left at the break is everything. Other people think it depends. Often there are worse things than getting left. Sometimes you get left into a perfect trip. Similarly, a lot of guys think every wide trip is bad, other guys don't. I think there are a lot worse things than wide trips—especially in a world where sheet players aren't differentiating. I don't worry that much about wide trips because other people worry too much about them, in my opinion."

RANDY GALLO: "I'm not just interested in whether or not a horse gets steadied. I want to know how much of an effect that his being steadied had on the race. Every horse that gets steadied the guy goes, 'Oh, he gets steadied on the far turn.' Well that doesn't mean he was going to win the race or even run a big race. You know, if he's seventh into the far turn and he checks him and drops out wide, sometimes you can interpret that either way. You can say he would have run forward. Other times you can say, 'Well, he checked but he wasn't getting there anyway.' So you have your own opinion as far as the trip goes."

DAVE CUSCUNA: "If a trouble-line comment says, 'Checked at the quarter pole,' what does that really mean? Was he tiring already and he checked and finished eighth, beaten 18, when he was going to finish sixth, beaten 12, because he was a tired dead piece anyway? Or was he checked making a potential winning move and he totally lost all chance? If you see it with the naked eye, it tells you more than if you just see it in the paper."

ERNIE DAHLMAN: "Once you understand how races are run, you have to be able to give the horses that had excuses excuses, and the horses that had no excuses no excuses. I started with harness racing, where you'd spend half your life betting horses that were blocked. They'd sit in the two hole until the top of the stretch and then get loose and win and everyone would say it was a perfect trip. With Thoroughbreds, they'll say, 'Did you see that? He was blocked the whole way!' And I'll say, 'Well, he got loose at the top of the stretch, that's good enough for me.' It was a whole different mind-set. I still don't think for most races it's a bad trip to sit like that in the two hole."

We heard from a couple of players that while trip handicapping is valuable for them, it's not something that's recommended for someone who isn't willing to really devote himself to it.

MARYLAND PLAYER: "In some ways, it's probably the worst thing for an occasional racegoer. It's a lot of work. It's subjective so it's not clear how much you'll get out of it. And a lot of people are doing it. All things considered, the market being what it is, it's probably not that great a place to spend your time. If I was just starting out I probably wouldn't be doing it, but this is what I do."

We asked for advice on how one could learn trip work.

ANDY SERLING: "You spend endless hours watching the races, you watch all the head-ons and you teach yourself and you learn. I don't know that I could sit down and teach a guy. Some people are going to get it and some people aren't. I think a lot of it comes down to watching a lot of races."

■ Track Bias

CARY FOTIAS: "I've seen days where of three competent handicappers, maybe one thinks it's an inside bias, another thinks there's no bias, and the third thinks it's an outside bias. It's a very subjective thing."

The discussion of track biases is inextricably interwoven with trips, and, as with trip handicapping, track bias is an area where subjectivity rules. The theory behind track bias is that at certain distances at certain tracks at certain times, there is something fundamental about the track or turf itself that helps or hurts horses with certain styles. One of the most impressive trips a horse can have comes when he's running against the grain of a bias and still runs credibly. A horse running on a dead Belmont rail in the spring could have a mediocre-looking last running line but still be a terrific bet-back up at Saratoga on a day when rail speed is king and he figures to get the inside again. And a horse who has an impressive figure from a perfect rail trip on the lead on the Aqueduct inner might be a terrible bet-back next time on a fair track. Of course, you don't want to be overzealous in ascribing a bias to a track:

95

ANDY SERLING: "Nowadays the whole world is carried away with biases that just don't exist. Some people seem to think, 'It can't be even, because if it was even, I didn't do any work.' Well, most racetracks are even, whether you like it or not. And people get carried away and that's just crap. You really have to be right if you're betting your own money and playing seriously."

CARY FOTIAS: "I think a lot of what people think is track bias really isn't. Some days speed horses are going to win not because there was a speed bias but because they were the best horses in the race. Or even if they weren't, it could just be random. Some days, a certain number of speed horses or closers are going to win just out of randomness and to ascribe that to bias is stupid.

"I think there's inherent bias, structural track biases. In other words, it's going to be difficult if you're trying to win from the one post at Belmont or out of the chute at Aqueduct. Or trying to win from the 12 post going two turns at Pimlico. That I would call a structural track bias. As for day-to-day biases, do they exist? Most definitely. Do they exist as much as people think? No."

ANDY SERLING: "There's this horrible misconception that there's a dead rail at Belmont all the time. I think that Belmont, because of its very nature as a track, because of the wide, sweeping turns, what it does isn't so much favor horses running on the outside so much as it doesn't give them a disadvantage—not nearly the disadvantage that a sharper-turned racetrack is going to do. Races are run in an outside-flow manner. Horses are herd animals. In general, they are much more comfortable making moves outside of horses than inside of horses or between horses. That doesn't mean a horse can't run on the inside. Belmont did have a dead rail for many years, but that's changed a lot. There can be an off rail but it's always going to be an outside-flow track."

MARYLAND PLAYER: "Track biases are definitely still a factor but they're less so, because track superintendents take this much more seriously now. Racetrack general managers and track supers used to insist 'There's no such thing as a track bias.' And this was at a time when you'd see race after race where the inside speed horses would run one-two-three all the way around the track. Pimlico, to take one example, was a highway. It still lives with that reputation even though it's pretty much gone. But the track bias lives on in people's minds because it was so overwhelming for so long.

"That was then, this is now. Today, persistent biases are rare. They don't happen unless there's nothing they can do to prevent it. The one hole breaking from a chute, for instance. In winter racing in the North, there's nothing they can do, they lose the racetrack from time to time. At Suffolk, the good horses will run six furlongs in 1:17. The other time when there's nothing they can do is with rain.

"Thirty years ago nobody was talking about track biases. Steve Davidowitz and Andy Beyer basically popularized it. But now it's gone to the opposite extreme, where two horses go wire to wire and people say it's a highway. They could have paid $4 and $6. It's not anywhere near where it used to be in terms of importance but there are still places, like Turfway in January, where it's nobody's fault but it just happens. It's five degrees in the middle of the night. It's hard to keep the track open. You've got to do things. At that point a track superintendent's job isn't to worry about a bias—it's to worry about whether or not the jockeys will ride."

We asked Cary Fotias how one might try and discern if the track was really biased.

CARY FOTIAS: "The clearest indication that there's a bias is when you start seeing unusual things happening. There was a day at Belmont earlier this month [September 2004] where outside closers were winning every sprint race and every horse was like 9-1 and up in five straight sprints. When you see horses at big prices winning with the same running style—not in two races but in five races—then you've got a bias. Or sometimes you'll see a horse who's a perpetual quitter and he gets on the lead and he doesn't win the race but maybe instead of fading to his usual eighth place, he hangs on for second or third only beaten a couple of lengths.

"To be able to have confidence in your ability to find biases, you've got to be a pretty good handicapper. You want to improve your ability to spot biases? Improve your handicapping. You should be thinking before the race, how is this race going to play out? And when race after race doesn't play out like you thought it was going to if it was an honest track, then you've probably got a bias."

Our Kentucky Player took the idea even a bit further.

KENTUCKY PLAYER: "I think that's really a skill that has to be developed. I watch people do that all the time and I watch people that get way off base with the bias. I think it's something that people have to practice; they have to do it a while before they're good at it. It goes back to experience again, it's something that you have to keep working at. I hear people say, 'I'm no good at bias.' Well, I don't know of any good horseplayer who doesn't understand bias. If you don't know bias, you don't know racing in my opinion. I don't think you can be a good handicapper without that and I think a lot of people get intimidated and give up on it too soon.

"You probably wish I'd say how you do it; well, I don't know exactly how you do it, I just know you have to be careful about it. I try to err on the side of not putting a bias into my notes unless I'm 90 percent sure that there was a bias. I try to make sure that I have good evidence that there was a bias before I put it into my notes. It's just a skill that's developed by being very aware, of constantly looking for bias at tracks and then going back and checking results and seeing what happens the next time out if you think there was a bias. If the rail was good and the horses run back out of that day you need to take the time to go back and look at what really happened. Did it hurt them to run on the outside the day you thought the rail was good? What happened when they came back? What happened with the horses that ran a big time on the rail that day?

"It's a process, and if you take the time to do those things, eventually you'll get better at spotting a bias. And it's another area where you have to be honest about it. You might have to say to yourself, 'Well, probably I was wrong here because this horse ran a big race on a rail and he came back and ran the same the next time on an honest track. So I was wrong about the rail being good that day.' You have to constantly go through that process and double-check yourself."

It seems almost contradictory to some of the points already made in this section, but that's the nature of handicapping. If you don't mind going out on a limb and you have an opinion about a bias existing, the results can be favorable.

CARY FOTIAS: "Analyzing the results after can help you excuse a horse or upgrade him or downgrade him based on a previous performance. But the biggest edge accrues to people who are able to spot a bias when it's happening. By the third race, all the evidence isn't in but nothing is 100 percent in this game. By the ninth race, everybody knows what's going on. You've got to have the courage if you see some unusual stuff happen in the first few races to believe it and go with it right then, in real time. That's when you can really crush them."

THAT LITTLE SOMETHING EXTRA

We're going to spend the next chapter concentrating on value and what it means to the horseplayer. Obviously, the best way to find value is to find an extra edge. Many players gain that edge simply by being fundamentally better than the crowd. But there can be more to that edge also.

STEVEN CRIST: "Anything that you do better than the competition— the other players—is an edge. Assuming that you have the basic knowledge and aptitude to play competitively, edges are almost always the result of extra work that other players do not do. They can take many forms. Maybe you make your own figures, giving you extra confidence in the quality of some performances and the ambiguities of others. Maybe you spend extra time watching replays, giving you information that others won't find in chart comments."

Sometimes that little something extra that gives you an edge is relatively easy to find—all it takes is a phone call.

DAVE GUTFREUND: "First-time geldings can be a good play. In Southern California a lot of times you can call their scratch line and they'll give you the first-time geldings and you can't find that information anywhere else."

No player is as famous for collecting additional pieces of information to add to the handicapping puzzle as Ernie Dahlman.

ERNIE DAHLMAN: "About three or four times in my life, I was in danger of going down and something happened that I figured out that other people hadn't figured out, which gave me an edge—ride it until the edge is over."

Dahlman explained to us that a big part of his handicapping philosophy is identifying and understanding change, something he mentioned in our introduction. Here, he elaborates:

ERNIE DAHLMAN: "When I was doing harness racing, I learned that the weight of the drivers was something very important. So a horse that's been ridden by a 200-pound driver and then a 100-pound driver gets on, the horse is going to run two seconds faster. But if a 100-pound driver is riding his horse right along for his last few starts and a 200-pound driver is riding his horse right along for his last few starts, then the 100-pound driver has no advantage because they're both put in a class where they run 2:02 or something, where they're comparable. I understood that it wasn't the weight that was as important. It was when there was change that it was very important."

We asked him how he applied his theories about change to the flat tracks.

ERNIE DAHLMAN: "Change is a crucial thing that most people don't understand. At the racetrack, you hear a lot of talk about first-time this and first-time that, but the important thing isn't that a horse is doing something for the first time; the important thing is that the horse is doing something different, that there's a change. If you can find a jockey that the horse has run faster for than other jockeys, well then you have an advantage because everybody else is thinking the horse is going to run a certain speed and you know that he's going to run faster than he has in the past. So you can make an adjustment that other people aren't making."

This interested us in particular because very few of the players we spoke with seemed to pay much attention at all to who was riding the horse. "I really don't consider the jockey at all in my handicapping," was a typical refrain.

ERNIE DAHLMAN: "The best thing is if you can figure out a jockey who horses are running for, like Patrick Valenzuela in California a couple of years ago [2002-2003]. When he's on a horse for the first time, when it's a change and the horse has been front-running and getting tired and just getting beat and then Patrick gets on it, well, assuming the horse looks okay you're going to have to do some talking to convince me from not betting that horse. He's going to have to have a horrible post or lots of other speed inside or something like that. I'm expecting that horse to run faster. And it's not that Patrick Valenzuela is smarter than the other jockeys who've been riding the horse, that means nothing. I think it has to do with aerodynamics myself, like the way a guy sits.

"I watched Jorge Chavez play softball once; he couldn't hit a ball. They say he's strong. I had a horse, Boom Towner, he couldn't ride him because he wasn't strong enough to ride him and Diane Nelson used to ride him. So I don't think strength has anything to do with it. And I don't think intelligence has anything to do with it either. Why do horses go faster for certain jocks? I think it has something to do with the jockey's center of gravity."

There are a couple of other areas that Dahlman makes sure he pays attention to as well. One involves adding a step when it comes to evaluating how a horse runs on a wet track.

ERNIE DAHLMAN: "I write down how wet I think a surface was every day. I don't really pay as much attention to what a track is listed as. I think a lot of racetracks in this country are a disgrace in the way they label racetracks. I've seen sloppy racetracks listed as fast; I have no idea why they'd do this but they do. I saw a race at Fair Grounds this year, where the announcer said the winner 'relished the going'—it was a horse who ran off by himself. Well, they had the track labeled as fast. It really is comical."

Famously, another angle Dahlman uses involves shoes. He explained how he discovered the importance of shoe changes in *Meadow's Racing Monthly*.

ERNIE DAHLMAN: "I started noticing that some trainers were using mud calks on their horses and getting good results, so I looked for horses switching from a stable that didn't use them. Then some guys started using turndowns on the horses' rear feet and they did great. [Turndowns are now prohibited at most tracks.] And nobody was picking up on this because it wasn't in the Form and it wasn't announced anywhere, and I made a fortune just betting these kinds of horses."

Hearing about all these different advanced strategies made us hungry for a way to come up with some proprietary angles of our own. One idea was to save the charts for every race at a meet and study them, looking for a new angle that might crop up. We asked our Kentucky Player if he thought it would be useful to clip the charts for the fall meet at Belmont and study them to prepare for next year's spring meet there.

KENTUCKY PLAYER: "I agree. I think that's a great thing to do. I would go back and do that same thing for the spring meet the year before. I think that would be at least as important as the fall meet. You might get more of an angle for who has the horses ready for earlier in the year and who doesn't. I think that's an absolute: The more you focus in, the better off you are. If you're an intelligent person and you go through some results and look at the charts, you can't help but learn something. If you're looking for patterns, looking for who won at prices, that's a quick way to find some gems on your circuit. Look at the horses who paid $20 or more, look at the winners and see why that happened. That's what you're looking for anyway, the good prices. See who won those races, see where that horse was on the track, when he last ran, what track he came from. If you do that diligently, you're going to see patterns. You're going to see the same people pop up or the same patterns pop up, the same preparations by the trainers pop up. There is going to be a rhythm and a reason to it; it's just digging in there and finding it."

There is a lot of information out there and the key is processing it in a way that is most effective for the way you play.

DAVE CUSCUNA: "There are a lot of people who think one thing or the other really doesn't matter. I know there's a small group of handicappers who can make a living looking at a horse's feet before they run on turf for the first time to see if their hoof is one that's going to be predisposed to being effective on grass as opposed to dirt. I don't know anything about that stuff. But I do know that the more information you have, assuming you have the intellectual ability to process it accurately, and not just allow yourself to swim in a sea of too much information, the better off you are."

THE PROCESS OF HANDICAPPING

We asked every single player we spoke with to describe the process of how they handicap a race. One thing they all shared was the idea that handicapping is a multi-step process. And while the early steps become intuitive as a player becomes more experienced, it's important to know that they're still there—though the more you know the horses on your circuit, the more quickly you'll be able to evaluate them in terms of the basics.

BRAD FREE: "When you are familiar with the horses and the trainers, as any expert handicapper should be on his or her circuit, some of those fundamentals come naturally. You don't have to go through and say 'Okay, who qualifies on form?' They all kind of meld together. I'll look at the horse and I'll know if this horse fits and that saves a lot of time. You have to eliminate the horses that have no shot and then you go from there."

In *Handicapping 101,* Brad Free writes about his basic process: "Examine the current condition of the entrants. Identify those in acceptable form, and those that are not. Ascertain the class level by reading the conditions of the race. Identify which horses are racing at an appropriate level, and those that are not. Know the speed-figure par for the type of race, and identify horses that have earned Beyer Speed Figures recently that are close to par. View the likely pace scenario, and identify which horses may be flattered or compromised."

Since this chapter has dealt with the building blocks of handicapping, it's important to see just how various successful players put the pieces of the puzzle together.

STEVEN CRIST: "In very broad terms, I begin by quickly looking through the past performances of an entire card—just the PPs, not anyone's picks or a graded handicap—to see who's running, if there are any horses I've been waiting to bet on or against, and what the flow of the card is like. I find this a very useful exercise in getting a handle on the depth and difficulty of a card and a sense of what kinds of races are in the pick four and pick six.

"I then handicap each race three separate times, looking for three very different things.

"The first time through, I am examining each entrant in a fairly traditional way in order to answer the basic question of who is capable of winning this race. My goal is to identify the true contenders based on raw ability, simple fitness, and suitability to today's distance and surface. At this point I am merely trying to eliminate overmatched entrants and get a sense of whether this is a race with a towering favorite, or two standouts, or a messy event where a majority of them are capable of winning.

"The second pass is an attempt to see how the race will be run, a step too many players leave out. Who's going to be on the lead? Will the pace be hot or cold? Is there a possibility of an aberrant situation, such as an uncontested front-runner or a likely meltdown? Can I eliminate more horses from serious contention, or do any of my initial throw-outs merit another look solely because their running style may fit the pace scenario?

"The third and most important step is to look at the race as a betting proposition. Only now do I look at the morning line and the DRF analysis and consensus picks. What I am of course hoping is that I have seen the race differently from the way the public is likely to—there's going to be an odds-on favorite I think is vulnerable, or I thought there was a standout in what others find an impossible event."

DAVE CUSCUNA: "I try to look at as much as I possibly can. I start off by looking at main trends, look at the conditions of today's race, and each horse running in today's race and just sort of mark off and circle things within each field of information. If today's race is a 1¹⁄₁₆ $25K claimer I'll circle the races where he's been running mostly in 1¹⁄₁₆ races. That helps me distinguish from what he has been doing in sprints. Is it a two-turn 1¹⁄₁₆ today, as opposed to a one-turn 1¹⁄₁₆ at Belmont? I'll look for two-turn 1¹⁄₁₆ races because I think there's a difference. The basic stuff is what I'll circle in the paper.

"Then I'll look at the claiming prices. I'll notice that a certain horse has been running in four allowance races in a row, I'll circle allowances, before that he was running in a couple of claiming races for $25K, I'll circle those, before that he was running for $45K, just so I can denote different groupings of distances, classes, that type of thing. Then I'll do some sort of fractional analysis. How fast is each horse running a half-mile? The idea is to get a sense of how today's race is going to be run. If a certain horse has run close to 48 every time, he obviously won't be ahead of a horse who runs 47's every time. The second horse will be four or five lengths ahead of the first horse at the half. A certain horse might usually be on the lead in 49 but he's five or six lengths behind when they run 47. And that information is going to help me plot out what's going to happen today.

"Then I'll look at common races in the company lines. That helps me see how the horses have done when they've run against each other.

"So I'll take that information and try and get a mental picture of how today's race is going to be run. Is there going to be a big speed duel or is one horse going to be loose on the lead or is it going to be a combination? Who's the most likely leader? Who's the strongest come-from-behind horse?

"Then maybe I'll look at the horses who I see as contenders in the race and see how they've done under today's circumstances. If a horse I like is a closer but I think the pace is going to be slow, I need to know how is this horse going to do when he's six lengths behind in 49? If the pace is going to be slow and a weak speed horse is going to be on the lead, how has the weak speed horse done when he's been able to slow down the pace?

"Then, time permitting, I might try and get deeper information than you can get out of the *Racing Form*, other speed figures, or maybe I'll watch a race replay if I have access to that."

PAUL BRASETH: "The first thing I do is look at who's training the horse. Then I figure the par times for each race. Let's say it's a race in Southern California for $10K claimers, I know what the par numbers are. I use Quirin-style figures; they're a combination of speed and pace numbers that quantify how fast a race was run to the pace call and for the final time. In this case, the pars would be $^{100}/_{100}$ because Quirin based his whole idea that $10K horses are $10K horses everywhere— that was the cornerstone of his system.

"Then I do Quirin speed points on every race, giving up to eight points based on how likely a certain horse is to go to the lead. I religiously use those and find them very beneficial because you can instantly see what the pace configuration of the race is going to be.

"Then, I take a ruler and I go back through each horse and I underline what I think are the key lines in the past-performance list, where the horse has won or run well or something. Then I go back and do figures on each of the races I think might be relevant to the race. I look back in my records to see what the figure was for the race it's coming out of so I can get some idea of, for example, who has the best pace figures early and who has the best final times. I look at the Beyer figures as well but I rely on my own figures probably more.

"And then I go back to step number one, which is looking at the trainer. And looking at the horses' recent races and how they might fit into some pattern I know about the trainers. And then I figure out who the logical contenders might be and where the value might be."

ANDY SERLING: "The first thing I do when I look at a race is try to figure out how a race is going to be run. Are there a lot of speed horses? Are there *really* a lot of speed horses? Is there one speed? You've got to think about how the race sets up. And you've got to think about that in terms of how the racetrack's playing, though generally we're going to assume that it's reasonably even. You decide from there which horses are going to be helped and which are going to be hindered by the way the race is going to be run. You're not going to be able to do this 10 times a day. You're going to find certain races that are interesting when you look at them in this manner. And then you're going to decide who the contenders are because of this, and who are the better contenders? And okay, are there horses that aren't contenders because of this who are going to be short prices? Or are there contenders who are going to be helped by this that don't necessarily look as good on paper?

"The biggest mistake you can make as a horseplayer is dismissing horses too readily. People are lazy. You want to look for horses with darkened form. You want to be able to have an excuse for their recent races. He didn't run well last time because he didn't like the wet track. He didn't run well the time before that because he really wants to go seven furlongs and that was 1⁄16 miles. The time before that it was an incredibly slow pace and he had an outside trip. And all of a sudden, you're not making excuses for the horse—he had real excuses. And before those four or five races, he ran races that were competitive with this group. Now you've got a darkened-form horse and a horse that fits the race. You've got a very interesting horse to bet on."

The handicapping process eventually leads to finding horses that offer value, a topic that is covered in Chapter 3. Our Kentucky Player mentioned this concept while describing how he looks to approach handicapping a race.

KENTUCKY PLAYER: "You always want to get a feel for the pace, to get a sense of what you can expect to unfold during the race. And then try to throw out the horses that aren't competitive in the race. Then look at what's left and if you see a horse that the public is going to overlook that has a chance or if a horse that looks like he has a real strong chance to win who maybe will be a bettable price, 3-1 or 4-1 in a race where they're betting three or four different horses, there could be an opportunity there. Or maybe there's a horse who fits but whose odds stand out to you; obviously that's a great betting opportunity. Or maybe you see a horse that may be 30-1 that you think can run third or fourth. Or a horse with odds anywhere between those two. The important thing is just seeing value somewhere, anywhere where you think your opinion may differ from what the public's going to do."

Part of Barry Meadow's process involves formalizing the search for value by actually writing a value line.

BARRY MEADOW: "The first thing I do is enter my own numbers. I do my own Power ratings for every horse that races in California and that's based on a number of factors, including the horse's recent speed and pace figures adjusted for bias and trip and track variant. It includes how consistent the horse is, if it looks like he's getting better or worse in his form, recent trainer changes, there's a lot of different factors. Then I wait until I get the track's morning line and the scratches because that gives me kind of a feel for who might get bet and who might not get bet because you don't want to waste an hour handicapping a race and you come up with the same 3-5 shot everybody else has.

"Every time a horse races, in addition to my numbers I also write comments. So then I punch each horse up on my screen and I transfer over anything relevant into my *Racing Form*, which is basically what I use to handicap. I watch the horses every time they race either live or on tape. Then I try to get a feel for how the race might set up, who might leave strongly from the gate, who might get forced wide, who might get a good trip, is the pace going to be fast or slow. After that I try and get an idea of who I might like best in the race, who I might like second best, third best, and I try to hang odds on them, fair odds for those horses. And then I'm looking for discrepancies between my odds and what the public puts up. If there's no discrepancy, there's nothing to bet."

108

Cary Fotias believes that his product, The Xtras, gives him enough of an information edge that it really takes center stage in his handicapping—though he doesn't ignore the basics altogether.

CARY FOTIAS: "If I have the time, I like to study *Daily Racing Form* before looking at the Xtras. I look to see what type of race I'm dealing with—the positional pace matchups, any relevant breeding or training stats, negative class drops, key jockey changes, bias notes, etc. Then I look at the Xtras, and the first thing I look for are conditioning patterns. It could be a new pace top, a turf decline line, or a compression line. I want to bet on horses that have something that is concealed from The Sheets players and conventional handicappers. The worse one of my horses looks in the *Form*, the more I like him.

"I then look at every horse in the race and predict what number (adjusted for weight) I expect it to run. These predictions are based on years of experience in reading the Xtras."

The specifics of what Fotias means when he talks about new pace tops and compression lines can be found in his book, *Blinkers Off*.

Dave Gutfreund talked about the importance of following various circuits.

DAVE GUTFREUND: "At this stage of my career, I follow four circuits religiously: Southern California, Kentucky, Chicago, and New York, and during the winter I pick up Fair Grounds and Gulfstream. Provided that I'm reading the *Racing Form* every day and I'm studying like I should be, when I look at a race, unless it's a baby race with all firsters, I know who the horses are and I know who the trainers are. Right now I'm looking at the seventh race from Hollywood, the first thing I'll do is look at the field and try and figure out where the speed is. Are there any specific trainer angles that are relevant to this race? Is there a Mike

Mitchell first-time claim? And then I'll just try and evaluate the ability level of the horses.

"Always, always, always take a look at what the pace scenario is going to be—absolutely it's a must. Figure out what the race shape is going to be. And then I hope that I can find a horse that's going to be a halfway decent price that is as good as the horse that's going to be the favorite."

ERNIE DAHLMAN: "I get the Ragozin Sheets and the past performances, which I use on the computer. Then I have a guy at the track who gets the shoe information; he sends me a program the night before that has all the information from the past about shoes the horses were wearing then. I like to see if there are any changes. Then I get the *Daily Racing Form*. And I won't make a bet that I don't like off The Sheets or off the *Form*.

"I look for recency. I pay more attention to recent races than I do to races back a ways, unless I can discard a number of races because of bad circumstances for the horse—like if the horse drew a bad post five times in a row in two-turn races and now he's got a good post. Post position means a lot to me. The most interesting thing I'm looking for is a horse that's in a good spot and fits the way the race is going to be run."

JAMES QUINN: "I'm a fundamentalist player in the first stage; I look at class conditions carefully. After class demands, I look for early speed and at the pace and final-time pars, to evaluate the horses in terms of form. Most horses are acceptable in these early stages of handicapping. Then I'll do an analysis of the early pace of the race; then I set a betting line after identifying the main contenders. I set the initial betting line based on fundamental handicapping, then juggle the line based on past trips, post positions, track biases, conditions, anything relevant. I use an $8/20$ line for contenders/noncontenders, meaning that a good handicapper should be able to have one of his contenders win four out of five bets in the straight pools—that's my standard of effectiveness. To sum up, I use fundamental handicapping, then I make my betting line, and then juggle the line based on situational factors."

As you can see from these quotes, not only are the handicapping factors themselves interwoven, but the entire process of handicapping is intertwined with the search for value—and that leads us to Chapter 3.

THE NEVER-ENDING
QUEST FOR VALUE

SECRET

They only bet when they have an edge.

UNDERSTANDING VALUE

CARY FOTIAS: "You should never play unless you're getting the best of it."

KEVIN BLACKWOOD: "Discernment—that's a key component for any line of gambling. You need to discern where the edge is before you make a bet."

If there's one key thing that separates winning players from losing players, it's an understanding of value. It's been written about in many places before but it still amazes us how ignored it is every day by a large section of players at every single racetrack in America. Perhaps that's because value is so subjective. Or maybe it's because most players are just lazy—after all, it's a lot easier to just say you "like" a certain horse and leave it at that. And that's the part of the problem that's ingrained in the very culture of the racetrack. All the time you hear people ask, "Who do you like?" It's a selection-oriented culture.

The real question they should ask is two-pronged: "Who do you like and at what price?"

Terrific public handicappers such as *Daily Racing Form*'s Brad Free in Southern California and Dave Litfin in New York are paid to tell you who they think is going to win each race—*not* at what price a certain horse would be a good bet. The latter question is the one you have to answer if you want to win.

112

> **STEVEN CRIST:** "People talk about value as if it is a 'factor' or an 'angle' when in fact it is the definition of success at parimutuel wagering. Every horse entered in a race has some chance of winning it, whether it's over 90 percent or under 1 percent, and the whole point of the game is for you to find situations where the public's assessment of that probability varies from yours. That's the definition of showing a profit. When someone says he 'likes' a horse in a race, it's a meaningless statement unless he is saying implicitly that he thinks the horse has a greater chance of winning than the likely tote-board price."

Before we get into a discussion of value, we must first start off with a discussion of probability. Then we'll go over the important concept of value-line handicapping, talk about the wisdom of the crowd, and listen to the players get into a debate about betting favorites.

■ Probability

What is it that separates a gambler from a speculator? The gambler is out to have a good time and bet some money and take a chance and maybe make a score. The speculator isn't interested in gambling at all—he's only playing if he has an edge. This is another concept that came up in every single interview we did. It was often illustrated with an example about tossing a coin.

> **MARYLAND PLAYER:** "If you want to ask me what the best bet in the world would be, I'd like to be flipping a coin for 51 cents. That to me is a great bet. You'd like to do that for the rest of your life. But that's not the way that horse racing is."

LAS VEGAS PLAYER: "I asked my father once: 'If you know that a flip of a coin was honest and you get $2 every time it's a head and you have to pay $1 every time it was a tail, how much would you bet?' He said, 'Nothing, because I could lose.' But if you could make a bet like that, who could ever bet on anything else? But he was very conservative, I don't think he ever bet $10 in his life. But that's basically what I'm looking for."

With a fair coin, you know that there's a 50-50 chance that it's going to be heads or tails. That's a constant. A fair gamble would be to bet your buddy 50 cents and toss the coin. You win the dollar if it comes up heads; he wins if it comes up tails. People who play the slots in Vegas would do a lot better if they took that bet. None of our players would touch it.

But what if, as our Maryland Player suggests, you were to receive 51 cents if you won but you only had to pay 50 cents if you lost? The tourist in Vegas looking for action would hardly notice the difference, but really, the whole nature of the venture has changed. Now there is a positive expectation—you're getting more out than you have to put in. Assuming that you could make that bet for as many times as you wanted, over hundreds of thousands of coin flips, you would surely get rich and your opponent would go poor. That's edge. That's what every professional gambler is looking for—situations where there is an *expected value* for every bet.

Phil Gordon, expert poker player and co-host of *Celebrity Poker Showdown*, defines expected value in his book *Poker: The Real Deal,* as: "The profit or loss that a certain strategy or game will generate, on average, over the long run." In other words, you're looking to indicate the average amount one would "expect" to win if allowed the same proposition many times.

As Richard Munchkin, the author of *Gambling Wizards*, observes, "It's just like a factory and every decision where you have an edge is just another widget going down the assembly line. And you want to have as many widgets going by an hour as you can. Winning and losing doesn't matter as long as you're playing with an edge.

"The most important thing, the most number-one important thing is the ability to identify an edge and then bet it. You have to be able to show me that you have an edge. When I used to talk to all these guys who are day-trading stocks and I asked them, 'Where is your edge and how can you demonstrate it?' And they all said, 'Well, I can't really tell because you've got to feel it and you've got to watch it . . .'

"Well, that's all bullshit and they're all broke now."

114

JAMES QUINN: "*Never* play the underlays because even when you win you lose. Think of it in terms of tossing a coin: When you win, you lose if you get 50 cents and your opponent gets a dollar."

Handicapping is all about assigning a precise probability to a given event. Just for an easy example, consider a horse whose true odds are even money. We're not talking about the tote board yet, we're saying that if a given race were run under these exact conditions 100 times, this horse would win 50 of them. The next step involves the tote board. What price are you being offered? Let's say the horse is 4-5 on the board. That means if you bet $2 on him, you'll get back $3.80. Well, for a horse whose true odds are even money, that's a lousy bet. If you make it, sure, you might win. But if you make that bet 100 times, you're nearly certain to lose overall because the wins can't make up for the losses. Even if you win in the short run, you'll lose in the long run.

On the other hand, what if you glance up at the tote board and see that your even-money horse is 8-5 on the board? That means he's going to pay around $5.20 for $2. And if he's going to win 50 percent of the time, that's a very good bet. The former situation, where the odds on the board are lower than the true possibility of the horse winning, is what's called an underlay, and the latter proposition, where the price on the board is larger than the chance of a horse winning, is an overlay.

■ Standard Deviation

Standard deviation is a key statistical concept for any successful player to understand. And while the specifics of the math are complicated, the theory behind the concept is simple enough. For the horseplayer, standard deviation is closely related to luck. Basically, standard deviation is a statistical concept used to measure the difference in a set of numbers. It measures how much the numbers differ from each other calculated using the average difference of each number from the mean of the group. This sounds tricky, but it's really not.

If you toss a coin an infinite number of times, the result is going to be heads 50 percent of the time and tails 50 percent of the time. But that doesn't mean if you toss a coin just 10 times that it's going to be heads exactly five times and tails exactly five times. If you tossed the coin enough times, five for every 10 would be the average, or "mean," number of times the coin came up heads. (That's what you'd call a normal distribution of data, or no standard deviation.) But on a given set of 10 coin flips, it could end up 10 heads or 10 tails. (That would be a high standard deviation because the result is so far away from what you'd expect to happen, given the average.) More often, for every 10 flips you'll have between three and seven heads, with a cluster around five.

So what's the point of all this math and coin tossing? The point is that because of standard deviation—or what you might just as easily call luck—you can be making all the right decisions and still lose (or more optimistically, be making the *wrong* decisions and still *win*). There is a ton of variance in gambling and just because you have an edge doesn't mean you're going to win all the time. Even the best players have losing days, weeks, months, even years. And that doesn't mean that they're suddenly no good—it could just mean that luck (or standard deviation) has gotten the best of them for a short period of time. That's why issues like capitalization (see Chapter 4) and the ability to keep emotionally level during the tough times (see Chapter 6) are so crucial to becoming a winning horseplayer.

But now let's move on to the big difference between coin tossing and horse racing. With a fair coin, the exact probability is a known quantity. The chance of any one toss being heads is 50 percent. Game, set, match. That's certain, and it's what's known as an objective probability.

Blackjack is another game that has set probabilities. And if you have the ability to count cards—to know when the odds are in your favor (when there are many high cards left in the deck)—and you bet more accordingly, you have a significant, built-in edge.

KEVIN BLACKWOOD: "There's a combination of factors for where and when I play: It takes into play how many decks, what the rules are, and what their level of penetration is. That will determine where I play.

Then when I get there, I'll bet higher amounts when the count is positive, but nothing or as little as possible when it's negative.

"If they dealt 4½ or five of a six-deck shoe, I would play. If less, I wouldn't even walk in the door."

In racing, we're dealing with what's known as subjective probability. We need to assess the probability of each horse winning. The better we are at doing this (that is, handicapping), the better we'll do at the track. That's obvious, right? We're trying to create our own objective probabilities out of the sea of subjectivity that is handicapping. We asked Howard Lederer if he thought this was possible.

HOWARD LEDERER: "Is it possible to create objective probabilities? Absolutely. That is what a true horse handicapper is doing.

"Degree of certainty, that's an issue. And certainly I can look at someone with a pair of aces and someone with a pair of sevens and give you with absolute certainty what are the probabilities of one hand beating the other. But in the same way, a handicapper can clearly state that Horse A is the most likely horse to win the race, and based on all the uncertainty functions that factor into horse racing, it's only going to win 22 percent of the time or whatever it is.

"I think the same thing happens in poker. I can give you an objective, certain probability of one hand beating another but that's not how you play poker. When I play poker, I know what I have, I then assess what I think my opponent has, and again I can say, 'Okay, I think he's going to have this kind of hand a certain percentage of the time and this kind of hand a certain percentage of the time and this kind of hand a third percentage of the time.' That's where the uncertainty is. I can give you absolute objective probabilities of my beating each of those hands but I can only place his hands in a range. So I have the exact same kinds of uncertainty issues that a horseplayer has.

"Blackjack is a completely different animal. If you have a perfect mind for blackjack, you know every card that's left in the deck. You could come up with a real-time model with certain probabilities of your chances of winning given your starting cards and the dealer's up-card because you know every card that's left in the deck if you have the perfect blackjack computer brain. It is a different animal than poker."

We asked our Baseball Bettor about how he operates. He uses a sophisticated computer model to assign exact probabilities to each team's chances of winning a certain game.

BASEBALL BETTOR: "On any given day, I'll take a look and run the numbers on every game on the schedule; then the computer objectively analyzes the games. It's like the computer players in the commodities market—that's a good analogy. They run a system.

"The casino sets up the money line; they take a vigorish. Let's say the Yanks are a 60 percent favorite, so they set up the money line that corresponds to that, which is Yanks minus 155, Anaheim plus 145. If I see a line like that, the public thinks the Yanks will win 60 percent of the time—the line reflects what they think the public thinks of the game.

"My computer analyzes the game based on my model (300 separate database files that go into it; it's a 3,000-line program; and it takes two minutes to analyze a game). The computer may come out and say that it thinks the Yanks will win the game 70 percent of the time or 50 percent of the time. When the number that the computer comes out with is some fairly arbitrary amount different, then I'll bet on the game one side or the other. Seventy percent, I might bet on the Yanks; if they say 50 percent, I might bet on the Angels. The difference has to be somewhat significant—arbitrarily but significantly different than what the casino comes up with. The more the difference is, the more money I'll bet because there's greater expected value.

"Same thing for the over/under totals. If the total is 10; you bet 11 to 10 on the totals—there's a higher vigorish than there is on the sides. In some sense it's a difficult obstacle to overcome. Sides is an initial disadvantage of about 2 percent; totals is about 4.5 percent disadvantage but it's a lot easier to get an edge on the totals. Oddsmakers are more wrong on the totals than they are on the sides; the totals are much more vulnerable than the sides.

"With baseball, there are 15 games almost every day. That's 30 potential bets (15 totals and sides). How many we bet is not a function of anything other than what the computer thinks of the games. On the average, we probably make about eight to 10 bets a day. Most sports bettors think that's crazy—too many. But I think we've got an edge on most of the bets. Some percentage of the time I'm wrong or the sports books are wrong. The idea is to catch them wrong a few times. If I'm 'wrong' on a game—and I mean 'wrong' in the philosophical sense that if God came down and told us what the 'real' line on the game is and if I'm off, then I'm wrong—I'm only giving up the casino average [juice] on those games. On the ones that I'm right, I may have a 6 to 10 percent advantage. So I don't mind having two games with a 2 percent disadvantage."

In our final chapter, we'll talk about how players are using similar computer models to beat horse racing, but for now our concern is discussing how horseplayers go about assigning probabilities on a day-to-day basis.

THE IMPORTANCE OF VALUE

In the previous section, our Baseball Bettor explained that one has a small percentage disadvantage to the casinos—the house take, or vigorish, on his bets. Compared to most gambling games, the takeout at the races is extremely, almost unfathomably, high. Roughly speaking, the track returns 80 cents to the bettors for every $1 bet. If our Baseball Bettor is just 10 percent better than the house, he'll make a killing; if you're 10 percent better than average at the races, however, you're still losing a dime on every $2 bet! The average bettor has got to be 20 percent better than average just to break even.

On the surface, you're betting a dollar on a coin flip and getting back 80 cents. No wonder it's so tough to win. But it's not impossible. Chapter 2 dealt with the factors players use to get an edge. But having that edge doesn't mean anything if you don't use it properly. As we started getting into earlier in this chapter, all successful players—whether they do it consciously or unconsciously—must assign a value to each horse in the race that they're willing to bet on.

GERRY OKUNEFF: "Value is the name of the game. There's a healthy takeout, so if you don't have the discipline to look for value then the vigorish is going to eat you up."

LAS VEGAS PLAYER: "Obviously, everything depends on the odds. Anybody who says, 'I'm going to go out and bet this horse' before the day starts, you can eliminate him as a serious player. You can have a feel for what you're going to do but you can't make a final judgment until you see a price. Horse racing is almost like you're in the insurance business. They insure millions of people. They could insure a 30-year-old guy who drops dead of a heart attack tomorrow. They'll lose a fortune on him, but in the long run they'll win a lot."

Our Las Vegas Player gave another example of value from the world of sports.

LAS VEGAS PLAYER: "In Vegas, the price on Annika Sorenstam making the cut (against males in the 2003 Colonial) was 4-1 against. A lot of people I talked to said she had zero chance. As it was she played pretty well, she only missed the cut by like five or six strokes. They had the odds of her winning that tournament at 500-1. The real odds of her winning a tournament against all males is probably 5,000,000-1. I made money on that."

Horesplayers are looking for the racing equivalent, when the price on the board is out of whack with the horse's actual chances of winning. They want to get on the overlays and toss the underlays. Of course, it's all very subjective.

ROXY ROXBOROUGH: "Beauty is in the eye of the beholder. You see a girl walking down the street who nine out of 10 guys won't pay attention to. But one guy will. The same is true in handicapping—it's subjective. One guy can make a horse 4-1; another guy can make the same horse 10-1. Who's right and who's wrong? Value is a tough concept to get a hold of. Better handicappers have a better aspect of value.

"I like to look for discrepancies between my line and the track odds, particularly if I'm playing a parlay. Since parlays are off the morning line, I'll find a separator. [In other words, you can't see the tote board for the second and third legs of a pick three, so Roxborough uses the morning line to find a spot where his opinion might "separate" him from the crowd.] If I've got a horse at 4-1, and his morning line is 10-1, that speaks to me. I always look for something that will separate me from the rest of the pack.

"Of course, everything is relative. If I've got a horse at 30-1, and he goes off at 50-1, I probably won't bet it. But you can be sure I'll bet a horse at 7-2 if I think he should be 5-2. The problem with long-priced horses is that it's pretty hard to assess horses between 30-1 and 70-1."

That last point Roxborough makes is important. You expect a 30-1 shot to win about three times out of 100. You expect a 50-1 shot to win two times out of 100. That's really not a significant difference and isn't worth risking a lot of money on such a tight margin. Plus, there is a higher standard deviation with longshots than there is with favorites, making them harder to assign dead-on proper odds. However, while there's little difference between 30-1 and 50-1, there's a big difference between 7-2 and 5-2. A 7-2 shot would be expected to win about 22 percent of the time. With a 5-2 shot, that number jumps to roughly 29 percent. That means that over the course of 100 tries, the 5-2 would be expected to win nearly seven times more than the 7-2 (remember, the difference between 30-1 and 50-1 was only one time per hundred). So if you've isolated a horse who should be 5-2 and he's 7-2, that's value and you should get to the window.

Of course, finding these discrepancies isn't easy. And to complicate matters further, the better a horse looks on paper, the harder it will be to find value.

PAUL BRASETH: "Another reason I think people who are good handicappers can sometimes lose is that they amass these vast amounts of information on whatever—speed, pace, trainer patterns, track bias, etc.—and they can paralyze themselves. I think Peter Lynch said it one time that good investors have to be able to make decisions on imperfect or incomplete information. You can't have all the ducks in a row. And if you do, then there's no value because everybody else does too. His contention was, and I agree at the racetrack, that a lot of times you're playing horses that they do have some downside to them; you don't know something but enough is there to allow you to bet on it.

"It's important to have the discipline to always play into value and not just play when you think a horse will win even if it doesn't offer any value."

VALUE-LINE HANDICAPPING

CARY FOTIAS: "Always put a price on a horse's head—and only bet when you're getting a couple of odds levels better. If you can't put a price on a horse's head, you have little chance of winning at this game. Everything comes back to the odds. Just because a horse is on a great pattern line doesn't mean he should automatically be bet. The price must still be right."

There are a number of good books that get into very specific discussions of how to use value lines. Barry Meadow's *Money Secrets at the Racetrack* and the works of Mark Cramer are good places to start if you're interested in reading more about value lines. The basic idea is this: In a value line, you assign each horse a probability of winning and you convert that possibility into an odds line (a 2-1 has a 33 percent chance; 3-1 has a 25 percent chance; 4-1 has a 20 percent chance, etc.). If you're doing it properly, you'll want your line to add up to 120 percent to account for the takeout.

So why, in the quote above, does Cary Fotias suggest betting only when you're getting a couple of odds levels better than the price on the board? This helps account for things like chaos, standard deviation, and just plain being wrong. By giving yourself a cushion, you increase your chances of winning over the long haul. The compromise is that you'll make fewer bets. But then again, a wise man once pointed out that the only way you lose playing the horses is when you bet on horses whose chances of winning are less than what you see on the tote board.

There's also a school of thought where you do a contenders' value line—you eliminate the horses you're not interested in at all, lumping them all together as having a 20 percent chance to account for the possibility of something unforeseen happening, and you then hang numbers on the remaining horses. This is what James Quinn talks about in his quote at the end of Chapter 2 when he walks us through his handicapping process.

We were curious to talk to the rest of our players about value lines—at their level, are they still useful? The answer is yes, although many of the biggest bettors we spoke with have an intuitive sense of value as opposed to formally writing it out.

DAVE CUSCUNA: "No, I don't make a formal line. I don't sit down and say, 'I'll bet this horse at 2-1 and this one at 11-1,' but I have a rough idea in my head. It's like if somebody asks you how long it's going to take you to get from your house to Bensonhurst at 5:00 P.M. on a Wednesday. You don't have it quantified exactly but you have a pretty good idea about the FDR Drive and which bridge you'll take and what 17 crossings they're doing construction on, so you don't have in your mind that it's going to be one hour and 17 minutes, but you know roughly how long it's going to take and you have a sense of when you better leave."

So how does he decide when to pull the trigger on a bet?

DAVE CUSCUNA: "I've been fortunate enough that I've never gone up to a betting window where there was someone with a gun forcing me to bet any particular horse. The way I look at it, every horse in the race is an eligible opportunity at some price. I don't know what that price is, and it could be an awful big number. At some price, I would have to bet that I'll go home with Cindy Crawford tonight. You know there's going to be a lot of commas in that particular number, but at some price, it's worth a shot."

But how does that theoretical example relate to day-to-day life playing the horses?

DAVE CUSCUNA: "So I think that on any race you should be willing to bet every horse, every exacta, and every trifecta at some price. Realistically, nobody's going to give me one penny versus Ross Perot's assets on my Cindy Crawford bet for tonight. That would probably be the price that would have to be and that person would probably still be getting the best of it. However, for one penny against Ross Perot's assets, I would have to take the shot. You don't get too many opportunities for returns like that at the track, so you know going in you're not going to bet certain horses because you're not going to get 27,000-1.

"But I have seen races where some hopeless horse that's 20 lengths slower than the rest of the field has won because four horses got into a spill and some jockeys fell off and somebody's left standing and wins. There is a chance that that's going to happen so you should be willing to bet anything and anyone at the right price.

"I'll look at the board and say, 'Here's what I think is going to happen, here's what's being offered to me,' and I can glance at the odds board pretty quickly and get an idea from where my opportunity is going to lie in this race."

Steven Crist makes an excellent point about the difficulty of trying to live and die solely by strictly adhering to a set line.

STEVEN CRIST: "I don't know a single horseplayer whose entire game consists of betting 4-1 shots who should be 3-1. That's a brutally rigorous way to play and not very entertaining. I'm also not convinced that anyone has got this thing down to a sufficiently exact science to say with certainty that a horse has precisely a 20 percent versus a 25 percent chance of victory. I have a 'correct price' for just about every horse in a race in my head after I'm done handicapping because that's how I think. It's a useful exercise to make a line of your own for each race if you don't normally think that way, but I'm at the point where I do that formally only with major races."

ANDREW BEYER: "I don't make a formal value line. I guess I've been doing this long enough that it's more or less instinctual. You have an idea in a race and suddenly the horses are 8-5 and 7-2 and you say, 'This is terrible.' Or sometimes you'll like it, and you'll say, '8-5 and 7-2, yeah, that's a square price.' But I don't have anything systematic, though there are obviously a lot of wise guys out there who do."

So what's the difference between Andrew Beyer and someone who relies more religiously on a value line?

ANDREW BEYER: "I'm selection-oriented. I generally will have my ideas on a race pretty well fixed and then I just need to make sure that the odds aren't ridiculously underlaid before I bet it. Sometimes you'll see cases where you've looked at a race and a horse you didn't pay much attention to, who is a marginal contender, is up there at 40-1 on the board inexplicably and you say, 'I've got to throw this one in.' I don't know if this is a right or wrong approach, but generally I just have my opinions rather than scanning the board and looking for overlays—maybe in this day and age the overlay approach might be the better route."

Another player who has a sense of value but gravitates to the selection-oriented approach is Ernie Dahlman.

ERNIE DAHLMAN: "It's intuitive for me and it's becoming more difficult because I see more and more numbers changing at the last minute. One minute an exacta pays $50, the next it's $34. One minute a number is 12, then it's 9.

"Sometimes I'll bet $2,000 to win on a horse when the window opens at a smaller track and the analyst they have will say, 'Wow, this horse is 1-9, there's no value there. . . .' Well, he's 1-9 because I bet $2K on him; he's not going to go off at 1-9. If he was then I wouldn't bet him either. So on TV he's giving out different horses than he would have because my horse is 1-9 and he might end up at 4-5, and then he'll win and they'll say, 'Well, if I knew he was going to be 4-5 I would have picked him.'

"With all the money coming in so late, you can't possibly know what the odds are going to be on the horse you're betting on so you better be betting live horses. Basically, I'm looking to bet live horses. I don't bet on many horses that don't run."

DAVE GUTFREUND: "I don't write down a number for each and every horse, but I have an idea what that might be—there is a breaking point clearly. If I think a horse should be 4-1 and it's 2-1 I'm not betting it straight, that's for sure."

PAUL BRASETH: "I'll say I'm going to play this horse if I get 4-1 or higher. I make some judgment as to what a horse's chances are of winning. I don't use formulas. I do it more intuitively and subjectively and make the line based on what I see as the competition in the race. And I'll mark down my top horse, and know that at 4-1 I'll play him. I'll say to myself, 'This is my other choice, I'll need 6-1 or 8-1,' or whatever it is."

GERRY OKUNEFF: "I make a line on the contenders that are key to the race; if I think it's a two-horse race and one horse is two or three times the price, that's a no-brainer. If I have an overlay or if I have an opinion, I'll get more involved."

JIM MAZUR: "I don't make a value line and I really should. I will do it intuitively, but not for every horse. A lot of times I'll look at a race like the 2003 Kentucky Derby. And I'll see that maybe a length or two separated a couple of the contenders in their previous race and then next time out, they're together again and Empire Maker is 2-1 and Funny Cide is 12-1 and that to me is distorted value. I don't have time to sit there and make a real value line for every horse, but you should."

CARY FOTIAS: "I don't always make a line on every race. It's very time-consuming converting all of these estimates into a 100 percent odds line that accurately reflects my opinion. When I have time to do it, my ROI skyrockets. All I have to do is normalize my line for late scratches or adjust it for track conditions, etc. Then I simply wait for a few minutes before post and see who is going off at a bigger price than my line."

PAUL CORNMAN: "I don't actually have a value line on paper but I think about it. A year ago I referred to myself as the world's worst line-maker. I think I'm up to about sixth from the bottom now because I've met a few people who are worse than I am. I'm not going to pinpoint what price my horse is going to be, but in a field of seven, I'll know if my horse is supposed to be the third or fourth choice or the favorite."

ROXY ROXBOROUGH: "One of the most important things for me is value. Whenever I handicap a race, I assess a price for each horse; I make a morning line/odds line and I use it as a gauge for betting. Successful gamblers have a good sense of what value is. I know 'value' is a vague term, but it's important to figure out what constitutes a bet where you'll win money in the long run."

JAMES QUINN: "I definitely make a line on the races I play. I can do it now intuitively to make an 80 percent line. I do it almost all the time and regret it when I don't do it. As for a horse's price—at first, it seemed crucial for me to get generous odds on my number-one horse. Then, in the mid-eighties, it changed and I bet second and third choices that were overlays and when my number-one choice was overbet.

"The concept of value is crucial; it's indispensable to winning the game.

"There are three reasons that players lose:

1. Players lose because they're not proficient handicappers.
2. They put too much emphasis on secondary factors.
3. But the main reason they lose is because they play too many underlays.

"So value is indispensable to making a profit.

"To me, there's only one axiom in racing: Avoid the underlays and play the overlays as intelligently as you can."

BARRY MEADOW: "I'm putting numbers on the horse or on the double or on the exacta that I need. Let's say I make a horse 4-1, which means I think he's got a 20 percent chance to win the race, I won't play him unless he's 6-1. I won't play unless there's some value in the race. I'm going to make a lot of mistakes, more mistakes than the public, so I have to have a safety margin that I'm going to win even though I may make money with some errors in judgment."

Interestingly, Meadow mentions that he expects to make more mistakes than the public. The "wisdom of crowds," as *New Yorker* columnist James Surowiecki titled his book about the importance of collective knowledge, will be addressed in more detail in the following section.

Another one of the most interesting responses we received about value lines was from Randy Gallo, who puts value at the forefront and makes a line but also, like Barry Meadow, has an intuitive respect for the wisdom of the crowd.

RANDY GALLO: "I write down the price I think every horse should be. Sometimes you have to use a little feel too because just because Randy Gallo writes down 3-1, that alone doesn't mean the horse should be

3-1. If I write him down at 3-1 and he's up on the board at 5-1 and he's absolutely dead, no movement in exactas, I may play him, I may not play him—because I may have written down a wrong price. But if I write down 3- or 4-1 and the horse is 10-, 11-, 12-, 13-1 or something like that, even if he's dead on the board I will play him. You look for small things too, like horses that are competitive with favorites. You can see in the black print in the *Form* or you can see it yourself. You might find a horse that's 15-1 or 20-1 or 25-1 and he was only beaten three lengths by a 2-1 in the race. And this horse may not be much better than the other horse. You don't have to hit many 20-1's to show a profit."

WHEN "VALUE" ISN'T VALUE— THE WISDOM OF THE CROWD

Even the best handicappers can't always pick more winners than the public. But as we've discussed, picking winners is only a piece of the larger equation. The public gets the winner right 33 percent of the time—a number that over the long haul is better than any individual handicapper—and yet the public still loses 20 cents on every dollar wagered!

Still, the impressive batting average of the public in picking winners—and codifying the chances of the other horses in the race—is something that is to be respected. You might think this is contradictory given that the name of the game is to beat the public when it's wrong. But in reality, this paradox is true and should be considered. We're not advocating using horses just because they get bet or anything as systematic and methodical as that. We're just suggesting that sometimes it's worth a second look at the past performances when your line is out of whack with what the crowd says. You're not always going to be right and they're not always going to be wrong. You want to be able to at least make an attempt to understand what the crowd is up to.

BARRY MEADOW: "The crowd is not that foolish. Every survey that's ever been done shows that the crowd's 6-5 shots win more than the crowd's 7-5 shots who in turn win more than their 8-5 shots. So the crowd's a pretty good handicapper. When you're deciding what to bet, you have to understand why the crowd is making the horse 7-5 and you only have the horse at 3-1. And vice versa. You have to have an understanding not only of the race and of those horses but of the crowd's behavior. Maybe a horse has had two straight perfect trips. So he's got two nice close-up finishes and the crowd likes that because it's obvious in the *Racing Form*. They may bet that horse but I might be able to say, 'Well, that horse had two lucky trips, is he going to get another lucky trip at 6-5? Probably not. I'm going to look elsewhere.'"

As discussed in Chapter 2, another common instance where a horse will take too much cash is when there is a speed-figure advantage that isn't necessarily backed up by the other fundamental factors. Steve Davidowitz makes the great point that value lines for all races aren't created equal—in some instances they're going to be more useful than others.

Maiden races are a place where the average player is going to want to give the crowd's opinion a bit more credence. Again, that's not to say you want to blindly follow the tote board, but it sure seems to us that early money showing at the windows is more valuable than any so-called tip we've received on the backstretch or in the press box. With maidens there's such a comparative scarcity of information that the tote board—which reflects the opinions of the people who own, train, and work with the horses and see them run every day—takes on added significance.

Davidowitz takes this idea even further, suggesting you pay attention to the connections of the horses being bet early and factor them in as well.

STEVE DAVIDOWITZ: "On certain races I do make a value line—high-profile races that will attract a lot of action. Then I can identify overlays in the win pool and for multi-race bets. A lot of races don't lend themselves to value lines, though. Look at a maiden race with all firsters. Old-school morning-line makers used to make all firsters 10-, 12-, or 15-1. There is value in knowing which horse is going to be bet, but there is more value in knowing which barns are successful when they bet a firster. Who are the guys who win and lose when the money shows? People are often too far swayed by the actions of others—it cuts both ways.

"You don't know what's in the other barns so you can't always trust that early money. You can have a barn think they've got a sure thing and run up against Citation first out. That happened; and, of course, Secretariat famously lost his first race.

"I trust my instincts, my feel for the board. There's a classic phrase, 'He's cold on the board.' When it's all there—good workouts, high-profile connections—and the horse who should be 4-5 is 9-5, then something is wrong."

Cary Fotias and Dave Cuscuna echoed this idea:

CARY FOTIAS: "When Todd Pletcher has a horse who's 5-2 on the morning line and he's 7-2 on the board, you have to look twice. If I can explain why a horse isn't bet, it doesn't bother me. Likewise, if a horse is taking a lot of action and I don't know why, I'll look at him more closely, though it won't necessarily change the way I play the race."

DAVE CUSCUNA: "Very rarely will I let the public influence the way I bet. Maybe in the case of a 2-year-old first-time starter from an outfit that usually gets bet and has decent works. And the works look good and he's 9-1. But I tend not to worry too much about what other people are doing because if you do that you're saying that a group of people knows more than you when you've done a lot of work and if that's the case, you shouldn't be risking your money. But in a race of first-time starters, I'm humble enough to say, 'I don't know, I've never seen them run.'

"But when there's a race where I have a lot of information and I make a horse my second choice and he pops up at 17-1 and I expected him to be 4-1, I'll go back in and ask myself, 'Did I make a mistake? Did I overlook something?' I might go off a horse if I find something I did wrong but I won't go off because the public's not betting him, I'll go off because I reconsidered my handicapping and reevaluated the race and reassessed the horse's chances of winning.

"Sometimes I will use other people's opinions, whether it is the public on the tote board or the guy on TV or if there's a good tout sheet, I'll take their opinions into account. I play a lot of tracks so I might miss something that another handicapper who only plays one track will see. Maybe the rail at seven furlongs is 1 for 47, there's a dead rail. I might miss that. And I'll reassess the situation if the guy on TV points out that it's a bad favorite because he's breaking on the rail at seven furlongs."

Some players, particularly those who use proprietary workout information, give the tote less consideration, but even there, there's some respect for the collective intelligence.

BARRY MEADOW: "If I don't have enough information on the race, I won't be playing it. If I believe I have plenty of information on the race and then some horse is getting bet and I wonder why and I look at the *Form* and can't seem to figure out a reason why, I might take a second look. But generally speaking, if nobody on the planet bets my horse but me, I'm very happy—even in a maiden race, because a lot of stables don't bet and some owners don't bet or maybe if they bet, $100 is a big step up for them, so if a horse doesn't get bet that doesn't bother me. I don't like horses to get bet. If a horse is getting pounded, I'm not going to bet. When I'm reduced to saying, 'Well, the crowd didn't bet this horse so what's wrong with me?' then maybe I shouldn't be playing that race at all. I don't want to depend on the board to make my decisions for me. I want to make my own decisions."

And Barry Meadow is not the only one who feels it's wrong to get scared away.

DAVE GUTFREUND: "Do I get off a maiden who I like that isn't being bet? Absolutely not. I know some of the people that you've talked to argue the other way but if there's a first-timer at a major track like New York or Southern California and it's 5-1 in the program and it drifts up to 12-1, and I thought the horse had a pedigree or the workouts or a trainer or there are three 10-time maidens in the race that are favored and they're all professional losers, I'd increase my bet. That's what you're supposed to do when you get better odds than you expect."

JAMES QUINN: "No, I don't get off a horse I like if he's not bet. I've never been a victim of that kind of pattern. For instance, I made a big bet on Congaree in the 2002 Cigar Mile. For whatever reason, he went off at 9-2 when he should have been no more than 2-1. I think Red Bullet was the favorite at even money. Congaree went off at 9-2. So I tripled the bet. It was a fortunate play for me. He looked like a stand-out and was a fantastic overlay. If you have a strong opinion and it's different than the public's opinion, that's when you have to play. That's when you have your edge."

131

BETTING FAVORITES

When we asked Paul Cornman about the process of how he handicaps, he introduced an important topic for discussion—what to do with favorites? Some players avoid them rigorously; others are inexorably drawn to them. As we discussed above, they can't be dismissed out of hand—but at the same time, no one in the horseplayer fraternity wants to be a chalk-sucking drone either. Here's what Cornman said about his process.

PAUL CORNMAN: "I've gotten to the point in the last year and a half where I don't even write in the *Form*—I'm blessed with a good memory. To me, everything is keyed off the favorite. You're either saying, 'Hey, maybe I can hook him up and make 6-1 out of 6-5.' Or if you don't have any opinion except that you don't like the favorite, you may spread around and try to catch a good number.

"However, I've found myself doing this and I've had to rein myself in, and many other people have done this as well. You can bet more in a race where your only opinion is that you don't like a horse or two than you will in a race where you do like somebody. How do you feel when the 3-5 you don't like runs fifth and you end up losing three times your normal unit because you couldn't come up with it? What's the solution there? Be smarter. Or else try to find someone who likes the favorite and bet them one-on-one."

The idea of betting one-on-one against someone who likes the favorite came up again in another interview.

GERRY OKUNEFF: "I've made match bets. I'll troll at the racetrack and say, 'Boy, I'd sure like to make a horse-for-horse bet against the fave.' If someone takes me up on it, I'll take it even if I don't get a price. I generally win that bet. The greatest compliment I ever got was when I bet another guy at the track head-up for $50 and I beat him; then I saw this guy again the next day. I didn't know him from Adam, but I saw him again and beat him again. Then, I saw him five days later—I asked if he wanted to get even and he said, 'Fuck you.' To me, that was a compliment."

We asked Paul Cornman if his idea of keying off the favorite (either for or against) has changed over the years.

PAUL CORNMAN: "I have no prejudice against betting a favorite straight. I know it's not a stylish thing to say but sometimes if a horse is 8-5 and I think he should be 2-5, I'll take 8-5. Of course the problem in the year 2003 is it could be 8-5 with two minutes to post and 3-5 when the race is over.

"One of the things about favorites to me is that horses who used to be 8-5 are now routinely even money. Even moneys are now routinely 1-5. There are 1-5 shots all over the place now, even in the worst races imaginable, where it used to be like twice a year there would be a 1-5 shot. So that should make the game easier but it's still impossible.

"To me, if I think I have a horse that falls through the cracks that I really have an opinion on—one who's lightly raced and I'm expecting a big, big race and I think I have a handle on what everyone can do—then I'll double or triple my play. But I'm not going to do that on a horse who's 8-5 that I think can't lose because I see them losing all the time."

Gerry Okuneff brought up another interesting point. If you can absolutely toss a horse who's taking more than 20 percent of the win pool, it's almost like betting with no takeout.

GERRY OKUNEFF: "I will bet a favorite if he's not overbet and if it appears to me that the horse will win even if he has some significant trouble during the race. One of the key things you're looking for is a false favorite. If a horse at 4-1 has the same chance as a horse at 6-5 then that's an easy call. You've negated the takeout if you're right most of the time—if your horse beats the favorite."

It all depends on your style of play, but to us the key idea seems to be that if your only conviction is that the favorite is bad—and you really don't like anyone else—you still might want to pass the race (unless you find someone to bet heads-up, either at the track or through on-line betting exchanges, which have become very popular of late).

ANDREW BEYER: "If I've got an idea, I'll make a play to beat the favorite. But if I don't know what the hell to do—sometimes if the favorite looks bad I'll spread around him, but taking real big spreads is not my game. It's not often I'll say, 'I hate this favorite so I'll box seven horses.' Even if you hit, your percentage return might not be that great. I prefer to have a conviction that I can hammer."

And that's where the biggest opportunities lie. When you don't like the favorite *and* you have a positive opinion on another horse in the race (or perhaps in the other legs of a double or pick three), then that's a chance to make a real score.

STEVEN CRIST: "I'm usually looking to beat favorites because that's how you make scores, and making scores quicker than you give them back is how you come out ahead. But knowing which favorites are reliable and offer value is often the key to those scores. When you hit a $5,000 pick four or a $20,000 pick six, sure, you beat some favorites along the way, but it's just as important that you narrowed or singled the right favorites in one or two legs. There's nothing inherently good or bad about a 3-2 favorite. If you think his true chances are 20 percent, he's a great play against, and if his true chances are 60 percent, he's a great bet. I usually get greedy and try to leverage an overlaid favorite in multiple-race pools, but I'm not ashamed to bet to win at 2-1 on a horse I think should be 3-5."

ANDY SERLING: "I'm a guy who's looking for decent-priced horses with a chance so I don't have to be right that often and still win. The best and most obvious situations to bet are when the public has a horse at even money and he probably shouldn't even be the favorite. I'll bet favorites, though. I'm not running to the window to bet horses that are short prices but in pick threes, things like that, of course. When I'm going to make a real bet, I'd like it to be in a situation where I find the favorite vulnerable. On the other hand, there are favorites at decent prices who can't possibly lose. I've been told that if I like a horse and he's a short price that my opinion is mediocre, and while my opinion has gotten better on favorites, I'm not insulted by that. I've got a good opinion on horses who are prices."

We asked Serling how he tries to identify bad favorites.

ANDY SERLING: "Ask yourself, 'Why is this horse being bet?' And if the reason the horse is being bet is something other than actual concrete handicapping, then you're on the right track. Like if a horse is being bet simply because he's trained by a certain trainer or ridden by a certain jockey. And that's certainly more true of a boutique meet like Saratoga or Keeneland. Or if a horse who Pat Day is riding would be two points higher if Joe Blow was riding, there's a start."

Of all the players we spoke with, none seemed as comfortable backing favorites as Ernie Dahlman.

ERNIE DAHLMAN: "I think there's a better chance that a favorite is an overlay than a 50-1 shot. And I think that's been proven. You lose less money betting every even-money horse than every 50-1. When people say this horse is an overlay because he's 30-1 or something, he might be and I'd bet him if I thought he was. But for the most part, there are enough people betting phone numbers and stuff like that that sometimes . . . Do you remember that horse in the Breeders' Cup a few years ago, the $5K claimer, Rick's Natural Star? He was like 40-1, and the real odds of him winning were way into the millions. Maybe he should have been a billion to one and people were betting on the horse."

So what's the shortest price Dahlman would accept on a favorite?

ERNIE DAHLMAN: "I bet a horse today who paid $2.10 but that was because of a dead heat, and when I bet I didn't think he'd go off that short. You can't control what price a horse will go off at. If I think a horse is an absolute certainty to win—like if Michael Jordan wants to challenge me to a game of one-on-one—and I could bet $100K on him to win $1K, I'd do it."

Other players also relate everything back to their value lines.

BARRY MEADOW: "Absolutely, I bet plenty of favorites. Maybe I have a horse at 6-5 and the crowd has him at 9-5. The good thing about betting favorites is that your losing streaks are going to be less, which is good for preservation of capital. The bad thing is that you're going to have to hit a lot of them. I bet favorites, I bet middle-priced horses, I bet longshots. I'm looking for anything where there's a discrepancy between my line and the tote board."

ROXY ROXBOROUGH: "I don't mind playing favorites if the price is right. In pick-six handicapping, it's pretty hard to not use a few favorites. Statistically, they win a third of the time; so if you leave them out of your exotics, you're leaving yourself a tall order. I don't have an aversion to favorites. I prefer not to play them if I don't have to, but if the price comes up right I will."

Steve Davidowitz has had some success betting favorites straight but doesn't seem comfortable taking short prices in general.

STEVE DAVIDOWITZ: "One of the best bets I ever made was on Fusaichi Pegasus in the Derby. He laid over that field and was value at that price. But generally I try to find scenarios to beat the favorite because over the long run, if I'm getting inflated value elsewhere, that will offset when the higher-percentage horse wins. I don't like to say 'never,' but I will never bet a horse straight who is less than 8-5. I might give in to impulse once in a while but I'll argue with myself about it.

"I can't remember a pick six where I singled a heavy favorite and didn't at least have a small backup ticket trying to beat him. Betting a single in the pick six is making a win bet and complicating it. I also try to improve the potential payoff by using a favorite I like in exotics."

A number of our players accept that betting favorites is a reality they must live with, and they try to get value out of the exotic pools if it doesn't exist in the win pool.

BARRY MEADOW: "Every situation is different and because of that you might find a race where an exacta offers the value in the race and maybe betting to win doesn't offer any value. I'll give you an example from the other day. There was a horse I liked at Golden Gate. I had him on my line at 9-2 and he got hammered. For some reason, the public decided they liked him. There were only four horses that could run second; the others were just too slow. By proper proportional betting, I was able to get 5-1 on the horse in the exacta where he only paid $9 to win. That race I played only exactas and didn't bet to win. Whereas if I were a player who said 'I'm only going to bet to win and that's that,' then I would have lost that opportunity. I'm only looking for what might be the best way to exploit my particular opinion—which might be the daily double, it could be the exacta, it could be anything."

ANDREW BEYER: "I don't bet favorites to win a lot. Let me give you an overview of my idea on betting. The one thing that makes horse-race betting an appealing form of gambling is the fact that you can take a shot for big returns with relatively little risk as opposed to laying 11-10 on a football game or sitting down at a poker game where you may regularly be put in the uncomfortable position of shoving all your chips into the pot because it's the right play. I like the leverage that exotic bets offer. In the old pre-exotic days, I'd bet $200 to win on a horse. Now that my bankroll is larger, I'm much less likely to make a bet like that. If I love a horse at 5-2 I'm much more likely to take $1,000 and key him in exactas and trifectas and try to hit a home run with him. I have no qualms about keying in on a 5-2 shot or an 8-5 shot. The issue for me is, what can I do with him? If the race is indecipherable beyond that horse then I'm not interested. If I say, 'Okay, this horse is 8-5 but there are only two horses who can run second,' then that 8-5 might be the basis of a bet that I find very attractive."

RANDY GALLO: "If you can find a favorite and a 15-1 shot that runs with him or a 25-1 shot that runs with him, that can be a good situation. As a matter of fact, we got a horse at Gulfstream today that went off at like 3-2, and believe it or not we liked a 35-1 shot with him and that horse ran second. We used the favorite with the 35-1 with a bunch of horses, and the favorite with a bunch of horses with the 35-1 shot. The favorite won and the longshot came in second, so we were pretty fortunate. All of a sudden we wound up turning a 3-2 shot into a 15-1 shot.

"You can't play a favorite to double your money. If you can find a favorite at even money and turn him into a 3- or 4-1 shot, you can do that. I like to bet a little to make a lot; I never like to bet a lot to make a little."

James Quinn is another who'll take the favorite straight but also emphasizes the opportunities that exist when you don't like the public's choice.

JAMES QUINN: "Most favorites are underlays, but an overlaid favorite is one of the best plays at the racetrack. Even money, 3-2, 2-1, 5-2 are all good plays. The ability to make profit on horses at 5-2 and below—that's a good player. You can distinguish false favorites from legitimate ones. You should only play when you're getting a bit of an edge. Barry Meadow bets a lot of money. He'll bet $5,000 on a 3-2 shot if he thinks the horse should be 4-5. Underbet favorites are a good play, because the probability of winning is very high. False favorites? Never play! Never play a favorite in a contentious race—where more than three horses have a reasonable probability of winning (12 percent to 15 percent). Always play the real contenders at the highest odds. Bet the highest overlays. Barry is good on money management and betting. We tend to overemphasize the horses we like best. Adjust that in your line. There's a larger error factor in the game and it bites when you have a favorite that loses outside of your analysis.

"If a race has a false favorite and if he's overbet to a fault, those are among the ripest opportunities in all of racing.

1. If you have an opinion on another horse, bet to win, more than you would normally do.
2. If you don't have a strong opinion, eliminate the favorite and

combine the contenders in exotics or play in pick threes going forward. The pick three pays best when the first leg has the overlay."

DAVE GUTFREUND: "Yes, I'll bet favorites. Since many of my plays are doubles or pick threes or pick fours, yes, you have to use favorites in those types of bets to keep those bets alive. It would take a very rare situation for me to bet one straight. I'll give you an example from December 7, 2003. Bare Necessities was in the feature at Hollywood against the Breeders' Cup Distaff winner Adoration. Everything that you read about the race was going on about Adoration, the Breeders' Cup Distaff winner, the champion. If Bare Necessities would have been 8-5 or 9-5 in that race, I probably would have played her because in my mind she was an even-money shot. But as it turned out the public had the betting right, but they got the result wrong. They made Bare Necessities 4-5 so I didn't bet her. [Bare Necessities ran third, Adoration second.] There are places where I'd bet a favorite straight but it would have to be a very, very strong situation."

Other times, if the value isn't there in any pool, you're just going to have to pass or you're going to have to accept that even though a certain horse might be the most likely winner of the race, the right play is to try and beat him.

CARY FOTIAS: "Sometimes you'll be setting yourself up to lose by trying to beat the favorite but that's exactly what you have to do when that favorite is overbet. When you win, you'll score out. You'll get paid."

Our Maryland Player and Paul Braseth will begrudgingly use a favorite to save with price horses they like, but only as a last resort.

MARYLAND PLAYER: "I was never any good with favorites. I just never liked betting them. I understand the old pricing model of the expected return on favorites. I don't think that's true anymore. The computer groups would have grabbed that inefficiency in a half a second. But I was always interested in the price end of the spectrum. I thought that it's a lot easier to hit .150 than it is to hit .350. So I wanted to be in a part of the world where I could hit .150 and be okay.

"I am not one of those persons who starts out with a 3-5 shot that I love and I say, 'Let's see if I can find an exacta.' More likely, it's, 'Gee, this 10-1 shot is cute but I can't beat the even-money shot.' It's the reverse process. I get to the favorite at the second level, not the first. When I think the favorite is the horse to beat, I just go to the next race. There are a lot of races where I just turn the page."

PAUL BRASETH: "No, I don't bet favorites, not unless I place it in a pick three or something if I have some value in the other races. I may use the favorite in an exacta if I have some sort of overlay that I can combine it with. But I have sort of a rule that I pretty much follow. I almost never play a horse that's not at least 4-1. And I pay close attention to all winners that are 4-1 or more. What I do is I cut the past performances out of the *Racing Form*—are you familiar with Brad Free? He does the same thing. You keep all the winning past performances and match them up with the charts and you get a good handle on what the trainers are doing right now at this meet. But favorites, no, I don't mess around with that. I don't agree with James Quinn. He'll come to the track and he'll say, 'God, this horse is 7-5 and it's an overlay.' I would never play that horse."

Jim Mazur is another one of our players who does his best work beating the favorites, which, according to him, he tries to do to a fault.

JIM MAZUR: "I'm in a bad place with that. I almost always play against favorites. One of my biggest downfalls is not being able to just walk away from a race where the favorite just looks unbeatable. I've gotten better at it in the last couple of years with experience but I still find myself reaching sometimes to beat a horse that just looks unbeatable on paper.

"Like any handicapper, I think the best situation you can be in is one where there's a vulnerable favorite. Over time, I've gotten better at finding those. There are a couple of little things you can look for. One is when you find a low-percentage trainer with a favorite that might be a good play against if they don't win a lot, period, and the stats show that he's not really superb with horses that are bet down to 5-2, then that's a good situation."

We asked Mazur to talk about some instances in which he's had success beating weak favorites.

JIM MAZUR: "I'll do similar stuff that a lot of people look at: a maiden special weight moving up to face winners. An older horse off a layoff that's run a really big race and might be set to regress. A lot of it is dealing with the trainers. Or maybe there's a bad jockey on the horse. Or a horse who has won and then a good jockey has gotten off and gone somewhere else."

As you can see from the wide array of responses about favorites, there is no one answer that successful players share—in fact, it is each player's ability to determine what works for him that makes them all winners, a subject we'll tackle in depth in Chapter 5. But for now let's look at the question of what to do once you've determined that value exists in a race.

4

IF I ONLY KNEW HOW TO BET . . .

SECRET

*They manage their money
to maximize their advantage.*

WHAT IS MONEY MANAGEMENT?

In this day and age of usurious takeout, it's more important than ever to manage your money effectively. Whole books have been written about money management, most notably Barry Meadow's *Money Secrets at the Racetrack,* but it's still a topic that most beginning handicappers know little about.

In order to take advantage of your edge and to maximize your value, you need to know what to do with your money. Some of the basic tenets of money management—like keeping sound accounting—seem so mundane, but good money management is more than just managing your money effectively, in strict accounting terms. It's about building your bankroll, betting wisely, taking advantage of overlays and not betting underlays (isolating value), and maximizing your edge. It's about managing your bankroll so it can grow. The more your bankroll grows, the more confidence you'll have at the track. All of our serious bettors know that they're in this game for the long haul and thus manage their bankroll accordingly.

As you'll see in Chapter 6, winning and losing affect the mental aspect of your game—sometimes positively, often negatively—and that's why it's of paramount importance to have sound money-management skills, so that you don't let short-term fluctuations of the game impact the way you spend your money at the racetrack. During losing streaks, you might have a tendency to press and double up your bets to try to get even. Don't! This is a surefire way to go broke. Similarly, when people are winning, they have a tendency to get too aggressive and throw their money away—or, perhaps even worse, get too conservative and leave big money on the table. Sound money-management skills will help you stay focused on your bankroll and what you need to do to keep it growing, without risking too much or not enough.

Before we get into the nuts and bolts of money management, it's important to discuss the distinction, if any, between the two fundamental elements of this game: handicapping (which, of course, is the actual process of picking contenders in any given race) and betting (using money to back up your convictions in a way that gives you the best chance to win and make money). The two certainly go hand in hand, but they're not as clear-cut as one might think. Or are they?

THE GREAT DEBATE: HANDICAPPING VS. BETTING

There are two factors that go into playing the horses: handicapping and betting. Some would say that these two factors are the same thing and that you can't be good at one without being good at the other—and they'd be right. And that's because with the takeout, most everything comes down to value. And if you can't select horses that offer value, and then bet in such a way that you're able to maximize that value, then you won't be able to beat the takeout over the long haul. Therefore, both factors are not mutually exclusive.

But in order to understand the importance of this concept, you must first look at them as separate entities: the art of handicapping and selecting winners, and the art of betting and using your money to maximum advantage.

We presented this topic to our players, asking them which factor they viewed as more important: handicapping or betting. Surprisingly, the answers were varied, but each player stressed the proper implementation of the two as a deciding factor for winning at the races.

■ Equal Parts Handicapping and Betting

Several of our players emphasized the importance of being proficient at both. Barry Meadow wrote the preeminent book on money management and he views them as equal endeavors. So does Steven Crist. They both stated that if you can't select winners, then it doesn't matter how good a bettor you are. And if you can't maximize your selections with creative bets, then you're not going to be able to beat the takeout. It's a fine line, but it also stresses the importance of integration in your game: There are many factors that make up a winning player, and it's vital to incorporate certain elements of each into your overall play so that you can win.

143

BARRY MEADOW: "I think they're both important. If you can't handicap, you don't have any way to assess whether you're getting any good value or not. On the other hand, if you're just trying to pick winners, that's not going to work either. If a horse should be 6-1 and you're taking 3-1, you're not going to win. They're both very important. There are many players who are good handicappers but will never win because they don't understand betting. There are probably fewer players who are great bettors who are not good handicappers. They're both important. If you can't handicap, how are you going to come to an assessment of the race?"

STEVEN CRIST: "You need to be good at both to succeed. A lousy handicapper, who bets on hopeless horses or takes the worst of prices, has no shot. A decent handicapper who makes idiotic bets won't do much better. A ton of players consider themselves excellent handicappers and poor bettors or money managers, but I think they may be kidding themselves by rationalizing their losses this way. What does it mean to be an excellent handicapper if you then consistently lose money betting on your opinions? The truth is that only a small number of people are 20 percent better than the market in order to beat the takeout, and that just gets you even. It's a tough, tough game to win."

Our Las Vegas Gambler and Roxy Roxborough, who, as a former oddsmaker, might just understand the concept of value better than anyone, had similar takes.

LAS VEGAS PLAYER: "You have to be a good handicapper *and* you have to know how to bet well; you have to do both. If you can't handicap, it doesn't matter how you bet, and if you can't bet, that's no good. You really have to know both."

ROXY ROXBOROUGH: "It's a well-balanced mix; it's like a recipe. It's hard to assess what's more important since it's a process that goes hand in hand. To me, handicapping and betting are equally important. I'm always thinking about price when I handicap. They're one and the same."

Paul Cornman saw the process as linear—starting with handicapping and leading into betting—but attached equal importance to both. His point is a good one: No matter which side of the debate you fall on, the first step in the process requires good handicapping. If you haven't done the work and isolated the potential winners, then there's just no way you can show up the next day and take advantage of your handicapping edge by betting smartly.

PAUL CORNMAN: "You can go out and acquire good information now, which you were not able to do when I started doing this 30 years ago. I've always created my own information so I'm always looking at it as a handicapper who thinks his betting sucks. So I always say, 'Gee, I wish I was a better bettor than handicapper,' but if somebody doesn't know how to handicap at all, I don't think they know what they're looking at to begin with. So you have to do the first one in order to be good at the second one."

Len Friedman spoke about the relationship between the two in a way that stressed the connection to another aspect of being a winning player (and the subject of our previous chapter)—value.

LEN FRIEDMAN: "There are some people I've seen who get results that are better than what their handicapping was—because they were very good about putting their plays together and are always insisting on value and not getting trapped into just liking the pattern on a horse that's maybe 6-1 on the morning line and he goes off at 3-1 and you bet it anyway because you got locked into it. If he had been listed at 3-1 originally, you might have just passed the race altogether and not even thought about it. That's a big problem for me. I get locked into approaches to a race based on the morning line and then I don't adjust well to what the final odds are and I'll play horses that may not even be overlays anymore. I need to be able to accept the situations where the horse I like wins and pays $7.80 and I didn't get to cash. Because it really wasn't supposed to be bet at 5-2."

More Handicapping

Several of our pros explained a linear approach similar to Cornman's, but eventually sided with handicapping as being slightly more important because without good horses you can't make good bets. So if it starts with handicapping, it could also very well end with handicapping.

As Dave Cuscuna notes, you need to know why a certain horse is good value at a certain price. The only way to do that is through solid handicapping.

DAVE CUSCUNA: "You can't have one without the other. For me, it's pretty equal, but if you boil it down to the basic elements, you have to say that handicapping is more important because if you can't handicap it's hard to bet. You have to know what you're betting on. You have to know why 3-1 is a good price or a bad price. I haven't bumped into the guy who picks 100 percent winners, so you better know what value is, otherwise you could be a good handicapper and lose money. But if you don't understand how to pick them, you could be a mathematician and not make money. So I think it's important to know a lot about both."

Ernie Dahlman was a lot stronger than most in his assessment, stressing the fact that if you can't pick winners then you can't win at the races—period!

ERNIE DAHLMAN: "There's no comparison. Handicapping is much more important than betting. I've read all kinds of stuff that says the opposite. But let's take it to the absurdity: If you know who's going to run one-two in every race, if you're such a good handicapper you can pick them one-two-three, what do you have to know about betting? All you need to know is that there's such a thing as an exacta or a trifecta. If you're a great handicapper, you have everything going in your favor—you have to be an imbecile not to win if you're a great handicapper.

146

"Most people think they're great handicappers and bad bettors and that's why they lose—where the reality is that people lose because they are bad handicappers. You let me sit next to a great handicapper every time, and you can go partners with a great bettor who doesn't have a clue about handicapping. In order to know value, you have to be a great handicapper anyway because you have to know what the horse's real chances are of winning."

Steve Davidowitz and Gerry Okuneff shared similar opinions.

STEVE DAVIDOWITZ: "A truly great bettor—a creative bettor—probably does not have to be the best handicapper on the grounds, but he has to be a *great* bettor; he has to be able to combine betting situations in a purely mathematical, empirical way, in a way that's better than everyone else.

"But the idea that betting is all there is is nonsense. Handicapping is still more important. If you don't have a good handicapping opinion, it doesn't make any difference how you bet—you need to combine these talents in a synaptic way that is instantaneous recognition. You need to know what bets are out there and learn how to manipulate your money.

"You need to have a feel for how to handicap, the accent is on having a good handicapping opinion, but you must know how to bet and the more knowledge of betting you have, the stronger your game will become."

GERRY OKUNEFF: "If you don't have live horses then you're never going to cash. How would you judge if a horse was a bigger price than it should be if you weren't able to handicap the race?"

More Betting

Some of our pros fell on the betting side of the debate, and that's because they stress the concept of value and maximizing your bets to increase your bankroll. James Quinn explained the latter part of this very well:

JAMES QUINN: "For a newcomer or a novice or for a losing player, it's on the order of 80 percent handicapping proficiency, 20 percent betting and money management.

"When you get to a point where you have an edge on the game, it's probably 40 percent/60 percent in favor of the betting. It's important to manage your money to appreciate your bankroll over time. You need to maximize profits. Until you become a proficient player, you should just make flat bets. If you don't know how to play, money management is less important. You need effective strategies when you're proficient because that will mean the difference of how much money you're going to make."

The other point these players made was that they've seen a lot of really good handicappers go broke—and that's because they didn't understand how to manage their bankroll.

RANDY GALLO: "Most people that go to the racetrack can handicap. I put more weight on money management; it's got to be 80 percent of it, if not higher. There's no question about it. I see a lot of guys with solid opinions that are always broke so obviously they don't know how to bet."

JIM MAZUR: "To me that's 50-50 or, if anything, skewed a little bit toward betting. You can be a great handicapper and pick five winners in a day and still come home a loser if you don't bet right. I have toyed with all sorts of different methods of wagering and I've found that your money management is a big part of the overall picture."

MONEY MANAGEMENT IN ACTION

As discussed above, money management is a crucial concept to grasp if you're going to win at the racetrack. "To put it real simply," said Dave Cuscuna, "you have to manage your money; you have to know

SIX SECRETS OF SUCCESSFUL BETTORS

there are nine more races tomorrow and there are 30 tracks running tomorrow."

Not surprisingly, our pros had some strong thoughts when it came to the topic of money management. Most of them have the luxury of having deep pockets and large bankrolls, so going broke isn't a big concern of theirs. But, like all of us, they had to build up their bankrolls some way, and thus, all were well aware of the importance of sound money-management skills.

Our Maryland Player talked about two general ways to manage your money. The first was the Kelly Criterion of money management, which, as explained on the Del Mar Thoroughbred Club website, states:

> The Kelly Criterion is a money management and dutching system that is designed to maximize the growth of your bankroll over the long term. Put another way, it gives bettors a method of calculating the optimal amount to bet on a horse and the best way to take advantage of overlays and underlays . . . The Kelly system works by leveraging the odds . . . finding spots where there are overlays and betting a portion of your bankroll based on how much of an overlay it is. . . . With the Kelly Criterion, you are always betting percentages of your bankroll so as your bankroll grows, so do your bets. Likewise, when your bankroll shrinks, your bets will shrink.

That's one way to effectively manage your bankroll, and you can easily find out the real math behind the method if you do a quick search online. But if your personality isn't structured enough or rigid enough to stick to Kelly's principles, there are other, easy, more general ways to manage your bankroll, as Our Maryland Player explained:

> **MARYLAND PLAYER:** "There are two mechanisms for dealing with probability. You can do it technically, a Kelly style where your betting is subjected to rules about how much you'll commit. The other doesn't have to be that fancy. You say, 'Okay, this is the bankroll; this is the amount of money I'm willing to lose this year on horse racing or on any activity. And this is my budget.' And once you have a budget you decide how much you are willing to bet on any given opportunity.

"One of the beautiful things about Kelly is that your bet size fluctuates with your bankroll. There's a connection between how much your bankroll is and how much you bet. If your bankroll goes down, your bet size goes down. It may not be linear because it's always a function of the opportunity but that's a standard discipline that people apply in most aspects of their life and they're crazy for not doing the same thing at the racetrack.

"One of the most depressing sights I see at a racetrack is when you see people lined at those cash-card machines they put in at the racetrack. The rates on those things are highway robbery and you see people lined up ten-deep. And that tells you that (1) not only are they playing a 17-20-25 percent takeout, but they're also throwing away 8 percent to get cash on top of it, and (2) these are people who walked into the racetrack with no idea of what they were willing to lose. And that's a classic model that you have no chance.

"I participate in a bulletin board of serious horseplayers who are casual bettors. They're pretty smart people and they all clearly have a good idea of the amount they want to risk. They never explicitly say it but you can see from the thought processes that go into devising bets that they get it—and you've got to get it. They are wagering relatively small amounts of money and thinking carefully about constructing their bets. The targeted reader of this book is someone who goes to the racetrack recreationally, who'd like to be more serious but who isn't at the bottom of the pyramid. People don't like to do this because it sounds boring, like accounting. But you really do need sound, basic principles. You should keep records, have a budget, and stay within the parameters of that budget. It's a discipline."

Andrew Beyer has always been an astute student of the game, constantly in tune with the changing nature of the sport and how it affects the way he plays. Here are his thoughts on money management.

ANDREW BEYER: "Thirty years ago, wise guys had an advantage, of knowledge and handicapping techniques. Nowadays there aren't many secrets left in terms of handicapping. That makes it more important than ever to handle your money well. You look at the computer guys and the sophisticated methods that they're using. But I think for any player, a rational betting or money-management strategy is important. I don't think it's necessary to have a system but in a game this competitive, you can't afford to sacrifice a few percentage points through irrational or compulsive betting. Handling your money right has always been important but today it's more important than ever."

Steven Crist talked about the value of unit plays when placing common exotic wagers, but stressed that the pick six is a completely different animal. A few of our other players emphasized the importance of setting aside a separate budget for pick-four and pick-six plays, since the risk-reward factor is much greater for those bets than for the more common types of wagers.

STEVEN CRIST: "For most bets, units and percentage-of-bankroll are useful concepts, because you have to decide whether you're making $5 or $100 exacta boxes. But with the pick six, the unit is always $2 and there's a correct total to invest that has nothing to do with how you did last week. There's not as much fluidity in bet-sizing. I put between $500 and $2,500 into pick-six carryovers because that's the range where I'm comfortable and effective, and I've determined through years of experience and analysis that this is the proper range for the way I play. My decision of whether it's closer to $500 or $2,500 on a given day is based on things like my confidence level in today's card and the size of the pool, not my morning bank balance or whether I've been having a good or bad month. If I started making $192 or $10,000 plays as a result of recent performance, I would be making plays that I have already decided are bad plays."

On the topic of risk-reward, Gerry Okuneff felt it was important to limit your losses, but not your winnings—and thus, he talked about making wagers where the goal is to get maximum reward for minimum outlay.

GERRY OKUNEFF: "I think it's critical if you can set a limit on what you can lose. You should have a rock-solid limit on what you can lose. You should try not to limit what you can win—don't be satisfied with an early profit and protect it. It's a point of pride not to lose everything in your pocket. You don't need money at the racetrack—you just need winners. A shrewd player can turn $50 into $100.

"I'm looking to make big scores with the least amount of capital outlay. In my view, there's no need to expose yourself. If you can bet $5K a horse, then that's good for you. You find your own comfort level.

"I think it's important to have the discipline of keeping an accurate daily count."

Our Las Vegas Player also stressed the importance of crushing overlays and avoiding underlays. With the purpose of this game being to build your bankroll, it's important to manage your money in such a way that you're able to make the most of your opportunities. Some of our biggest players also talked about the importance of unit play and percentage-of-bankroll play, but stressed that it wasn't the type of money-management approach for them.

The beauty of this game is that it's different for everyone, so you need to find a money-management approach that works for you. The reason some of our pros don't care about unit plays is because they have a never-ending cash flow and it's more important for them to isolate and crush opportunities than to limit what they can lose. For the casual player who is looking to get serious, however, it's critical to have a sound money-management approach that is going to allow you to play this game for a long time, and build your bankroll systematically.

LAS VEGAS PLAYER: "Money management is really making big bets on something you have really got the best of and making small bets on something you just have marginally the best of. That's money management, not what other people think, which is bet X percent of your bankroll on each bet—that's nonsense.

"You have to be able to distinguish the real good bets from the marginal bets and not be afraid. Betting $30K of your $100K bankroll, you don't want to do that either but you certainly want to vary your bets because of how much the best of it you have. Each play is a different situation. Sometimes you might have 500 percent the best of it. Another time you might have 5 percent the best of it. Five percent is still a bet but you're not going to bet as much.

"Unit play doesn't really exist for me. But the parimutuel system doesn't allow for bets where you have a huge percentage the best of it."

Dave Cuscuna and Randy Gallo reiterated the importance of value—of taking advantage of opportunities, but also of having the patience to wait for the right opportunities. It's critical to take advantage of scenarios where you have edge, and all of our players have been able to recognize those opportunities and make the most of them.

DAVE CUSCUNA: "A part of money management is knowing how much you want to invest in terms of any one opportunity, and knowing how that might affect you with other opportunities.

"Take a great real-estate deal. You might have one opportunity to buy a property that you have a pretty good idea will make money over the course of many years but it'll mean tying up 75 percent of your income and there'll be an opportunity cost because something else might come up but you won't have the money to do it—maybe a great job in Tokyo, but you won't have the money to cover your moving expenses.

"There are going to be opportunities tomorrow so you have to be careful about risking too large a percentage of your bankroll today. If there's a great perceived edge, how do you allocate your bankroll?

"Over time you build up a bankroll and it's good game theory not to risk too large a percentage of that bankroll."

RANDY GALLO: "You may not know what you're going to play until you see prices. I'm saying you handicap the card at night and you write down what you like and you have in your mind how much you want to bet on these races if these horses are at a particular price. I don't know if that's the correct way of doing it, but that's the way I do it.

"It all depends on how much you want to make, what your goal is. You need money management and you have to be methodical in what you're doing. To me, that's the name of the game.

"I've heard philosophies where people say you should never bet more than a certain percentage of your bankroll, 5 percent or whatever it is, but I don't want to get locked into something like that.

"But you do have to find where the value is and just stay methodical in what you're doing because no matter how much you win or lose you have to have money management—that to me is 95 percent of the game. Because a lot of people get to the racetrack and they're betting $20, $20, $20, and all of a sudden they hit a race for a thousand and they're betting $500. How much you win or lose should have no bearing on what your plan of attack should be."

THE IMPORTANCE OF HAVING A BANKROLL
AND BEING CAPITALIZED

As we briefly touched on above, it's impossible to play this game well without being capitalized and having a bankroll. Sure, you're not all going to have bankrolls the size of our pro players' bankrolls, but you have to start somewhere. By playing well and systematically increasing the size of your bankroll, you'll be able to take your game to a whole new level. As Randy Gallo said, "Successful gamblers have to be capitalized."

Part of systematically growing your bankroll is understanding that this is one long game. Though we go into this topic in much more detail in Chapter 6, it's important to mention it here because short-term fluctuation can affect your play, and thus your bankroll. By maintaining an even keel and having sound money-management skills, you can play this game consistently for a long time—and that's the goal of this book: to help casual players pick winners, beat the takeout, maximize edge, and make money in the long run.

Our Maryland Player talked about the difference between the big-time players and the casual-serious player, and how it's important to understand your budget and how to manage it effectively.

MARYLAND PLAYER: "A lot of big players don't necessarily have a set bankroll because they're so capitalized. But even if you don't have a budget you have an intuitive idea. I can't tell you what a quart of milk costs in the grocery store, couldn't get within 50 cents of the right price probably, but I can probably give you a decent guess on how much I'll spend on groceries this year.

"The same kind of approach works in gambling. Why would it be different? Why wouldn't you have a budget and a plan? At the high end, it doesn't matter. The high end, they know how much money they have and they know how much they're willing to lose in a year. They've had years to develop intuition and they're not likely to go broke. Whereas a lot of your readers, were they to decide tomorrow that they want to be full-time professional horseplayers, would be in danger of going broke. And therefore they don't have the luxury of being casual."

Several of our other players, including Steven Crist, Andy Serling, Jim Mazur, and Paul Braseth, talked about the importance of being capitalized. It seems so obvious, but it's a topic that most casual players don't think about. If you show up at the track with $500 and you whittle it down to $100 by the fourth race, you're not going to play smartly and you might as well just throw that money away. Thus, a key component to sound money management is sound betting strategy— it's all part of one long game and if you're in a bad money situation, it's going to affect your mental state. And if your mental state is being affected, it's going to affect your play.

STEVEN CRIST: "Undercapitalization is one of the biggest reasons players lose. Playing with scared money never works because you start cutting corners and playing defensively. The more you can think of your bankroll as chips rather than money, the better."

ANDY SERLING: "Of course being capitalized is important and this is the problem that a lot of people face. If you don't have much money, you're going to be worried about what you're betting. It's the same in any gambling enterprise whether it's trading in the stock markets or playing poker. You have to be thinking about these things as chips, not money. You can't think, 'I just bet two months' rent on this horse.' Or 'Wow, that was a week's worth of dinners at a nice restaurant.' You have to think of money as a tool. If you're undercapitalized, you're dead."

JIM MAZUR: "It's also important that there aren't any financial constraints that restrict you in your handicapping."

PAUL BRASETH: "Have a lot of money to start with. That's hugely important. Anyone who is thinking about doing serious betting, you just have to have the capital."

■ Having a Set Bankroll

155

How important is it to have a set bankroll—a certain amount of money that you use to play the races? This topic didn't really affect our pros too much because capitalization wasn't a problem for them and they don't need to operate with a set bankroll. But for the player who is just starting to get serious, having a set bankroll is a good way to ensure longevity in this game, especially if you're only risking a certain percentage of your bankroll on any given wager. By doing it this way, you eliminate the risk of going broke quickly, but you also give yourself a good chance to increase your bankroll.

Cary Fotias, Paul Braseth, and Len Friedman thought it was important to have a set bankroll and to base your play on the amount of money you have. Notice how this kind of approach allows you to distance yourself emotionally from short-term fluctuations since you know that if you're losing, you're going to scale back your action, and if you're winning, you're going to increase your action a bit. This is an important side of money management that many people take for granted. In fact, it's *the* reason why money management is so important—it helps keep your emotional side in check, and as you'll see in Chapter 6, winning players know how to handle their emotions as well as their money.

CARY FOTIAS: "Players should have a bankroll. That bankroll should usually be about 50 times your bet on a given race. So if your unit play is $20, your bankroll would be $1,000. Based on how you're doing, you change your unit play. If your bankroll dips to $800, drop your unit play to $15. If it climbs to $1,200, start betting $25."

PAUL BRASETH: "Yes. My top play is probably 5 percent of that bankroll. Very rarely would I do the top play. Having a set bankroll gives me peace of mind. I like to know what I'm going to do. I will vary a small percentage, true, but I just feel comfortable doing it that way. And if you don't feel comfortable, well, you're going to have problems."

LEN FRIEDMAN: "I absolutely believe that your unit play should be a specific percentage of your bankroll. In the old days, our basic view was that you shouldn't play more than one-fiftieth of your bankroll. I think Ragozin was the one who worked that out. Assuming that you had a 5 percent edge, then it was too dangerous [because of standard deviation] to be betting more than one-fiftieth of your bankroll, that you could bust out too easily.

"For me, I discovered in the early days when I did not have a set unit that I used to play—I used to vary my handle tremendously from race to race—I found that the variation had nothing to do with my results. So I figured that for my sanity it would be better if I just bet basically the same thing every race because it was much too annoying to have the small bet come in and the big bet lose.

"When I was beginning to play I had much more limited funds and I had to have some unit that related to what I could afford to lose. In later years, my unit was based more on what the pools were."

Jim Mazur talked about one's comfort level and how it's important to know what you can and cannot afford to lose.

JIM MAZUR: "Money management is the type of thing that's very individual, based on your financial situation. What you don't want to do is spend your rent money. It's got to be totally discretionary money. Instead of going to a show, you take $200 and spend it at the track. After that, you have to learn what's best for your own demeanor. Some people love to play the favorites and cash a lot of tickets. You have to find a wager that you're comfortable with—are you going to be a win player or an exacta player or a trifecta player or a pick-three player? Then you concentrate on that and then you evolve.

"You have to get comfortable with your bankroll and what you can afford, and learn from your mistakes. I find that the pie-in-the-sky moves are not the ones to go for. You're far better off concentrating on a trainer who wins a lot, who's maybe at 6-1 or 7-1. That's a good play because you're getting the best of both worlds. You're getting a pretty good price and you're getting a trainer or maybe even a horse who knows how to win. Sometimes on big days I'm just going to follow trainers and jockeys who know how to win."

Brad Free talked about having a bankroll and how important it was to *not* play with scared money.

BRAD FREE: "Let me ask you this: What's the definition of 'bankroll'? You hear people talk about bankroll and I always used to think that a bankroll was all this money lying in your drawer with a rubber band around it and that's what you play from. It doesn't have to be like that. And for me it's not.

"A portion of my regular income goes to playing the horses. Conversely, when money is coming back the other way, that goes into the budget as well. A bankroll can be either money that you've set aside or a percentage of income that you've set aside for doing what you like to do.

"As for its importance, it's incredibly important. Because once you're fooling around with money that is earmarked for something else—the mortgage, or your kids' college, or food, or whatever— once you start losing money that you can't afford to lose, you're dead. You're just dead. That's scared money and scared money never wins. That just doesn't happen. You second-guess yourself enough in this game as it is. Once you add the pressure of having to win, it makes your head spin. If you have to win, it makes you risk-averse and you don't take chances that you should take. And then you're playing safe. And once you're playing safe, you're just doing what everybody else does."

As mentioned above, most of our big players don't operate with a set bankroll because capital isn't a concern of theirs and they know that they're in this game for the long haul. But they all had some interesting things to say about the concept of bankroll and how it's necessary for aspiring professionals to grasp the idea of money management.

RANDY GALLO: "I don't operate with a set bankroll. That's the correct way to do it, but I have a pretty big bankroll so I have in mind what I'm doing and I stick to that, and whether you're right or wrong, if you stick with it and you have some kind of game plan that's solid, then you should show a profit."

ANDREW BEYER: "I don't operate with a set bankroll. One of the things I think horseplayers need to have is a proper time frame for looking at their results. Too many people go to the track and they focus on what happened today or what happened at a given meeting. In terms of my money management, I keep it on an annual basis. I have a spreadsheet on my computer and my whole focus is the year's bottom line, and aside from that I don't have it that structured."

BARRY MEADOW: "I don't operate with a set bankroll. I have a pretty good idea of what I can and can't do but I don't say, 'Well, I lost yesterday so my bankroll is $3,000 less than what it was so I'm going to cut my bets.' At the beginning of each year I evaluate and see what I want to do."

ERNIE DAHLMAN: "I don't have a standard unit of play. I found out that over the course of time my betting hasn't increased as much as I would have expected it to. I've talked to some people who are very wealthy and they don't bet much more than when they weren't wealthy. I think it's a personal thing how much you can tolerate, and I had a high tolerance early on. I was betting big money then. I was so damn sure of myself. At that age, you don't know how wrong you can be. I was right a lot. It was harness races and I'd win and I'd say, 'I should have had more on that.' There came a time soon after when I said, 'I should have had more on that,' and people would laugh because of what I did have on it! People knew I was kidding around when I said, 'I should have had more on that.'

"No, I don't have a set bankroll."

ROXY ROXBOROUGH: "I don't have a set bankroll. My bets are restricted—not by my bankroll but by how much I'm allowed to bet. I usually want to bet the maximum. My limit is set by the type of bets. Ninety-five percent of the time I bet the maximum of what they'll take."

DECIDING HOW MUCH TO BET

With all of the choices at the racetrack, it's easy to get sucked into playing races you don't want to play. In Chapter 6, we'll talk about having the discipline to maintain focus. Also, in Chapter 3, we talked about the importance of having an edge and maximizing value. This section goes hand in hand with those two concepts: You need to decide how much you want to bet on a given race. With fancy exotic wagers and the overwhelming short prices on favorites, it's more important than ever to know how much to bet on a given race.

This is a fundamental aspect of money management, and the answer is: it depends. Some players like to bet a percentage of their bankroll; others like to take real advantage of their edge and aren't afraid to step out and bet a lot if they have conviction. As Jim Mazur mentioned above, it's all about one's comfort level.

One thing to note before we hear from our experts: There are many systems out there that claim to work. Most of them are based on due-column bets, which is a system of betting where a financial goal is set for the day and bet sizes are increased until that profit goal is reached. While any system may work at times, in the long run, they are recipes for disaster. No system like that is going to work in a parimutuel system (the size of your wager will affect your odds), just the same way that progressing your bets doesn't work in roulette because the house limits the amount of money you can bet in order to get the money back that you've already lost—or your bankroll runs out.

While we know that systems don't work in the long run, this is not to say that your betting should not, on the whole, be *systematic*. By that we mean that you need to have a strategy that's going to work for the way you bet and the size of your bankroll. As Randy Gallo said, "The first way to improve is to try and stay methodical in what you're doing. Keep the highs and lows basically in the same level if you can so that they have no effect on what you're doing. If you have in your mind that you're going to bet $300 in the third race, $600 in the eighth race, and $200 in the tenth race, the results should have no bearing on what you're doing. If you hit the third race for $10K, $600 is still the correct bet for the eighth race. And if you hit for another $5K, $200 is still the correct bet for the last race. Don't step up your action because you had a couple of winners.

"And vice versa, if a guy loses two or three in a row, he might say, 'I'm due to hit this race.' Instead of betting $20, he bets $40 or $100."

While this quote also has to do with pressing, which we discuss later in this chapter, it's just as relevant here. You need to have a game plan that works for you, and you have to stick to that plan if you want to be in this game for a long time.

160

Paul Cornman echoed Randy Gallo's sentiments about staying methodical, but he stressed the emotion factor, which is crucial to the psychological makeup of a successful bettor.

> **PAUL CORNMAN:** "I'm never one who bets a frightening amount of money. I keep my middle-of-the-road play and my top unit the same all the time. I'm in it for the long run. I've seen too many weird results. I think part of it is not to get down on yourself. This is a very psychological game, betting, all the decisions we have to make. If you get down on yourself because you've lost too much, you are going to make some bad decisions along the way."

As we mentioned above, progression bets and due-column bets are ultimately doomed to fail. On paper, they look good, but they don't really work in reality. Jim Mazur talked about his experience with a series of progression bets.

> **JIM MAZUR:** "I'm not a great money manager; I'll just come out and say it. A couple of times I've set up a progression: setting aside a certain percentage for pick threes and then with the win bets, doing a progression. I would start with a $20 or $30 bet, and each time I'd lose I'd increase the bet 20 percent. If you bet $20 and lose, then you bet $25, then $30, that kind of thing. After losing 10 in a row, that's a $250 win bet, which was way out of character, and what I found was I was totally frozen. At age 47, I have a good stock portfolio and I could lose $5K or $10K from that overnight and not even notice it in the stock market, but the thought of betting $250 on a horse totally paralyzed me.
>
> "At that point I was sitting out lots of races and making just action plays until I finally found a horse to bet $250 on. Fortunately, it did win—a Christophe Clement horse that was a high-percentage play. But I wasn't comfortable with that process."

James Quinn and Steve Davidowitz play systematically and their opinions on this topic should serve the casual-serious player very well, as most of their approaches should apply to bettors who are finally starting to get serious about playing for a living.

16

JAMES QUINN: "When I'm playing for profit, I use a fixed-percentage approach: 3 percent of $10,000 in straight wagers. That doesn't vary at all. It's systematic. I'm a grinder; I've always been. I don't have risk-taking skills and I probably left money on the table. I play a small percentage of a large bankroll and run that through X number of wagers.

"On straight wagering, I'll play 3 percent of a $10,000 bankroll. I'll double or triple in certain situations, but that's infrequent. In order to max the profits in straight bets, you have to run it through a large number of wagers. Then I'll stop. I'll usually win $12K to $20K at Santa Anita; a good season might be $30K. A bad season might be $5K or $6K. This is straight bet with a bankroll. Exotics are more of an X factor. I'll put aside $5K and use it as a nonrefundable bank of exotic wagering. If I lose, I'm playing out-of-pocket in exotics. I want to put a cap on the losses. You don't put a cap on the winnings, so if you make a big score, it overcompensates for the losses if you play that way.

"There's not too much variance on my handle. It's the same year after year. When you're learning how to play, and if you have success, you should increase your handle and the size of your wagers. Then you reach a certain threshold—stay there. I don't escalate the bets dramatically because I don't want to put it back. You should also put aside a number of dollars per month for Breeders' Cup Day. You need the bankroll to play and you could walk out with a big score. Save up. If you're going to put profits back, put them back on that day."

STEVE DAVIDOWITZ: "I have a certain amount of money I'm willing to lose in pursuit of a bomb, even if I don't have that strong of a feeling. But I just have a little nugget.

"When I'm at the track playing seriously, I expect to bet $2K to $3K in a day. I may not use it but I'm prepared to bet it. It's a significant amount to me; it isn't significant for some. Betting also keeps me sharp for the writing I do about the game and makes me write about the game in a way that I couldn't otherwise.

"I keep a separate bankroll available—which I use for no other purpose—specifically for wagering. When I get over a certain amount, I will transfer money to my checking account or use it for expenses. I don't distinguish from my racing money and other gambling money. My living and traveling money, however, is separate.

"I have a range of different units I'll play depending on my confidence level. Low-level exotic bets are sometimes my action bets. Maybe I'll spend $24. But in a multi-race situation to key on one or two horses, I'll put hundreds—between $24 and $2,000. I keep my pick six separate. I manage a small pick-six syndicate and I get a generous cut if we win, but I don't put in my own money.

"The structuring of these smaller plays means that the one I hit can pay for all the ones that don't. My opinion is stronger, and I feel more confident and have a better win percentage on the real plays."

Cary Fotias bets a percentage of his bankroll.

CARY FOTIAS: "I'm only playing about 2 percent of my bankroll on a given race . . . I might double that if I'm really getting an edge. I bet between $200 and $400 a race. I know guys who I advise who bet more like $2,000 to $4,000."

As Fotias mentioned, he might increase his bet if he feels he has a substantial edge. Dave Cuscuna felt the same way, stressing value as a major indicator of how much to bet on any given race (as opposed to using a percentage-of-bankroll approach). He also talked about betting into certain pools, which a lot of these big bettors have to be careful about. If their money hits a small pool, they're not going to get any kind of price.

DAVE CUSCUNA: "Essentially I'll bet proportionally to the opportunity and the size of the pool. That doesn't come into play for me when I bet in New York. I don't bet enough to hurt my price there; you'd need to bet $10K to win, and I'm not that big of a bettor. But if you're playing a smaller track, if I'm at Tampa Bay Downs and there's $20K in the trifecta pool and you like an 8-1 shot in the race, it doesn't make sense to bet $1K in trifectas off the 8-1—all you're doing is hurting your own price.

"It is good gambling theory to not risk too much of your bankroll on any one play. I'm not in that situation in life but at some point I was, and that does make sense."

Brad Free stressed the importance of knowing just how much you're willing to lose—and never exceeding that amount.

BRAD FREE: "I think using the Kelly Criterion is a good way to do it but I don't do it that way. I'm not that scientific. I know what I am comfortable losing on a particular race and how many bets I'm likely to lose betting the way that I do. But there are times when I'll step out. Future wagers to me have been an absolute treasure chest over the last six years or so, so I don't mind stepping out on those quite a bit.

"How do you know how much to bet? I don't know the answer to that. I know how much I'm willing to lose and I know that I have a limit of how much I'll lose in one day. And in a typical day I won't make more than four serious bets, and even that would be a lot. I do know this: If you're betting the same amount of money on every single race, that's a ridiculous thing to do also. So there's probably a happy medium in there. I've read Barry Meadow's stuff and I know what I'm good at and if I made an analysis of every wager I've made in the last five years I could probably come up with a system of betting to help me maximize my profits. But a lot of the game is flat intuition and I don't want to get bogged down in that to that extent. I know from record keeping what I do well at, I know what I'm not good at, and I know what I'm comfortable losing."

Here are some other quotes about what our pros handle and how much they like to bet on a given race.

ERNIE DAHLMAN: "Right now I start getting nervous if I bet more than $8K in one race—that gets me a little nervous. I usually bet like $5K to $6K on a race in New York and less elsewhere. I bet $3,500 on a race at Churchill today and $5K on another race. If I was losing in New York I'm not looking to bet $5K at Churchill, and if I'm winning in New York I'm not looking to piss it away at Churchill either. That was more of a case of New York being closed and trying to make a good day's pay. I wanted to earn something today and I did. But I could have got out of there real quick with a couple of losing bets."

RANDY GALLO: "On the dogs, I probably make anywhere from 10 to 12 bets a week, from as small as $1,500 to as large as $8K or $9K, depending on the size of the carryover and how much each jackpot is worth to what the crowd is betting.

"On the horses, depending what the exactas are in the race, I could bet $600 to win and $3K in exactas, or I could bet $3K to win and nothing in exactas. If I have a particular horse that I say should be 2-1 and he's 5-2, if I want to take that, I can take that and bet win money.

"I got a horse the other day, I ended up betting $6K; I didn't have a dollar to win on him, I bet it all in exactas and trifectas. And he ended up winning and paying $8; I had him at like 5-1, and I ended up breaking even on the race. Obviously, I didn't do well in that race."

STEVEN CRIST: "At Saratoga in 2003, I played 34 out of 36 cards and my daily handle was anywhere between $300 and $5,000. The low end were days when it poured and the track was a mess, or sunny days where I just didn't see any opportunities and made a token early pick-three and late pick-four play just to make myself pay attention and have a little entertainment. High-end days were when I made a four-figure investment in a pick-six carryover and also attacked individual races with gusto."

BASEBALL BETTOR: "I bet either 1 to 3 percent of my bankroll on any given bet, depending on how strong the given bet is. It's very arbitrary.

"Dollar-wise over the course of a season, in the past few years, we were betting about $20,000 to $100,000 per game. In baseball it's very difficult to bet a lot of money on totals. The casinos take a half to a quarter of the amount of money on totals than they do on sides. The casinos limit the action. They don't like to take as much action on baseball. The only reason they take baseball is because there's nothing to do when the other sports are not in season. And the popularity of baseball betting is nowhere near what it is in other sports. Football is four times more popular; basketball is two times more popular in terms of handle—and that's with less games!

"We probably have close to a thousand bets in the course of a year—15 percent of all betting opportunities. What do we put into action in the course of a year? About $25 or $30 million in action."

KEVIN BLACKWOOD: "My top bet was always a thousand dollars in blackjack, and depending on one, two, or six decks, it would range up and down. Each game required a slightly different spread in order to beat it.

"I had a set bankroll when I was playing professionally. And that was a hundred thousand dollars.

"In blackjack, you never get a real big edge on one hand so I would never risk more than one percent of the bankroll on any one bet.

"In blackjack, you're playing hundreds of hands over the course of a day. You could put a hundred thousand in action each day. That would be reasonable, but it's in such small increments over time."

BETTING ITSELF AS AN EDGE:
HOW TO CONSTRUCT A GOOD BET

Another important idea to consider when thinking about how to manage your money is that the specific way in which you construct a bet can either contribute to—or take away from—your overall edge. The pick six is probably the best place to illustrate how important it is to know how to construct a ticket properly. That particular skill is just one of the things that has made Steven Crist famous.

STEVEN CRIST: "An edge can also simply be a method that others are too lazy to use, such as making out multiple tickets in multi-race wagers rather than just putting as many horses as you can afford on a single ticket."

In *Betting on Myself,* Steven Crist writes about the evolution of his pick-six play. When he was involved as an investor in Andrew Beyer's syndicate in Florida in the mid-eighties (a group that also included Paul

Cornman), the strategy was to construct "main" and "backup" tickets. Rather than play every horse on every ticket (which would quickly become prohibitively expensive), they'd play three separate tickets: one narrowed down to just their main horses, one that had main horses in five legs but spread out in, say, the fourth leg, and yet another that had mains in five legs but spread out in a sixth.

STEVEN CRIST: "What we were basically doing was creating an old-time Chinese-restaurant menu and saying that we were allowed either six selections from Column A or five from Column A and one from Column B. You could only have one backup horse win, and if he did, A's had to win the other five races."

Later in the book, Crist talked about how this strategy evolved over time to maximize his edge. "Rather than buying backup tickets in two races a day," Crist wrote, "what if you had backups and contingencies in virtually every race? Instead of demanding that your Chinese menu consist of six A's or five A's and a B, what if you could construct a more elaborate dinner in which you could get four items from Column A and up to two from Column B? Might there even be a Column C, exotic side horses you could add to the menu if everything else worked out perfectly?

"The nuisance factor in this approach was making out so many tickets—usually at least 10 and as many as 30 with a particularly complicated play . . . What made all the paperwork tolerable was knowing that no one else was approaching the bet this way and that all the permutations had to give us an edge."

Randy Gallo also plays the pick six in a creative way to maximize his advantage.

RANDY GALLO: I've been playing the pick six for 30 years now. I'm playing much harder tickets now. One-ticket, two-ticket, three-ticket outcomes [he's looking to hold tickets where only one, two, or three tickets have the winning combination]. Whereas before, I wouldn't hesitate to bet $4,000 to hit a $20,000 ticket. If I'm betting $4,000 now, I'm looking to get anywhere from $80,000 to $100,000 and up."

In other words, Gallo isn't interested in hitting the tickets that he knows other pick-six players are going to have, and he eliminates those combinations from his tickets even though they are much more likely to hit than combinations that remain on his tickets.

RANDY GALLO: "I think the margin of error now is much smaller than it was 25 or 30 years ago simply because the public has learned how to bet. The basic overlays in pick sixes are the tickets that the public is not going to have, the one-, two-, and three-ticket outcomes where you're outside the crowd. That's where I think the overlay is. In other words, if the winner pays anything between $6 and $10 for six races and you figure out the parlay price is 23,000-1, the ticket usually pays between $40,000 and $60,000. Because that's where the money is saturated so the predictability is pretty much there.

"If you get tickets outside of that, that's where the overlay is. In other words, a lot of the groups [syndicates who are playing the pick six regularly] are playing tickets that are likely to pay anywhere from $4,000 to $20,000—winning-ticket payouts within those groups are pretty predictable; that is, they come back reasonably close to the parlay and are not huge overlays. If you get outside of that [if you have tickets that include more long prices], you might find a ticket that parlays out to 100K to 1 and it actually pays $300K. We had a ticket at Del Mar in 2001, in late August, and the parlay price on it was, I think, 77,000-1 and it paid $630,000. I consider that a big overlay."

We asked Gallo to talk more about how he puts his tickets together.

RANDY GALLO: "If I'm looking at the card and I say, 'There's two bullets, one of them is probably going to win, and if the other one doesn't win, you can't go past three deep, and there are a couple of other races where I don't think it's going to go past three horses,' I'm not going to play. I'm not going to invest $15K or $20K, praying for two 20-1 shots in the other two races. I'm not going to play any ticket that the crowd's going to be on. You can't be betting that kind of money and end up betting $12K and cashing for $19K. There's too much risk.

"If I think the card is probably going to run chalk, I'm not going to play regardless of the carryover. And believe it or not, I would say my success rate is pretty high in doing that, by not playing and saving money. If I get a card that I can't pick, I want to play. I want to play in a heartbeat. Because if I can't handicap it, I know these other guys are going to have trouble. Then I want to get in a range that's outside the crowd. Once I set an odd on every horse, if I'm going to spend $20K, I'll eliminate every ticket that parlays out to $50K or less, according to my odds. And I'll only play tickets that are higher than that.

"So in other words, if I'm with the crowd according to what the odds are going to be on the board, I say to myself, 'I don't want to play any tickets that figure to pay less than 50,000-1.' So I eliminate those tickets with the computer program I have. I want a hard ticket. So I might play tickets that figure to parlay out from $50K to $80K or maybe $50K to $100K or something along there. That doesn't mean it's going to come in. If I hit, the value is going to be there."

As for intra-race wagers, the same idea of betting in a way to maximize your advantage applies to vertical wagers as well. Most of the public is box happy—they'll box the three favorites in the exacta and trifecta, and when these horses come in, the result is almost always an underlay. A better way to play is to write your bets in a way that more precisely reflects what you think is going to happen. Of the three horses in your exacta box, do you like one of them a bit more? Okay, then take your 4-1 key horse and play him top and bottom with the other contenders. Sure, there will be times when the two horses you left out will run one-two and you get nothing. But the extra money you get when you win should make up for it.

Our Kentucky Player illustrated this point perfectly.

KENTUCKY PLAYER: "The actual way I play has changed over the years too—maybe not a lot, but I've refined the way I bet, becoming more efficient in allocating each dollar of my bet to the proper combination in the proper amount. The way I like to think of it is that I want my bet to represent my exact opinion of the race, of the horses involved versus the odds. When I finish my bet—I might bet an exacta, trifecta, superfecta, all in the same race—I want to walk away from the window and feel like I took advantage of everything I know about the horses involved and about the odds involved, and the money I bet on each combination is an accurate representation of where I feel the value is in the race."

This thought was echoed by Len Friedman, who feels that many players use poor management as an excuse for why they lose, when the real problem is that they're not handicapping well enough and/or are unable to convert their real opinion into a sensible wager.

LEN FRIEDMAN: "People often say, 'I handicapped the race well but I bet it wrong.' But that shouldn't happen because you should bet the race in accordance with what your handicapping opinion was. That's going to require your actually thinking it through. You're going to have to say, 'In this race my real opinion is I don't like the favorite.' Or in another race you might say, 'My real opinion is that this longshot looks good and while the favorite might be an underlay, he's not bad.' And in the latter case, you should use the favorite with your longshot. And in the former case, you shouldn't. The way you construct your play should depend on what your real handicapping opinion is.

"Depending on what your opinion is, you should use different parts of the wagering pools. If your basic opinion is that the favorite is no good, you want to play bets that enable you to throw out the favorite in as many positions as possible. You want to be playing trifectas and superfectas if you're playing against what you think is a very weak favorite. Because every race you throw the favorite out of, you're multiplying your edge if you're right. Whereas on the other hand, if your opinion is that you really like a 6-1 shot in the race, you ought to have at least two-thirds of your play to win on him. You don't want to have to be dependent on some other horse coming in, if your real opinion is on a particular horse. You don't want to get too smart and try to correctly handicap every horse in the race.

"Putting your bets together in accordance with your opinion is an important part of winning. It doesn't do any good if you have a really strong handicapping opinion and then you don't really cash it because you threw out horses that you didn't really have an opinion on and those horses didn't run to the way you played the race. Even though the horse you did like did run to the way you expected him too."

BRAD FREE: "Bet construction obviously applies to exotic wagers and it's a huge factor. Whatever edge you may already have by being a good handicapper can only be magnified by structuring your bet properly. If you're playing a pick three that goes three by three by three, you've got no edge. You can't weight every horse the same in all three legs. You need to take a stand somewhere and allow yourself a chance to be wrong along the way. And that's just in horizontal wagers.

"I love vertical wagers because you can find horses that you don't necessarily expect to win the race, but you can build wagers around crazy horses to finish second and third. And that's my favorite way to do it. Find a horse that for whatever reason has a real good chance to outrun his odds. He's probably not going to win, maybe he's some clunk-up closer. But if you build your trifecta from the bottom up, he could be the one to construct the whole thing around.

"I know a lot of people who do their trifectas 1-2-3 with 1-2-3 with ALL and every time I hear that I just cringe. What's the point? I hate the ALL button. When you hit the ALL button, you're admitting defeat and you're inviting the whole process of luck into your decision making. I don't want to set out to get lucky and hope that maybe a longshot finishes third. I'll key that longshot to do just that and use the logical contenders to finish first and second. Or first and third. There are smart ways to construct bets and there are idiot ways to do it. You need to weigh horses differently and you also need to key horses, and I would very rarely hit the ALL button."

CARY FOTIAS: "Bet your opinions concisely—make surgical strikes. Too many good handicappers squander money by boxing and wheeling out of laziness or a fear of not cashing.

"Most players bet more money on races where they have a smaller edge. They'll bet a lot on an 8-5 and less on a 10-1. You should have the courage to bet just as much on your 10-1's as your 5-2's."

Fotias's last point is true in the sense that if your edge is the same, you should bet as much on an overlaid longshot you like as on an overlaid favorite. But it can also be more complicated than that.

BARRY MEADOW: "We all want to bet $1,000 on a 50-1 that wins and $2 to show on a 4-5 shot who finishes out of the money. But that's not the way it works. What I do is use the bet charts from my book so I'm going to bet more if the value is greater—but is the value greater? Say one horse is 8-1 on the board, and I might have him on my value line at 6-1, so there's value. But if I have him at 4-1 that's more value, so I'm going to bet more on that horse I have at 4-1 than the one I have at 6-1. I'm going to play more money on the shorter-priced horses for two reasons.

"First of all, they win more often so that helps with bankroll preservation and leads to shorter losing streaks.

"Second, your bet doesn't affect the odds as much. You can't be betting a zillion dollars on these wacky longshots. You have a much greater standard deviation on horses that are 10-1 than horses that are 2-1. And if you get lucky and win on those 10-1 shots, that's great, but what happens if you don't? You're going to have some serious, serious streaks of badness there."

■ Imagination

With the topic of bet construction comes the interesting aspect of imagination—having the ability to see things differently from the public.

PAUL CORNMAN: "A good imagination is one of the most important things you can have. This is where it comes into play. Everyone is looking at the same problem and you have to have some thought process, some creativity where you can maybe anticipate something that the other people aren't. I believe that comes from the power of imagination. You have to know the game; you can't imagine what you don't know. You have to be mentally sharp to do that."

Brad Free also talked about the importance of having imagination—of being able to see things a little differently from everyone else as a way to give yourself an edge. This topic can be applied to any facet of the game, particularly handicapping, but it's also very crucial to the way you construct your bets.

172

BRAD FREE: "Imagination is what sets you aside from every other person in the grandstand. If you don't have a unique opinion—if you're not able to stand alone from doing what everybody else does—you're in the wrong game. If you can employ imagination in your handicapping and/or in the way you construct wagers, you are going to stand apart from the crowd, for better or worse.

"One of the most imaginative handicappers I've ever met is Mark Cramer. He is phenomenal. Imagination is a very good topic that hasn't been written about enough. If you're just doing what everybody else is doing, what's the point? You need to have unique ideas and unique ways of looking at things, and if you don't, over time, the takeout is going to eat you alive. You could get lucky for a while. Or maybe some people out there are so brilliant that they're just the world's greatest handicappers, and they can win just because they're smarter than everybody else. I'm not. So I know that I have to be as imaginative and creative as possible—without getting too out there.

"You have to be able to stand apart. You can't be afraid to be wrong. Being imaginative is part of the whole process, especially when you remember that there are no black-and-white answers. Two great handicappers can look at the same race and come to two completely different conclusions. Being unique is what makes this such a fascinating game. It's okay to be wrong a lot more than you're right as long as the times you're right, you've bet the race the right way. In the long run, you'll be doing okay."

David Sklansky, a famous poker player and the author of *Getting the Best of It* and *Hold 'em Poker* (among other best-selling poker-strategy books), wrote a related online story about thinking outside the box:

"Many years ago, Jeff Yass asked me what I thought the best strategy would be for a particular situation on fifth street in seven-card stud. When I answered, he then asked me if the same would be true for *eight*-card stud! At that moment I knew I was talking to a man who was going places. Many of you know that he went on after a short successful poker career to be the premier options trader in the world. (To this day every employee of his firm Susquehanna Securities is required to read my *Getting the Best of It.*) The fact that he asked me about a nonexistent game showed me he was aware of the concept that looking at hypothetical examples could be very useful to get a handle on something."

TO PRESS OR NOT TO PRESS

While we have a whole chapter dedicated to the emotional aspect of the game, we felt it was important to specifically discuss pressing in this chapter. Some players step out and bet more when they're ahead. Others bet more when they're down in order to get even or turn a small profit. We feel this concept is germane to a discussion of money management. If you can't manage your money effectively—and you stray from the amount you're willing to lose—you're going to find yourself in dire situations more often than not. And if that's case, you're not long for this game.

There's a fine line between being aggressive in certain optimal situations and pressing just because you're on a win streak. If you've isolated great value and have an edge, then it's important to bet with more conviction. You need to have the discipline to pick your spots when betting more money than you're used to—and not get sucked into increasing your bets just because you've been winning that day, even though you might not have a distinct edge.

GERRY OKUNEFF: "I certainly do try to be more aggressive when I'm winning. When I'm in a losing streak, I'll back off—that's fundamental to surviving. I never consider the last race of the day as having any more significance than the first race of the day. There is no finish line—trying to get even is a foolish thing to do. It's just the 48,600th race I've seen and I'll see the next one tomorrow. You have to set a limit on what you'll allow yourself to lose and *not* set a limit on how much you can win."

BRAD FREE: "I do bet more when I'm going well. And I'm not sure that that's the right thing to do but I do. I don't think there's anything wrong with that. When you're going well, you have the freedom to play a little more loose than you should. And sometimes by pressing you can magnify a particularly clever streak of handicapping. But you have to be careful about it. Even as I'm talking about it, I'm realizing that it's probably not the right thing to do.

"When I'm going poorly, I back way down. And I know when I'm going bad. When I start going bad, it becomes very simple for me. I have my own little system that I do to try and shake a slump or ride it out. When I'm in a slump, I know it because I write down what I've done in my program every day and I transcribe it onto my hard drive when I get home every night so I know exactly what happened at the end of every day. When that happens, I just stick to win bets on my top three picks in the paper. I set an odds line: 3-1 on the top choice, 6-1 on the second choice, 10-1 on the third choice, and I bet according to that. It's so simple and basic and it works. If any of my choices is higher than those odds, I'll bet it. It reemphasizes the whole idea of a betting line. And that's really the only time I use a hard-and-fast betting line."

LAS VEGAS PLAYER: "I won't make bad bets. Some guys get a tough beat in poker and the next hand they want to raise no matter what to get their money back. You shouldn't *not* bet, but whatever the next hand is that would warrant betting, you should bet. For me to want to make a big bet I really have to think I have way the best of it. I'm not looking to gamble, I'm looking to get the best of it."

ROXY ROXBOROUGH: "When I'm winning, I bet more; when I'm losing, I bet less. I have a strong aversion to losing.

"Most people are much better players when they're winning and worse players when they're losing. In poker, if a player is playing well, stay out of his way. When he's losing, then people can't line up fast enough to play against him. I hate losing. I'm losing-averse, so I back off when things are going bad. When I win, I'll play like I normally do and maybe start betting more.

"In the early seventies, before I became an oddsmaker, I was betting sports. I had a mentor who told me that you have to leap at good opportunities. If you want to be a pro gambler you can't have bad habits and you have to take advantage of opportunities—take calculated risks. Don't take your bankroll and put it all on black—that's not a calculated risk. Instead, bet a sizable amount of money to take advantage of edge. Make the most of your opportunities.

"Fortunately, I found that out early in my gambling career, so I was able to really capitalize on favorable situations. When most gamblers start out and want to become pros, they find the hardest part is pulling the trigger; the easiest part is finding loopholes and edges. But putting the money down and making the bet, that's the hard part."

BASEBALL BETTOR: "When I'm losing . . . I resist the temptation to press; it's just a matter of fortitude. The more structured it is the easier it is to resist something outside of your realm. Blackjack was very easy to resist temptations. I take that experience with me. Blackjack is set up in a structured way—it's the same with sports. If you have a set bankroll and get in the right habits, it's easier to resist the temptation to lower or raise your bets."

KEVIN BLACKWOOD: "No, I don't bet more to try and get even. But that is a temptation. I don't think it affects serious pros. But if you're going to be successful, that's something you have to purge out of your system early on.

"In blackjack, there's nothing mentally that's going to change the cards or affect the way you play as long as you're going by the correct mathematical decisions.

"So no, I don't play differently if I've won or lost five in a row.

"I usually try to play as long as I can as long as the game is good. I think we're all human and there's a bit of tendency—if you're near the end of a day—to cut the session a little short. I'd play as many hours as I could."

DAVE GUTFREUND: "There's definitely truth to the following cliché: When you're going well you're supposed to bet more and when you're going badly you're supposed to bet less. And it is much easier to say that than to actually do that. When I've lost badly for two or three days I take a day off from betting. That doesn't mean I don't read *Daily Racing Form* or don't study, and it doesn't mean I don't keep up with what goes on at the track that day; it just means some days you need to take a little freshening, like a horse."

AMARILLO SLIM PRESTON: "Discipline is very important. I don't believe in luck, but I think that people do go in streaks. And I know they do playing cards. When I'm going bad, I'll limit my wagers. I don't know what I want to win on any given day, but I sure as hell know what I'll lose. If I didn't, I wouldn't be in business."

PAUL BRASETH: "Confidence is very important. I definitely play with more confidence when I'm winning, increasing my bets but not by much. And if I'm in a losing streak I will back off and I won't start betting my usual amount until I start winning. I'll still do all the same work, I just won't bet as much. Any player who says they don't change, I think that's a mistake. We all go through times when we're playing well and when we're not playing well—if we knew the answer we'd be geniuses. It's like trying to figure out why a hitter goes into a slump. Nobody knows. You can try to figure it out. A ballplayer might go back and watch films. I do the same thing: I go back and say, 'Okay, how did I make this wrong decision?' Most players I know, when they're not going well, they back off on their bets."

Paul Cornman talked about the importance of consistency.

PAUL CORNMAN: "I'm in for the big picture. If God tapped me on the shoulder and said, 'Paul, if you don't win today, this is your last day on Earth,' I think I'd have a different approach of double up and get even. But other than that I plan on being there for the first race tomorrow.

"I've known some characters at the track. I knew a guy when I was starting out, if he didn't win the last race, he wasn't going to win. I don't think that's a strategy that's going to work. If somebody told me I was smarter in the late races than in the earlier ones, I'd think about doing that but for me, uh-uh, that's not for me."

■ Quitting Winners

One side aspect of this topic is "quitting winners." Is it okay to walk away from a winning streak even though you might be leaving money on the table? As you'll see in Chapter 6, the fact that our players know that it's one long game allows them to keep a systematic approach to the task at hand—making money in the long run.

JAMES QUINN: "I'm a grinder and always have been up until recent years. I'm disciplined and systematic in play. I regret leaving money on the table and should have been more aggressive when I wasn't. I would make $20K to $40K a year and more than half of that was during Santa Anita. That was okay but it wasn't the kind of money a lot of players would have been satisfied with.

"I was a winner right away and that convinced me I could play well enough to win. Confidence has never been a problem for me. I don't play differently. I don't recognize a hot streak. I play my hand the same way. So I'm not so good at recognizing hot streaks. That's one regret. I don't have those skills. But losing doesn't affect me. I know what the expectations are. I do computer simulations so I know what the expectations are. You can lose 22 in a row and still make a profit betting the way I like to play.

"Losing doesn't affect my play or my confidence; I'm good at coming back from losing runs. Also, I'm not a chaser. I don't make due-column bets, which means I won't try to win a thousand dollars by betting a hundred on a horse just to try and get a thousand dollars to win on the day. I'm not a stabber."

BASEBALL BETTOR: "Quitting and pressing are individual things and they are tremendous temptations to gamblers and it goes in all directions. Some people have a strong desire to quit when they're ahead. I'm like that. There are a lot of people worse than that. For baseball, historically, I've quit at the end of August or middle of August if we've had a successful season. I can take a month off because it's stressful. For me, that's my tendency. Others are opposite; when people are losing, they'll quit. After winning, they'll bet more and keep betting more money. Compulsion, allure, temptation all have to do with the fluctuations of gambling. If I quit early, I can justify it rationally. Sure, I could be leaving money on the table where I have a positive expectation percentage-wise and dollar-wise. It's no different than taking an unpaid vacation from your job.

"It's all about personal utility. It's not only about money. It's about stress, time, etc.—so many issues that are varied and complex."

ERNIE DAHLMAN: "If I've won five in a row because I notice some bias or I've picked up on something, like the inside was dead, that would give me all kinds of confidence. If I won five in a row but I was more or less stabbing, felt I had a little thing going for me, that wouldn't make me bet any more money. I kind of have a good idea of when I love something. If I love something and it wins and then I love something and it wins and then I love something and it wins, well, I'm expecting the next horse I love to win. I think that's human nature. I'm liable to be betting through the ceiling by the time the sixth horse that I love comes in.

"In the other direction, I'll back off. I'll think I'm missing something. I didn't think that horse could lose and he ran fifth. What did I miss? Why did that happen? If that starts happening a lot, I back off a lot."

5

WOULDA . . . COULDA . . . SHOULDA . . . DOESN'T GET IT DONE

SECRET

They know how to handicap themselves.

Handicapping is both an art and a science. Like art, it's purely subjective—some aspects of the game, like pace or paddock inspection, have more or less importance depending on the type of player you are. Like science, there are certain immutable laws, or hard-and-fast facts, that can't be ignored when you're handicapping a race—like how fast a horse is, or a trainer's record with turf horses. It's the handicapper's job to mix art with science in order to pick winners and profit from those selections over the long haul. This chapter concerns itself with the subjective aspect of the game, i.e., the proficiency with different elements of handicapping that each player brings to the table.

Since there are so many elements to handicapping and betting, it's important to figure out which of those elements of the game work best for you. How long should you take to handicap? Should you go to the track or stay at home and play on the computer? Which tracks should you play and how many races should you bet? Should you bet exactas and trifectas or stick to sequential bets like pick threes and pick fours? Is it better to play dirt or turf races? Is it okay to make action bets? All successful gamblers have a comprehensive approach toward handicapping and betting that works best for them—and that's why they're able to win in the long run.

This isn't something you can figure out right away—it takes years to understand all of the nuances of the game, and then to figure out which elements you understand more than others—and most important, it takes courage and fortitude to be honest with yourself, especially when you're losing or making mistakes. There are so many different ways to play the game that you need to be systematic and honest with yourself in figuring out what works best for you. As Dave Gutfreund said, "Self-analysis is the key to success."

By keeping records of your play (and your wins and losses) and by analyzing your strengths and weaknesses, you can become a better player. In horse racing, there is no room for excuses—you need to learn, adjust, and move on.

GERRY OKUNEFF: "At some point, I realized that 'woulda . . . coulda . . . shoulda' just wasn't going to cut it anymore."

Our Las Vegas Player had a similar take.

LAS VEGAS PLAYER: "The most successful people in life are always willing to learn. They're the ones who don't think they have all the answers. If you really think you're great and you're just unlucky, then you have no chance. You have to understand what a tough game this is and try to learn from your mistakes and don't blame it on bad luck.

"Here's a key to what losers do: After the race they red-board. 'Oh, I should've done that,' they say. I don't think I've ever done that. A lot of times I'll say, 'Ah, I should've bet more,' but I don't think I should even do that.

"You'll never hear a successful player say after a race that he should have bet a different horse. He might say that he missed something. But if you've put a lot of analysis into it and then after the race you say, 'I should've bet something else,' well, then you really should be doing something else. You have to be comfortable with what you bet and accept what you bet; I give a little leverage to saying, 'I should've bet a little more or a little less,' but not to 'I should've bet a different horse.' If you should have bet a different horse, then you shouldn't be playing the game in the first place. You don't know what you're doing."

It sounds so simple and clichéd, but being honest with yourself is the only way to win at the races.

How many people do you know who cheat on their golf score? Why? How many people say that they "just broke even" at the track when you know they had a losing day? To some, this might be a method of positive reinforcement—but it's positive reinforcement for *losers.* Winners are honest with themselves—and if they're losing, they understand that and make the necessary adjustments so that they're only losing in the short run and not over the long haul.

All of our players are brutally honest—and not only with themselves, but also with those around them.

They're also very established in knowing what works best for them and using that knowledge to maximize their advantage.

WHAT IT MEANS TO HANDICAP YOURSELF

There's no sense playing this game if you can't sit back after a long day of racing and analyze your play. If you can't learn from your mistakes or accentuate your strengths, then there is just no way you can be a winning horseplayer. In horse racing, honesty really is the best policy. If you're deceiving yourself—either in terms of your handicapping ability, your proficiency at making smart bets, or your money ledger at the end of a meet—then you're destined for the poorhouse. To win consistently over time, you need to be honest and analytical about the way you play the game. As Dave Gutfreund said, "Be aware of what you're doing. Handicap yourself."

Steve Davidowitz summed this up perfectly. "We all tell little tales about the whale that got away; we all exaggerate our life stories over time for gratification and the approval of others," he said. "But even when we do that we have to be honest with ourselves to be successful in the gambling world. You have to keep records and review what you're doing or that will undermine you."

Our Kentucky Gambler concurred.

KENTUCKY GAMBLER: "One thing I say to people when they ask me about gambling is that it's really important to be honest with yourself—to look at the bottom line at some point and say, 'Okay, this is where I am,' and to not allow yourself to have any excuses. You teach yourself to overcome the problems that occur along the way and you stay focused on that end result of being a winning player. And you keep that focus point while you're riding the ups and downs that a horse-player goes through.

"You have to be honest. If you lose that honesty with yourself it opens up all kinds of bad things that can happen to you. As long as you're being honest with yourself, as long as you're saying, 'Hey, I lost $50K at the races last year; I made $70K in my job; this is not a good thing. I either need to improve or I just need to be a recreational player.' As long as you're on that path, and then the next year you only lose $20K, well, a logical man can sit down and say, 'Okay, I'll give it another year.' An illogical man can start betting another $100K a year and go bankrupt and start embezzling from his company. I've seen that happen. And I'm pretty sure you have too if you've been around the racetrack. It's not something we want to promote but I think it's a real thing. Some people just don't handle it and that needs to be in print too. Not everybody's cut out for that. Not everybody, no matter how much training, or how long they've been doing it or how hard they try, not everybody is necessarily a candidate to be comfortable gambling or to be successful gambling. I've seen several lives ruined by gambling. You have to respect it."

Ernie Dahlman recognizes that it's important not to make excuses. It's easy to blame your losses on external factors—bad trips, jockey error, a tough DQ—but at the end of the day, it's all part of the game.

ERNIE DAHLMAN: "You have to be very good at analyzing. I see a lot of people who are bad players and every time they lose they blame the jockey or they blame some outside force and you can't do that. You have to be evaluating your horse just like the other horses because when they run back you've got to know whether this horse ran a good race or a bad race, and if it duplicates that last race, can it win today? You have to be objective in every race. You can't be blaming jockeys or trainers. You have to be able to put a good analysis on the horses you picked and the horses you didn't like. If you thought a horse had no shot, then you've got to be able to say, 'Wow, did he improve! He was a lot better than I thought he'd be.' So, either he improved and there was a reason you missed it, or you were wrong about him—you've got to be willing to accept that.

"I think the less you're surprised, the better a player you are, but you're still going to be surprised no matter who you are. When you get surprised a lot, you're not thinking clearly or you don't understand the game well enough or something. If you're constantly being amazed at what just happened, you're missing something."

Dahlman also finds it important to analyze your play—regardless of whether you've won or lost. There's always something to be learned from analyzing a race, and if you're able to figure out what went wrong or confirm why something went right, then you've advanced in your play.

ERNIE DAHLMAN: "The casual bettor, after the race, should try to figure out what he thought before the race, what he thought after the race, why he thinks he lost, and what did he learn? A lot of times you're between a couple of horses and the other one wins; you drive yourself crazy. But you have to constantly be reevaluating, constantly trying to figure out the game. What did you miss? What didn't you give enough weight to? Were there any changes there you didn't think about, was there a trainer change on the winner, was there a jockey change? Who was it?"

Amarillo Slim likes to say that the best woodcutter is the one with the most chips. Our Las Vegas Player, who regards Dahlman as one of the best players in the game, agrees.

LAS VEGAS PLAYER: "To me, the best player is the one with the most money. I play tennis a lot and I have a lot better strokes than one of the guys I play with and I don't think I've ever beaten him. They all say, 'You're better than him.' I say, 'Better than him? The guy beats me all the time. Who cares if my strokes *look* better?'

"If you play poker you'll hear this: 'I'm much better than the guys who play higher than me, I just don't have a high enough bankroll.'

Think of the absurdity of that! The guys with big bankrolls started with small bankrolls and built up!"

It's true. Every one of our big players had to start somewhere. And they've gotten to this point in their careers because they consistently evaluate their game. Dave Cuscuna was open about his handicapping ability. He knows that there are people out there who might be better at him when it comes to one specific thing. But he also knows that his overall game is what's important, and he works hard to be the best he can be, concentrating on the aspects that make him such a great player.

DAVE CUSCUNA: "I find my edge from being very good at a lot of things. I wish I could be great at everything. I'm not. I'm probably not great at any one thing. But I'm probably very good at a lot of the things we're talking about: handicapping, money management, discipline, and all those things. And I think that my edge comes from being above average in every aspect.

"If you throw something out to me at any one aspect—handicapping, mathematics, money management—I can tell you one or two people who I know personally that are better at it than I am. But they might be a lot worse than me at the other areas. My edge comes from being pretty good at a lot of different things.

"I played the Saratoga meet nine years ago. The first week I lost multiple five figures and along the way I just missed a pick six; I lost a photo in a pick six that was going to cash $78K. I lost $20K, but if one of five things had gone my way I'd have had a real good week, so I said, 'Okay, let's get 'em next week.'

"I went back the next week and lost again, same story—a lost photo here and there. By the time it got to be the end of the fourth week, I was stuck big money. And I started looking back at these photos and I realized that these photos that I took these tough breaks on couldn't get me back to even. One of my favorite quotes by Bill Parcells is: 'You are what you are.'

"There gets to be a point as a sports team where you can say, 'Yeah, well we're six and six but if the ref didn't blow that call, if we hadn't fumbled on the one, if the kicker hadn't squibbed that kick out of bounds, we would be nine and three.'

"But you know, you're six and six. And what I was was minus many times five figures. At some point, you have to take a look at your results, see what you are. At that point I put an asterisk next to my name and it said, 'I suck,' because I did. You can sugarcoat things and say I got unlucky and this or that happened, but the bottom line is what I am is a multiple-five-figure loser with a lot of work. It's time to sit down and revamp the game plan."

So how did Dave Cuscuna handle it?

DAVE CUSCUNA: "I did two things. I made a state-of-mind choice. And then I showed some discipline. The state-of-mind choice was that I said to myself, 'I can afford this and I'm not going to feel any worse if I blow another $25K, but I'll feel a hell of a lot better if I can get out from underneath this.' This is poor gambling theory and I don't necessarily recommend this. But what I decided to do was take another $25K and throw it at the last week.

"But I said to myself, 'No matter what happens, even if I end up winning $200K, I'm not going to get fooled into thinking I had a winning system all along. If I lose the other $25K, which I probably will because I'm going sour right now, I'm not going to feel any worse or any stupider than I do already. I'm going to take the shot with the $25K. It's bad gambling theory but I'll feel a lot better if I can get out of this meet close to even. Then, no matter what, win or lose, I'm going to go back to the drawing board. I'm not going to play this type of betting for a couple of months and see if I can figure out what I need to do differently.'

"What ended up happening was I ended up winning money the last week but not enough to get me out for the whole meet. I won back maybe a third of my losses. And then I showed some discipline. I took a lot of time off and revamped the game plan; I knew I had to do a lot of things differently. I started over and got out of the slump by reevaluating my play, trying to replicate my successes and eliminate my failures."

Your play should be no different. If you're losing at the races, step back, look at your past plays, and try to figure out why you're not winning. If you're winning, make sure you understand why you're winning, so that when you have a few losing streaks, you don't start doubting your ability as a handicapper. If you can continually analyze your game, and be honest in your analysis, you'll know where you stand at the end of the day.

Being honest with yourself is the first step. Then, once you know what your strengths and weaknesses are, it's important to continue to do what works best for you.

DOING WHAT WORKS FOR YOU

No two players are the same, and different players focus on different things in order to win. Some guys use The Sheets; others focus on training patterns; some are just damn good handicappers and understand the fundamentals of the game—speed, pace, class, condition—on an intuitive level; still others rely on sophisticated computer models to beat the races. They're all successful, yet they have a variety of different approaches. So which way is the right way?

The correct answer is that there is no right way—just plenty of wrong ways. But another way of looking at it is this: The right way is your way. Each of these guys, over decades, has established a method of handicapping that suits his own skills. It didn't happen overnight; it came about through trial and error and years and years of hard work. Over time, they figured out which aspects of the game they were most proficient at and used that to their advantage.

You can learn from all of these different approaches. You can try to make your own speed figures to complement, or use instead of, the Beyer Speed Figures that are printed in the *Daily Racing Form*. You can study pedigrees for turf races, distance races, and off tracks in order to give yourself an edge. You can keep your own trainer stats, or watch replays of every race and write up trip notes. You might have the time to do all these things, or you might have the time to do just some of them; that, combined with a simple trip down to the paddock to thoroughly inspect the horses up close, might give you your edge.

Do what works for you. That's how you become a winning player in the long run.

One other important thing to note here: While it's important to do what works for you, it's also important to consistently adapt your game to your surroundings—to new information that might become available, to changes that are inevitable in the game. Doing what works for you *does not mean* being narrow-minded. Quite the contrary: It means adapting and adjusting your game to your own comfort level so that you factor in the information that will allow you to be a consistent winner. Doing what works for you goes hand in hand with being honest with yourself.

Steve Davidowitz had some excellent comments about the general nature of handicapping and how it's important to do what works for you, but at the same time, how it's important to understand and be aware of all of the different facets of the game.

STEVE DAVIDOWITZ: "I've always resisted labels. They are poor excuses to dismiss what's really going on. When someone calls a ballplayer a Punch and Judy hitter, a fastball pitcher, etc., they never tell the whole story. But people do tend to come from certain directions. I recommend that people new to the game should find out what their strengths are. Are you visually inclined? Can you recognize talent visually? If so, go to the paddock, evaluate horses as visual athletes.

"Can you see Gestalt-type patterns? If you're really good at synthesizing data, like the past performances in *Daily Racing Form*, maybe you want to look at speed and pace as your starting point.

"Are you really good at puzzle solving? Maybe you want to examine training patterns.

"Take stock in yourself and go from there. Even if you do have a specialty, you shouldn't just stop there. You should pick and choose and build a full arsenal of knowledge.

"A speed or pace bent could lead you to being successful but it's more lucrative and reliable to branch out from there. But it isn't a bad idea to have an area of specialization that you're better at than most everyone else.

"The right way is to get a solid foundation based on your own inherent skills, and based on racing as it is conducted now and will be in the future. You need to understand the history of the game—who the best trainers and jockeys are. The whole gamut is what you need to understand to improve as a player.

"When I met Andy Beyer, he wasn't a speed handicapper yet, and he wasn't yet a winning player. But he had a passion for the game and spending a month at the races in Saratoga, he began to see how you could win, and how speed could become a tool to lead him way up the scale in his abilities.

"Find something that you do really well and focus on that—branch out from there.

"How many really successful writers, doctors, ballplayers are there? It's no different in horse racing.

"In my life, I have stepped away from the game a few times and it always took me at least a year to feel I could play professionally again when I came back. I could see that the game had changed in each of those times—trainer patterns, the racing surface, etc.—and I had to relearn the whole pecking order of horses."

The evolution of a horseplayer is natural. As we talked about in Chapter 1, if you don't evolve, you can't survive.

GERRY OKUNEFF: "Learning to handicap is an evolutionary process— everyone begins as a neophyte. The general progression is you start out knowing nothing and then you learn everything—and then you cull out the things that are not important. There's a lot of trial and error."

ERNIE DAHLMAN: "I wouldn't be a person who would ever say I'm a great gambler. I think I come up with more winners than the average person, a lot more contenders. But I know some people who are great gamblers and I wouldn't put myself in their class.

"Here's an example. I was playing tennis with a guy [who happens to be our Las Vegas Player] and he says, 'What do you think the odds are that Mark McGwire will hit more than 60 home runs this year [1998]?'

"He had 28 at the time, and I said, 'I'd make him a 3-5 shot.'

"'Well, you can get 2-1 at Caesars Palace,' he said.

"I tell him, 'I don't bet sports.'

"He said, 'What if it was 40 home runs, would you bet sports then?'

"So I thought about it and I said to myself, 'Yeah, he's right. If I think it's a 3-5 shot and I'm getting 2-1, I should bet on him.' So I went over and I bet. I got home and there was a report on *SportsCenter* that Mark McGwire had been taken out of the game in the first inning, and I yelled to the wife, 'I just killed Mark McGwire!'

"But he came back and he hit 70 homers and Sosa hit 65, so I won my bet. But it's a bet that this other guy picked up on immediately, and I don't think that way. I'm not looking for, what are the real odds of this, what are the real odds of that? I'm thinking about who's going to win this race, who's the speed, how can I make the most money? The exacta, the double, the trifecta? Usually I'll bet one race at a time, maybe the double. But I don't like to bet pick threes, pick fours."

So what are some of the things that work for winners?

ERNIE DAHLMAN: "I don't use labels. I do some of everything. The Sheets don't count pace but I think pace is very important, so there are some ways I differ from The Sheets. I believe in track biases so I'm always looking for that. I like two-turn races. I don't like Belmont's 1⅛; I'd rather go to Aqueduct's 1⅛ because I think my harness-racing background gives me a better understanding about what being wide on turns means, how important it is to save ground. You're kind of stuck with what you've learned to begin with and I started for 20 years doing harness racing."

Ernie Dahlman and our Las Vegas Player are friends—friends who respect each other's ability to handicap and win at the races.

LAS VEGAS PLAYER: "Ernie Dahlman says he's not a great gambler but I don't think that's right. The important thing is that he's in a groove and his bets might not be the greatest bets but he's comfortable with what he bets, which is much more important than making a bet that's 2 percent or 4 percent better because you'd be thinking more about that than what you've done over the years. Don't knock yourself, just keep doing what you're doing."

One of the challenges of handicapping is processing all of the information, but not allowing an overload of information to sway your judgment one way or the other. That's why doing what works for *you* is so important. If you're at the track and you're allowing yourself to get talked off or onto horses, then you're going to be a losing player. So, what should you do?

JIM MAZUR: "I certainly look to see who the classiest horses are. One of the ways I determine that—and it's something that's very helpful—is looking at company lines of horses to see who they ran against to get a feel for the class of the horse.

"As far as speed figures go, I use the Beyers. If I'm lucky enough to get a look at the Ragozin Sheets or the Thorograph sheets I'll look at those. Sometimes they can be confusing to me, and you should stick with what you do best—and what I do best is trainer angles.

"Not to digress, but sometimes I'll look at horses on the track—and I'm not a visual-handicapper type person—and I can't tell you how many times that's screwed me up because it's not what I do for a living and it's not what my specialty is, and you should stick to what you do best unless you're with an expert who can tell you, 'This is a horse who isn't going to win.'

"It's the same thing with the Ragozins and the Thorographs. I'm much better off when I'm dealing with friends and we can converse and say, 'Well, you know his sheet number's good but here are some negatives on the trainer side that we need to talk about.'

"Other than that I use the Beyers and make adjustments for trouble lines and horses going wide. I think a lot of people forget about that."

GERRY OKUNEFF: "I believe there are a number of ways to get to a live horse. You could come from several opposite directions and still land on the same horse. Until I find someone who's got more winners than I do, then I rely on what I do and don't begrudge other people their wins. The worst thing you can be is a weather vane—if you've got rabbit ears and are knocked off horses, then you're lost."

CARY FOTIAS: "Don't base your final decision on anyone's opinion but your own—listen to what other good handicappers have to say and if it makes sense, then factor it in, but don't listen to 'the clocker said . . .' or 'the barn bet . . .' or other such nonsense. I get upset when someone tells me, 'You talked me off a horse.' That's not right. Maybe you talked yourself off him based on my opinion."

IT'S NOT HOW LONG YOU WORK;
IT'S HOW SMART YOU WORK

With all of the information available, and all of the different facets of handicapping, it's important to use your time wisely. You can handi-cap a card for hours, but if you're not working efficiently, you're going to leave yourself with a lot to do come race day—and that's giv-ing yourself an impossible task, because on race day, a whole new set of variables will present itself. Thus, it's important to work smartly.

> **BASEBALL BETTOR:** "During baseball season, my investors and my workers play every day as long as there is one game going. Prior to base-ball season, I spend a lot of time working on the computer model and updating my programs and databases, etc. I'll spend several hundred hours doing that. Then it runs by itself, and I spend little time analyz-ing the games. It's not how hard you work; it's how smart you work."

It's similar in the realm of horse racing. If you're playing every day, you're going to be in tune with what's going on at a particular circuit, and, hopefully, the handicapping will come more easily because you're familiar with the horses and the types of races they've been running. You're also aware of which trainers are winning and which jockeys are 0 for 31 on the turf. The actual process of handicapping the races shouldn't be all that time-consuming if you're doing the work in a smart way.

We asked several of our pros how long it took them to handicap a card. The answers varied, as we expected, because each person has his own method of handicapping that works for him. But most pros have perfected the art of handicapping in such a way that it doesn't really take them all that long to effectively analyze a race.

> **CARY FOTIAS:** "Ideally, 10 to 15 minutes per race. You don't want to over-cap. There's a certain Zen to the game and you don't want to worry too much about outside factors."

> **DAVE GUTFREUND:** "This is going to sound strange but if you're watching the races and you're in synch with what's going on, the amount of time that you actually have to do on races isn't as much as

when you're not doing it. There are plenty of days I can do a whole card in 15 or 20 minutes and come up with one or two races and then maybe go back and look at those one or two races for a few more minutes. I'm a spot-play type of guy and I'm looking for hidden situations or unique situations where I feel I might have an edge."

JAMES QUINN: "I get *Daily Racing Form* or download it beforehand. I strongly believe in doing your homework off-track; I spend about 90 minutes to two hours to do it. I used to take three hours.

"After the races, 30 minutes of record keeping is important. I also make speed and pace figures. I do track profiles. Always keep your info files up to date."

GERRY OKUNEFF: "Before I can even begin separating horses, I have to get my *Form* into shape—delete unimportant things, highlight others, check trouble lines. All that takes two or three hours. Then I get my chart books and workout information. Then it's about 20 minutes a race."

KENTUCKY PLAYER: "I had a fellow write a program for me 10 years ago and he did a really good job. Basically, all I had to do was enter my trip notes, my biases, and download the charts from the *Racing Form* and this program would do the rest. I did it that way for a while but I didn't think it was as good as what I did by hand. I spent as much time just on the input and dealing with the program when it didn't work or if I had trouble downloading the chart. I did this for two years, and I ended up spending the same amount of time to get information that wasn't as good. So I gave up on doing it on the computer after a while.

"I still use the Horse Watch feature with the *Racing Form*. I keep a list of horses that I'm interested in that I want to know when they run at a track that maybe I'm not watching but that's about all I use the computer for now. I do it all by hand. I keep stacks of DRF *Simulcast Weekly*; I keep a couple of years of programs where I have my trip notes in; I have access to the replays of most of the tracks around the country so I can go back and check on that. So if there's a horse I'm interested in I can check on its last trip.

"It's very time-consuming but I think it sinks in better and I don't make as many mistakes when I do it by hand, and I'm really in touch with the figures I'm doing. A lot of times I'll know even before I put my figures in; I'll see the name of the horse or I'll see the race he came out of and then it immediately clicks in my head, 'Hey, that was a fast-paced race,' or 'Hey, that race had no pace or there was a bias that day or this horse was wide.' And I know even before I handicap the race that this is a horse I'm going to be interested in."

Brad Free felt strongly about the amount of preparation it takes to win at the races, and that's because you never know what's going to happen on race day—so, you need to be prepared for anything. In other words, in a handicapper's constant search for value, it's important to focus on handicapping throughout the day.

BRAD FREE: "You've got to spend the time to handicap. If you're showing up at the track and you're buying a *Form* on the way in, you're dead. Long term, you've got no shot. You might get lucky that day. You might get lucky that week. But you cannot show up at the track and do the necessary handicapping in the 25 minutes between races. In my opinion, it's just not possible to make an intelligent wager based on such short handicapping.

"You have to handicap the day before, and then you have to do it again after the scratches, and then do it again between races. This is one game where preparation means everything. Because you never know when the board is going to be screwed up, and that's when you can take advantage. You're not going to know if the board is screwed up unless you've done the homework—unless you know which five of those horses in that 10-horse field have some sort of chance to win. The only way to know that is to do the homework. I'm not smart enough to do it any other way.

"I don't know how people wager on multiple tracks at the same time; that's a different world to me. How they do that, I have no idea. That's something I could never do."

WHERE TO PLAY?
GOING TO THE TRACK VS. STAYING AT HOME

With so many choices for today's player, it's important to pick a venue where you feel most comfortable playing. Is that going to the track or local simulcast facility? Or is it playing in the privacy of your home, with the use of phone-betting accounts or Internet-wagering accounts? Clearly, this is a matter of personal preference and each particular venue has its pros and cons.

Roxy Roxborough laughed at the notion of going to the track if one is to bet seriously. "Who goes to the track anymore?" he asked. "I don't know any serious professional players who go to the track day in and day out. They're usually playing from home—because of the convenience factor. And because of an expense factor—but that's not that important. I find it's a lot easier to assess information at home—I can check the odds on the Internet or on the horse-racing channels.

"But if a serious player thought he could gain an edge by being at the track," Roxborough added, "then he would be there and pay to be there." That's the defining factor of a serious player—taking advantage of whatever edge he might have. If a player can be successful going to the track on a regular basis, then that's great. If he's apt to be more successful at home, that's fine too. The important thing is finding out which venue works best for you.

ANDREW BEYER: "To me, it's more of a function of the pleasantness of the racetrack. I love being at racetracks if the tracks happen to be Gulfstream or Del Mar. But to drive out 30 minutes each way on the Beltway to get to Laurel, where you don't have much in the way of aesthetics, is just a waste of time. When I'm here in Washington, D.C., I pretty much play from my desk. I've got two TV networks plus Youbet if I need it and all of my reference materials in case I need to look up something at the last minute. Really it's more convenient to play from home, but I'm a traditionalist: I love the atmosphere of the racetrack, so for two months I won't miss a day at Gulfstream."

194

PAUL BRASETH: "I don't go to the track every day, but I do go every day when I'm at Del Mar. My favorite track is Del Mar. Perhaps I'm influenced by the surroundings, and it's such a great place. At Del Mar, they start at 2:00 P.M.; it's wonderful. I sit in a box at the finish line with my friend Gibson. I'll get up early in the morning and go bike riding and then lie in the sun and then go to the track.

"Here in the Bay Area, where I live, I seldom go to the track. I play on the Internet and go maybe 25 percent of the time to the track, depending on what kind of bets I want to make."

JIM MAZUR: "I can't go to the track and play every day, but with the Internet I can watch every day, and the question becomes, do I have time to handicap a card? When time constraints are pulling me, I do a half-baked job and that's when you start missing things that can help you. That's why I developed the Daily Sheet, to save time. It's an Internet product that looks up the key stats—high and low—and that saves a lot of time.

"I do a seminar at Gulfstream on Wednesdays so I'll spend all day there, and then the rest of the week I'll watch from home and look for maybe a sequence of races for a pick three, perhaps on a Friday afternoon, and maybe go out then. But when you have phone accounts and the Internet, you really don't have to be there anymore. But that's not as much for me because I like to go out to the track with a couple of my friends and handicap the races with them. I really enjoy getting that other perspective."

JAMES QUINN: "At the track itself, there's a social aspect to it that's important because social interaction is important. But the more lonely the handicapping process is, the more successful it is.

"I always had a box at the track, and I liked that—the give and take and exchange. Then I went to the turf club and had my own table. You pay more attention to the board and odds and are more mentally involved.

"Your preoccupation should be finding overlays and overlay combos. Some social interaction is okay, though. It's a long day and mentally it can be tiring. You get a little bit of a burnout factor if you go too long."

WHAT TYPES OF TRACKS TO PLAY

It's also important to isolate certain meets that you might have an advantage at. Most of our players bet at the bigger tracks. But that doesn't mean you have to, especially if you think there's a perceived edge betting at a smaller venue.

ANDREW BEYER: "In terms of tracks, I see very little need to gravitate automatically to the big tracks that everybody plays. If all the wise guys and the computer guys and the rebate guys are playing New York and California and Kentucky, that creates a disincentive to go into those pools and tackle them. Last winter I played Tampa Bay Downs in addition to Gulfstream and I actually paid more attention to Tampa Bay simply because it's a track that doesn't attract a lot of wise guys.

"Because I love going to Florida, I've always made that one of my main focuses. Around this time of year [November], I start following Calder and gearing up, and then when Gulfstream opens I'll be in high gear and I'll play Tampa Bay Downs as well. I may even look a little bit at a third track like Maryland. I'll bet quite a few races during the day, maybe 10 to 15.

"Once Florida's done, I'll just kind of coast for the remainder of the spring and the Triple Crown season. I'll look at the Form every day but I'm not going to do it at the same intensity level. Traditionally in the summer, I always used to gear up for Saratoga. A couple of recent years I played Monmouth instead.

"In the old days, I'd go up to Saratoga and that would be my only focus, the only track I'd be doing. I've had enough bad situations over the years where I got locked into a particular track and for some reason that track just turned out to be unpromising. Maybe there was bad weather, maybe there was a Michael Gill screwing up the races, maybe it was inscrutable for reasons I didn't understand. I never like to have all of my intellectual investment nowadays in one single track. If I'm going to Gulfstream, I'll do Gulfstream and Tampa.

"This summer when I went to Saratoga, I did Saratoga and Monmouth. Just so on those days when there's nothing good at one track, you've got a reasonable fall-back option."

RANDY GALLO: "I like bigger fields with shippers from more than one place—not like a Calder meet where they just keep running the same horses over and over again against each other, and they take turns beating each other. I would rather have a Churchill or a Keeneland or a Gulfstream meet where you get horses coming from four or five different tracks. You find a lot better prices that way. At least I think so.

"Horses from Delta right now are running better at Fair Grounds than they ever have, so they get overlooked. Or horses from Turfway coming in to Churchill. Or Keeneland coming to Churchill. You always have an assortment and there seems to be bigger overlays. I think that Southern California is very hard to beat race to race. I've never been fond of that. Churchill and Gulfstream are probably my two favorite tracks."

PAUL CORNMAN: "New York is my bread and butter because I'm acquainted with all the players and it's more of a people game than anything else because of the high-percentage and the low-percentage people. I also play Gulfstream Park, then after Gulfstream I'll play a little Calder. When Delaware is open I'll look at their better horses; the same goes for Maryland. I play Keeneland just about every race during the spring, then in the fall when the quality is not as good, I have certain groups, as I do at Churchill and Fair Grounds. I do not do the West Coast. My day must end. I enjoy the handicapping. It's my passion. It's ruined the rest of my life but it's fun doing that!"

JAMES QUINN: "I play every day at Santa Anita; then weekends following their winter season. I'll play Saratoga during the summer. From 1971 through 1984 I played year-round. After *The Handicapper's Condition Book* was a success, I wrote other books. But I play full-time at Santa Anita, Saratoga, and Del Mar; weekends and spot plays otherwise."

ERNIE DAHLMAN: "I know New York racing because that's where I've played the most. I'm much more comfortable doing New York than anywhere else. I've had an okay record in California, a bad record in Kentucky. I believe that's because Kentucky is so liberal in their drug laws that people don't even need to cheat to change a horse's performance dramatically. They've got like 16 drugs that are legal there that aren't legal elsewhere, and they always defend it fiercely when anybody tries to do anything that's better for the horse.

"But they don't consider that they have bettors out there that find their races too difficult to bet and won't bet on their races. The last thing that racetracks ever think about is the customer, the bettor. And I think Kentucky is the number one area in the country that says to hell with the bettor. So I've cut way down on my betting in Kentucky.

"New York's my number one place and then probably Florida. I don't mind the Maryland circuit, although it's hard to find value there because a couple of sharp players are there and the pools are small—so it's hard to get much value there."

STEVEN CRIST: "I'm a throwback player. More than 90 percent of my annual handle is on New York racing. It's what I feel comfortable and confident playing seriously. Almost all the rest is on elite stakes racing, which I try to follow on a national level. My hat is off to people who can follow several circuits diligently enough. Even when I was playing full-time for a living I found that following just New York was a full-time job."

JIM MAZUR: "My basic meets that I tackle are Gulfstream and Saratoga and then the big events. And if I happen to be giving a seminar at a track, of course I'll handicap that day and see if we can come up with something.

"As the Gulfstream Park meet wears on, I wear out. My advantage there is at the beginning of the meet—when I can look at trainers who have historically gotten off to a good start and I can look for value plays—and then again at the end, when some of the form has settled and I can use the stats in the book."

THE PROS AND CONS OF SIMULCAST, OR HOW MANY RACES SHOULD YOU PLAY?

With the advent of simulcast wagering, your next great bet is only a few minutes away. That's either a blessing or a curse, depending on how you like to play. If you're able to play multiple tracks—and play them well—then there are plenty of opportunities to make big scores. If, however, you fall into the trap of playing more tracks than you should, it's important to recognize that and concentrate on the one track you're most comfortable playing.

Steven Crist, who focuses on the NYRA circuit, summed up the pitfalls of simulcasting brilliantly, as did Roxy Roxborough, who outlined why simulcasting can be tough if you don't have the discipline it requires.

199

STEVEN CRIST: "I don't think people who are making a simulcast bet every five or 10 minutes at several different tracks can be making that many thoughtful bets, but more power to them if they're enjoying themselves and can afford it. Knowing practically every horse on the grounds and remembering everyone's recent starts is just a huge advantage, because most of your competition is playing solely off what they see on paper and don't know the nuances that you do. So I stick to New York and the better races at a couple of key 'feeder' meetings like Gulfstream and Keeneland, because I'm going to have to deal with those horses by the time Belmont opens."

ROXY ROXBOROUGH: "I find that I play less races when I'm at home. The casual player will play more, which is the worst decision. The real pros play less. There's no compulsion. If you drive 20 miles to get to a simulcast facility and you're following two tracks—say Santa Anita and Churchill—then a lot of time goes by between races. Naturally, you want to fill that time with action."

Jim Mazur, like Crist, prefers to play one track whenever possible.

JIM MAZUR: "Even with all the data I have, trying to spread myself out is just too daunting. I'll concentrate on one track and if there's a series of races where I'm totally bored, if there's no value or something, I will then take a look at what's going on at the other tracks. Or if my assistant will point something out to me at another track, if there's a high-percentage play, then maybe I'll look at that race and the races around it to see if I can put together a pick three. Overall, I can't play three or four races at a time. At most, one or two."

MARYLAND PLAYER: "The most tracks I will ever do at any given time is three. I intensely dislike doing three. I try to keep it to two. Occasionally, in transition periods it's impossible to keep it to two. Let's take March 15, 2004, to April 1, 2004. A lot of the Gulfstream horses had gone to Kentucky. A lot of the New York horses had returned to Aqueduct. And you still had the locals running in Florida. So in that situation, I was forced—in the sense that I had horses from Gulfstream that I was interested in—into playing three tracks. But I hate doing that.

"I much prefer to play one—and I'm thrilled when I'm just playing one. I used to be much more conservative but these days I'd say if I play a third of the races on a card, that would be a lot of activity for me. Two or three races out of a 10-race card would probably be the norm. On a card with a lot of grass races maybe I'll play more because I do like grass races. I just think you get better opportunities in grass races because of the larger field size."

Ernie Dahlman and Dave Cuscuna look for spots at the available tracks and play accordingly. Dahlman focuses most of his action on New York, but if a play shows up at another track, he's not averse to acting on it. Dave Cuscuna figures out his game plan and then plays accordingly. The key here is: Don't play for the sake of playing. Play when you've got an edge.

ERNIE DAHLMAN: "It varies. Last week I was in New York so I didn't bet one track outside of New York; I just bet New York races. Today I bet a couple of Churchill races because New York was canceled because of wind. Churchill wins when there's no other competition. I also bet a Laurel race. I was going to bet Golden Gate but it rained so late in the day that nobody was using mud calks and I didn't feel like waiting around.

"I'll probably average—if New York has nine races—betting on seven of them, maybe eight. Some days I'll play all of them if I think I have an edge. But when it comes to New York I'm very opinionated. Other places I'm very selective. I try to be careful because the one thing that drives me crazy is to have a good day in New York and lose it on other tracks. That gets me so I don't have a good night's sleep, so I try to avoid that happening."

DAVE CUSCUNA: "I play probably four or five days a week. There's a huge variation in the number of bets I make. There aren't too many 30's for me. Those tend to be hard on the pocketbook. Probably six or eight. I've tried the 30-race game plan but I wrote those figures in with a red pen so I stopped doing that. Sometimes I'll play simulcast, sometimes I'll play them all at the same track. It varies. The number of tracks I handicap varies. It all varies based on my game plan and what I'm looking to accomplish."

Paul Cornman's take on this is similar, but he reemphasizes the importance of knowing a given track and all of its players. It's one thing to sit down and handicap a day's races on Saturdays or Sundays—it's a completely different thing when you follow a meet daily, picking up on the hot trainers and cold jockeys and knowing which horses are ready to run their best races.

PAUL CORNMAN: "In this day and age, with all the tracks, I'm not one of these people who can sit out a day. I'll find something to play. Some days, in New York, I can be active in eight of nine races; other times, three of nine. Moving out to Vegas I had the opportunity to look at every track. At first it was a new toy. But then I found that not knowing the players, not knowing the trainers' moves and everything else . . . I'm just better at following races in certain circuits and all of New York."

Randy Gallo lives and breathes simulcasting because a lot of his action comes at the dog tracks. But, like most of our other players, he stresses that betting in the right spots is the key to successful simulcast wagering.

RANDY GALLO: "First of all, I play dogs four days a week. There are probably 10 to 12 tracks between Wonderland and Jacksonville and Derby Lane and Palm Beach and Phoenix Greyhounds, where they have twin-trifecta carryovers and tri supers every week. So I'm playing those; my brother does the tape work on those. We're playing those through my betting shop.

"With horses, race-to-race stuff, I may play three to four bets a day, if that, on horses that I think have value."

WHAT TYPES OF RACES TO PLAY

Part of handicapping oneself is understanding what types of races to play. Some of our players preferred turf races, with bigger fields; others preferred dirt sprints because of the much larger sample size. The point here is that it's crucial to find out which races you have an eye for and which ones you don't.

If you're showing a solid profit on dirt sprints, then look to focus more of your action on dirt sprints. Similarly, if you're getting crushed betting turf stakes races, either cut back your action or try to figure out what you might be doing wrong and adapt accordingly.

It's all part of the evolution process of a handicapper, and knowing which races you can beat is a great way to improve your skills and fatten your bankroll. If you're honest with yourself, you can focus on the races that are going to make you the most money in the long run.

Steve Davidowitz spoke about the different types of races, and specifically stated that he stays away from middle-priced claimers.

STEVE DAVIDOWITZ: "Six furlongs on the dirt; long races on the grass; I bet a lot of types of races. There are very few types of races I don't like—but I don't like middle-priced claimers, which are of course the bread and butter of the game.

"When I was learning the game, the subtle variations in the levels of claiming meant something; now they don't really mean enough—with all the medications and form-cycle reversals, these races have become very tough to play. But I do like their unpredictability when it comes to playing a pick six.

"I love to follow the good 2-year-olds at Saratoga and Del Mar and through the fall stakes and the next season's Triple Crown races, all the time paying attention to the other races on those cards: grass races, allowance races, stakes for older horses. The year has a regular beginning, middle, and end."

Steven Crist is another player who looks for certain opportunities.

STEVEN CRIST: "There are three situations that always pique my interest because I have had success with them over the years. The first is a race with a probable pace-collapse scenario. If my visual observation of horses' unrateability and my analysis of likely early fractions suggest there is going to be a monstrous early fight for the lead, I will try to make closers run one-two in the exacta or one-two-three in the trifecta. The beauty of these situations is that the public is playing the speed horses on their individual merits and I may well be tossing the first, second, and fourth choices in the race.

203

"I have found that three- or four-horse boxes of the closers in these races have a decent strike rate at big numbers. Plenty of times one or two of the speeds don't break and my scenario doesn't materialize, but it's a play where you don't have to be right a high percentage of the time because the payoffs are so good. Two other things that always catch my eye are turn-backs in distance and horses moving from grass to dirt. In both cases, horses may have gained a foundation or a freshening that may allow them to perform better at their optimal distance and surface, and bettors overly focused on recent final-time speed figures often ignore these horses."

Dave Gutfreund simplified the issue when he said, "There are really two separate kinds of races: dirt races and grass races."

And our pros know which surface they'd rather bet. They also know the nuances of both games. Gutfreund continued, "I think there's a pace factor involved. On dirt they run fast early, slow late; on turf it's slow early, fast late. Most turf races are routes so you're dealing with more two-turn races versus one-turn races; post positions and jockeys come into play more on turf than they do on the main track."

So which races should you play? Obviously, you should play whichever ones you're better at, but here is what some of our experts had to say on the topic of dirt versus turf.

■ Dirt

DAVE CUSCUNA: "I prefer sprint races on dirt because it takes some of the guesswork out of it. Two-turn races and turf races are much more of a jockey's game—they're as much of a jockey's game as a horse's game. In a six-furlong race, the gates open, they run fast from the time the gate opens up until they cross the wire. Some run faster early, some run faster late, but in a three-quarter-mile race, there's no margin for error, there are no time-outs, there are no breaks. Essentially what you're getting is effort the whole way.

"In a two-turn race, there's a little more strategy involved: How do you ration out the horse's energy? And that's where the jockeys make decisions. I haven't succeeded in my lifetime sneaking inside a jockey's head too well to figure out what he's going to do. One race a horse is on the lead in 47, the next race at a similar track, they go 49 and the horse is four lengths off the lead—stuff like that makes me scratch my head and gets me frustrated.

"On the other hand, one of my best friends only handicaps distance races on grass—that's what he makes his living at, that's where he feels the most comfortable. My hat's off to him and his hat's off to me—he doesn't make a dime on dirt sprints. I guess we all have our thing that we feel best in and that's it for me."

ERNIE DAHLMAN: "I like all dirt tracks; I like sloppy, muddy, anything. I don't like soft grass because usually when it rains, the races are taken off the turf so you really don't have enough of a past performance on soft turf. A lot of times if they're running on soft turf, I might just pass the races. Even if I like something, I might say, 'It's soft turf, just forget about it.' There are all degrees of soft turf. This time of year [November], you might get a turf course where the horses are running six seconds slower than normal, or soft turf where it's three seconds slower. I kind of stay away from them.

"I like dirt races better because there are more past performances. I don't seem to be good at knowing which horses are going to be good turf horses; if I did I'd claim more of them. I kind of go with horses in a grass race who have established form over those who are trying it for the first time. I have a definite bias toward established form. And that works for me, over the course of time."

ANDREW BEYER: "I prefer dirt to turf. I don't bet grass races a lot because speed figures are a much more useful tool on dirt rather than grass, and that's the way I've always been oriented."

GERRY OKUNEFF: "I prefer sprint races, because speed generally plays better at most tracks in sprints and it is the most often-run distance."

04

KENTUCKY GAMBLER: "Probably the weakest part of my game is turf handicapping—I'm not a big believer in class, and that might be why. I've had a lot of people observe my game and tell me that something I need to improve on is that I don't give class enough weight in turf races, and it may be true because I know from handicapping myself that I'm better on the dirt than I am on the turf."

■ Turf

DAVE GUTFREUND: "I like turf races with horses going for the first time on grass. I'm not averse to playing first-time starters in maiden races on the turf if the breeding and the trainer warrant it. There are so many different things. The race I'm looking at now, there's a horse that came in from Europe; it cost $1.8 million; it was a winning selection of mine yesterday. The mother was Halo America, who was, if I remember correctly, a pretty good horse in this country. The horse was switching into a good barn and it kept better company in Europe. It paid $9—nothing to be too proud of.

"The things that I'm best at are grass races, especially maiden grass races, because there's a lot more thinking outside the box in those; there's so much speculation as to who might run on the grass, who might not run on the grass, whereas the sheets players and the numbers players are just looking at it from a numerical standpoint. I'm trying to project improvement at that point."

JIM MAZUR: "I always look forward to turf races. I think those are races that I have a good interest in; I have an advantage with the trainer analysis."

PAUL CORNMAN: "I like betting turf. I think I get little subtleties in turf races as far as the trips are concerned that one doesn't necessarily get in dirt races because they're shorter and they have short fields and it's tough to come up with a trip in a sprint race that the whole world doesn't see."

JAMES QUINN: "I prefer grass races and features and the nonclaiming races in particular. I do extremely well on the grass. I have an aptitude for class and I like the better races and grass races."

BARRY MEADOW: "I like grass races generally because the fields consist of better-class horses at most tracks—because you don't want to tear up the grass with slow horses so they don't card that many of them and the grass is usually in pretty good shape. I like those because I'm an observer of trips and looking for who might have gotten a bad trip last time, who might have gotten a good trip last time, and I have a good way of evaluating those horses.

"But I certainly play a lot more dirt races because there are a lot more dirt races available and I'll certainly play sprints, routes, anything where I think I have an advantage."

Some of our pros talked about the importance of being proficient at a certain condition of race, whether it be maiden races, claiming races, allowance races, or stakes races. The reason was no different from why they liked dirt over turf, or vice versa: They feel they have an edge in a certain type of race.

■ Claiming Races

PAUL BRASETH: "I grew up in my handicapping days at Longacres and Portland Meadows, which are smaller tracks where 85 percent of the races were some kind of claiming race. We had very few allowance and stakes races. So my bread and butter is betting on older horses in claiming races—that would be number one. I don't care if it's a route or a sprint.

"With claiming races there's more established form and also a lot of room for trainer manipulation, which is what I specialize in knowing, so I like that."

JAMES QUINN: "I detest 3-year-old claiming races. In the 1990's, when the older claiming game was de-emphasized in California, I made the mistake of trying to beat those races. The horses were inconsistent. January to June and into the fall, I limit my play to allowance drop-downs; nonclaiming drop-downs. Those I can beat, if I limit my play to allowance drop-downs."

BARRY MEADOW: "I prefer races where I have enough information on the horses that I can make some kind of intelligent judgment. I don't like races where there's a lot of conflicting information. For example, you might have a $12.5K claimer where two horses are taking massive class drops, two other horses are coming off layoffs, and you got two other horses that are very inconsistent—they run a big number and then a bad number.

"Sometimes those races are based on who's feeling well that day, and that's difficult for me to handicap. I prefer races where I pretty much have a good idea of what each horse is doing."

■ Young Horses and Maidens

CARY FOTIAS: "Younger horses have more volatility, which leads to value."

PAUL CORNMAN: "I prefer betting lightly raced horses because their form is more accurate as far as what I look for than a 6-year-old horse that runs lights-out and then doesn't run well for three races and then runs lights-out again.

"Another reason I like lightly raced horses is I also like to look at the horse, and the body language of the horse, to see if it looks like an athlete. I think I know enough about it to see if there's going to be improvement in the horse's early races."

JAMES QUINN: "In maidens and maiden-claiming races, I know exactly what I'm looking for. If I don't find what I'm looking for, it's tough. I use three conditions for first-time starters in maiden races. Note that in these races, par is crucial; first-time starters have a hard time beating experienced horses who run par, which is 88 at Santa Anita and 79 at Gulfstream. The horse also has to have run par more than twice, though I do know that second-starters improve dramatically.

"The criteria for first-time starters: The horse needs to have an acceptable sire (meaning, 11 percent or better for their first-time starters); an acceptable trainer (11 percent or better); and two or more sharp workouts (which means: in Southern California, faster than 48⅗; other places, add a second).

"The 11 percent number represents one horse in a nine-horse field.

"Usually, two of these factors will be positive; one will be negative. In that case, I won't play the horse if it's the favorite or a low-priced contender. I will play if 8-1 or higher. If it's a below-par field, I'll play.

"Note that second-time starters improve dramatically. Three-year-olds improve three to five lengths. Two-year-olds improve five to seven lengths. The real appeal here is that the public underbets second-time starters. They'll overbet a first-time starter and a horse with a high par figure. Even if a horse has an ugly line first time out and you can't really project him to par, if the surrounding data were good, that's usually a good play.

"D. Wayne Lukas is a good example. When he was a relative newcomer in Southern California—even after he developed a reputation—he would start a horse and it would be a no-go first time out. But six weeks later, the horse would come back and the second start would be good.

"In maiden-claiming races, it's textbook: a maiden drop-down who showed any ability against straight maidens. Sometimes you can get a fair price. But a better play is any drop in maiden-claiming price in a below-par field, and with the high-pace figure. It's a hidden figure play, and you get good odds, especially in Southern California."

LAS VEGAS PLAYER: "A lot of people don't want to bet a maiden race. To me, that's the best kind of race to bet where half the horses can't walk. I want to bet fast horses that are healthy. But there's not much going for you if you have to bet parimutuelly."

■ Stakes Races

JIM MAZUR: "I find stakes races are very difficult except on the big races when I've had a lot of time to analyze, like the Triple Crown races and the Breeders' Cup."

ROXY ROXBOROUGH: "I used to play a lot of different meets, but now I tend to look strictly at big races—the Triple Crown, the Breeders' Cup, and other big stakes races. I do that because with these big races there is now a different component because of online wagering—the bookies on the Internet offer proposition bets, head-to-head wagers, and other interesting betting opportunities.

"I don't play like I used to because I'm in Bangkok. But I focus on the Triple Crown and Breeders' Cup races, and I get interested in playing leading up to those events. I might not play a race from November to January. Then, after the Triple Crown, I won't look at a race again until August. I focus all of my playing around big races, including preps and the entire card of those preps, too. I feel it's better when I'm fresh."

STEVE DAVIDOWITZ: "On Breeders' Cup Day I'll make bets in all the races and accent two or three plays to play more seriously. I like the big days, and I'll kill the card on those days, like Kentucky Derby Day. There's a little cushion in the odds those days that creates opportunities.

"The ambiance of the situation and my attitude on the day are big factors in how much I'm going to play. After the Breeders' Cup, I recoup and take a little break where I'm not invested in playing every day but I'll handicap and play pick sixes with a carryover until mid-February. The old-fashioned clock is still my clock."

WHAT TYPES OF BETS TO MAKE

As we mentioned earlier, handicapping is just one facet of winning at the races. You need to back up your selections with your hard-earned money: That's where betting comes into play. We asked our pros if they thought having a set wager was a good way to go, or if it was important to vary your play. We also asked them what types of wagers they liked to make, knowing that after many years of self-analysis, most of these guys would have a pretty good idea where they liked to focus most of their action.

The answers varied—some liked the intra-race wagering of exactas and trifectas, while others preferred inter-race parlays—but one theme remained constant: the importance of betting smartly to maximize value.

BRAD FREE: "First of all, you've got to keep things simple. If you're just a novice starting out, there's nothing wrong with just betting to win—

even if you're betting more than one horse in a race, just to get your feet wet and learn the game. There's a fairly steep learning curve in handicapping and betting horses. You don't learn it overnight. You don't learn it in a week, a month, or even a year. I've been doing this for 25 years and I'm still learning.

"My suggestion to a relative newcomer would be to find big fields. I wouldn't waste time on small fields because the chances of there being a mistake in the odds are a lot less. Mistakes are more likely to happen in large fields. After that, I'd go race by race. Start with win betting, and then if you want to get a bit more creative, play exactas, and then if you want to get more creative than that, play trifectas."

■ Set Wagers

GERRY OKUNEFF: "I do think it's a good idea that players have a set type of wager. You should handicap yourself and see where your past successes have been and why. Eliminate the ones that never get it done for you. Try to figure out why certain bets you make have a higher yield."

STEVEN CRIST: "It's a very good idea for a bettor to concentrate on the bet types that he is technically good at. I think my strength is in making out multiple pick-four and pick-six tickets and I think a lot of otherwise perfectly good handicappers play these bets simplistically and poorly and I therefore have an edge. I have studied the optimal ways to play these bets and am willing to put in the extra time and effort to make out multiple tickets.

"I also just think I'm better at saying who can and cannot win a race than I am at saying who can or cannot finish third or fourth. This makes me clueless about playing superfectas. I don't know where the edge is. So supers account for less than half of one percent of my annual handle and I only play them when I truly despise a big favorite I think could well be fifth or worse."

JAMES QUINN: "I don't think that set wagers or varying your play are mutually exclusive. I think both are important—I think it's an excellent idea for players to understand where they're particularly strong and where they get positive results, and make that kind of play. Tom

Brohammer is an expert on pace; midlevel to high-level claiming races for older horses using speed and pace. He plays aggressively to that edge.

"Late speed for me on the grass in comparable class—I'll bet more aggressively; same goes for featured races.

"It's good to have a set type of play that has been profitable and play that aggressively.

"And yes, it's also important to vary things depending on the situation. Let the situation dictate the wager. Use it to your advantage. Exacta or serial bets? I used to do well on pick threes and thought this would be my bet and I would make my fortune, just rolling pick threes through the card. I had two good years, then got crushed in '96 and became more selective."

CARY FOTIAS: "Betting is idiosyncratic; different people are comfortable with one type of bet or another—there's no one style. I will say this: If you're not showing a flat profit on win bets, it'll be tough to have anything work for you.

"My favorite wagers are good old-fashioned win-place bets, especially in New York and California with the low takeouts. I have no qualms about betting two or even three horses to win in the same race if the prices are right. I just don't believe in giving away another 5 or 6 percent in takeout in exactas unless I have a strong negative opinion on one of the favorites. I will use exactas and even occasionally trifectas to cover my key horses in second and third with other logical contenders. Or if I play two or three horses I'll box them in an exacta. I like to keep 80 percent of my money as win-place."

PAUL CORNMAN: "I think racing is such a situational game. If you wanted to have a set wager you have to have such discipline. I'm not saying there are people out there who couldn't do that but I couldn't be one of them. I think you have to be ready to act."

■ Intra-Race (Exactas and Trifectas) or Inter-Race (Pick Threes and Pick Fours) or Both?

ANDREW BEYER: "I prefer exactas and trifectas. I don't make win bets too often unless a horse is an irresistible price. I prefer single-race bets to sequential bets like the pick threes and pick fours. There are times when you'll see a single race pretty clearly. Maybe it's a race where there are five faint-hearted speed horses you think are going to collapse, or maybe it's a race where the favorite has no chance. If you've got the right insight and understanding into a race, if that insight leads you to be able to pick the winner, it may well lead you to the second and third horses as well. Again if your premise in the race is that there's an abundance of speed and there's going to be a hot pace, the speed is going to collapse, so you're going for a closer, well, you may as well not just bet the closer to win, but look to hit closers one-two-three in the trifecta.

"Conversely, in a series of races, it is seldom, if ever, in a pick three or a pick four where you're going to have ironclad convictions in all three or four. You're going to be guessing. You're going to be at the mercy of a race where you really don't have an insight and that can kind of blow everything. That's why my preference is to bet individual races where I've just got a strong insight into that race."

GERRY OKUNEFF: "I think the exacta is the best opportunity. It's my opinion that I am more likely to fully understand a single race, as opposed to feeling as strongly in races going forward. In the exacta I can visualize the result, and if I can eliminate three-quarters of the field quickly, and if my key horse is 3-1 or 4-1 and if I can leave out a contender, I can get a good payoff. Good handicappers can do that a reasonable percentage of the time if they have a strong opinion.

"I think boxing or baseballing is weak because it doesn't reflect your opinion. You're going to throw five combos away in a three-horse box. Instead, if you key and you're right, you'll cash two times out of the six.

"[Movie director] Marty Ritt would make three one-way exactas for $40 ($120) and he wouldn't turn it around for a dime. You need real discipline to do that—to put your top horse on top only. It's tough to see your second horse win and your key horse run second and you don't cash. So I've weakened to the point that I put it in the two-hole, but on a two-to-one ratio.

"I admire the kind of player who backs up his opinion. People who save, generally, are showing a sign of weakness."

212

MARYLAND PLAYER: "There are very few pools I don't play in. I don't make a lot of place bets and I don't make just about any show bets, but outside of those two pools, I'll play anything. These days I tend to play a bit more in what I call the vertical pools than the horizontal pools. Because a lot of times, embarrassingly enough, I may not have gotten to all those races, like in the pick four or something. There are times when I'm betting the seventh race and I may not have looked at the tenth enough to construct a bet. And it's not that I think the vertical bets are better than the horizontal bets; it's just that there are times when you're looking at two or three tracks and it's easy to get in that situation where you really haven't looked at the rest of the races.

213

"Say I'm betting a Gulfstream horse at Aqueduct in the seventh race in April. I'm very unlikely to have looked at races eight, nine, and ten at Aqueduct so I'm very unlikely to be involved in those pools. But I don't buy into any philosophy that X bet is better than Y bet, that a win bet is better than an exacta or that an exacta is better than a win . . . with one exception—and that is that, and this is something that people recklessly disregard, when you play that 25 percent trifecta as opposed to a 15 percent win bet, you better have a much better opinion. You're talking about an extra 10 points of takeout. If you look at the percentages, you'd be well served to keep that in mind. It's a high price to pay.

"Most of my activity, except Fair Grounds, I try to play with the cheaper takeouts, Kentucky, New York, Gulfstream, not Philadelphia. I've moved my business to tracks with better prices.

"People just don't get how expensive that is, 25 percent. Sit down at poker with five guys and have the person running the game take 25 percent out of every dollar bet. It's one thing to take a percentage out of the ante but in racing that percentage is taken out of every dollar. When 25 cents are taken out, think about how good you have to be to win. The average player has no sense how big that bite is. It depresses me to see the typical guy bringing $200 to the races and betting it all on trifectas."

BARRY MEADOW: "Win, place, show, and exactas are what I play the most. Less on the daily doubles, less on trifectas, less on pick threes, pick fours, and pick sixes. It all depends on the setup of the races. Let's say I think there's going to be a discrepancy in races four and six. Well, those are two of the three legs of the pick three, so I might play a pick three because I have some advantage in two of the three races. I have a list of the races I believe I might be betting, but of course I don't know until it actually happens. Occasionally, I'll make a bet on a race that I didn't have listed in the first place, because suddenly the people aren't betting a horse I thought was obvious. Or maybe there are three obvious horses and one of them they decide they just don't want to bet."

ERNIE DAHLMAN: "I don't keep records on what types of races I do well on, but I have a *sense* of how I do. A lot of times I'll use the exacta like a win bet—try to get a little more than the win price if the horses I like run second or get a little less than the win price if they don't. I can make a 4-5 shot into a 6-5 shot if one of the ones I like comes in second, or make it into a 3-5 shot or 2-5 shot otherwise.

"But in maiden races, maiden-claiming races especially, a lot of the horses have no chance whatsoever, no chance for second, so I'll discard them; but with the contenders I'll bet them in a certain way, going for shots on certain horses to run second. But I'm not looking to lose my whole bet because early on I found I couldn't tolerate having a big bet on a horse, having him win and then lose my whole bet. I can tolerate breaking even or losing a little but I never got to where I could tolerate losing a whole bet when I like a horse."

PAUL CORNMAN: "I clearly bet exactas more than others."

JAMES QUINN: "I'll play two or three key bets to win; five or six exotic bets. I no longer roll pick threes, but I wind up playing three or four pick threes."

PAUL BRASETH: "I like to make win bets. Then I look to the exacta, if I have overlays that have a chance to win. Then I would look to the pick threes. In that order."

DAVE CUSCUNA: "I bet across all pools. I tend to like playing the exotic bets; the higher the degree of difficulty, the more I like it because it allows for a combination of strategy and handicapping."

DAVE GUTFREUND: "I play exactas and pick threes. When it comes to a given race, I'm too unconservative to just want to make straight bets mostly. And I'm too afraid in races to try and figure out who the third and fourth horses are going to be to suck up for the back end of a tri or a super. If I can get a favorite out of the exacta or something, if I'm going to play a race individually, it's mostly going to be through the exactas. And the pick threes and the pick fours; I'm more of a pick-three guy because there are more of them around the country; if you can get a couple of races without the favorites you can usually get a lot more value than what the parlay pays."

CARY FOTIAS: "I feel that the pick three and pick four are good options for the little player if you can get an overlay in the first leg because most people overspread in the first leg."

JIM MAZUR: "I really focus most of my betting on pick threes. There are going to be races where you get several conflicting angles, trainers with good numbers in certain categories and they are all in the same race. Then you look at the horses but sometimes they are tough to separate and they are all good odds and that's a perfect play for a pick three. Then maybe single a horse in the second race and spread out thereafter."

■ The Pick Six

The pick six, given its complication and potential for huge payoffs, is a different animal completely because it requires an entirely different mind-set from your typical wager. If you're going to play the pick six seriously, you have to be resilient, inured to losing, and flush with capital so that you can cover your preferred combinations. It's not a bet for the faint-hearted and it takes strong commitment and resolve to play this wager seriously. Like anything in life, however, with great risk comes the potential for great reward. It's up to you to decide if this is a wager you can play successfully.

One aspect of the pick six, however, makes it undeniably better than the rest of the wagering menu: carryovers. There are times when you'll have a situation in which the track will pay back more to the bettors than the bettors put into it.

RANDY GALLO: "I used to handicap plenty but I was always interested in the jackpots because your dollar was always worth more than a dollar. In a trifecta race, they take out 25 percent, some tracks take less, some tracks take more, but let's just use 25 percent as an example. So if there's $10,000 in the pool, in the regular trifecta race, they pay back $7,500, which means that your dollar is worth 75 cents.

"With carryover jackpots, unless they all bet the jackpot, which occasionally they do now in Southern California, in the twin trifecta or a pick six, there can be a $50,000 carryover and let's say they bet $100,000 into it. Well, once 25 percent is taken off the $100,000, there's still $75,000 plus the $50,000 in the carryover, so the crowd is betting $100,000 and they're paying back $125,000. So your dollar becomes $1.25, so that gives you an edge—it becomes a positive-expectation game."

But Gallo warns that not every pick-six carryover will lead to a positive expectation.

RANDY GALLO: "I know what each jackpot calls for—how much they'll bet in a carryover in all different situations. I'm not being wise but I know how much they're going to bet so I know how much the jackpot's worth.

"Say there's a $100,000 carryover on a Thursday afternoon at Del Mar. They're going to bet probably $600,000 the next day. If you take 20 percent of 600, it's 120. If there's only $100K carryover and they're taking out $120,000, now the pool is $600,000 and they're paying back $580,000. So even though there's a carryover of $100,000 your dollar is still only worth 93 cents."

He might still play in that situation, though.

RANDY GALLO: "If you think you can beat an even-money shot, or if you've got a 10-1 shot you like a lot, now all of a sudden you're turning it back in the other direction. But as far as head-to-head with the crowd, with no opinion, you're 93 cents."

BARRY MEADOW: "When you're playing the pick six, you're going to have monster days. You might win $100K but that's not something you can count on. Generally for me, if I win more than $5K it's a good day; if I lose more than $5K it's a bad day.

"I don't play the pick six unless there's a carryover and sometimes I won't play even then, if it looks too obvious or I have no feel for a bunch of the races."

ERNIE DAHLMAN: "Contrary to what I've read about myself, I'm not a big pick-six player. I will play the pick six seriously but I don't put a lot of money in. A few years ago when the pick six started I made my living off the pick six and that's probably why I got the reputation as a big pick-six player. For some reason as I got more into Thoroughbred racing and got more opinionated, I started hitting less pick sixes. Instead of using five horses, I'd use two horses and I just didn't do as well, so I started cutting down because I was doing very well on race-to-race bets.

"Last week I was alive in the pick six in New York and a horse I liked, Ryan Is Flying, came out and was using the shoes that I like in the last race—and I wasn't alive with him! So here I am alive with two horses, one ran second and one ran out, and I'm putting a good bet on Ryan Is Flying and I don't even have him in the pick six. He wins, he pays $14, and I think to myself, 'Why do I bet pick sixes?'

"How can I bet more than a token bet when in any given race I might change my mind as to what I'm betting on?"

STEVEN CRIST: "As a multi-race bettor, I have to get through races I don't like and would not bet on individually. I can't possibly have six consecutive great insights on the races that constitute a pick six. One of the things you learn to do over time is to become a good 'defensive' player to get through the weak legs. Sometimes survival is victory."

ROXY ROXBOROUGH: "When I'm not chasing the proposition bets and head-to-head matchups and future books, my bets are more toward getting a big score, playing pick-six carryovers and keying mid-priced horses in trifectas. That's evolved for me over time, because two generations ago, when I first started playing, you could only bet win-place-show and daily doubles. When I first started, all I did was win betting, and it took me a long time to get away from that.

"The new generation has been interested in overlays in exotic pools right from the beginning—it's second nature to them. Playing the pick six causes mental problems. Pick-six players walk away losers a lot. To go from playing 3-1 shots in the win pool to playing the pick six on a regular basis, you have to have a certain disposition to take that type of losing—every time you play you're a big favorite to walk away with nothing. There's a lot of losing that goes along with the exotics, and if you can't handle losing, then stick to win bets. You don't grind out a profit with exotics, and for a lot of people that's unnerving."

■ Proposition Bets

As Roxborough mentioned, he makes quite a decent living betting in areas where a lot of uninformed bettors are playing—proposition bets. With the advent of online gaming, proposition bets offer good value. A proposition bet can be anything from head-to-head matchups between horses (who will place better in the Breeders' Cup Classic, Perfect Drift or Evening Attire?) to betting who will have more Breeders' Cup winners, the United States or Europe? Any good gaming site or Vegas casino will have a wide menu of proposition-betting choices, and if you have a strong opinion, there is a big opportunity for the smart player to make a lot of money.

ROXY ROXBOROUGH: "I look at proposition bets for two reasons:
1. I can handicap them much better.
2. The takeout is much smaller.

"The Las Vegas books are the same way: The more betting selections a bettor has the more chances he has to find value. A proposition bet might be an over/under on how many Euros will win on Breeders' Cup Day, or will Frankie Dettori win more than one race, or will even-numbered horses win more on a given day than odd-numbered horses? If my top horses are all even-numbered, then I've found a good spot to put my money."

ACTION BETS

If you're going to win at the track over the long haul, is it okay to make an action bet, just for the thrill of the gamble? Making action bets doesn't really seem like a recipe for success, but surprisingly, most of our pros were in favor of action bets for the simple reason that they force you to continually analyze your play. Action bets allow you to experiment and learn from your mistakes. They also keep you involved and focused on the races. The important thing to note here is that *if you're going to make action bets, make sure that they are a small part of your handle.* It sounds like common sense, but it's easy to get carried away at the racetrack—giving back your winnings or doubling your losses—by craving action on every race.

■ Yes to Action Bets

ANDREW BEYER: "If I've got an opinion and maybe I love a horse, maybe I'll put $1,000 into a race and the next race I'll play a $20 exacta box. I just feel that there's no necessarily right way or wrong way in terms of betting strategy except for this—you're supposed to keep your bets proportionate to your convictions about a race. If you love a race, you bet $1,000; if you're screwing around, you bet $20 to $40. There are a million ways to deviate from that prescription. Players get carried away by a win or else they are in a hole and then they start escalating. Those are the traps that get bettors into trouble. I'll always make small action bets when I have a marginal opinion."

STEVEN CRIST: "There is nothing wrong with making tiny bets on other races for the entertainment value and to make yourself pay attention. If you break even or show a small loss on these investments, they probably pay for themselves in terms of mental equilibrium, relaxation, and forcing you to watch a race more carefully than you otherwise would, perhaps creating a future opportunity. The trick is to keep these plays very small relative to your serious bets."

ROXY ROXBOROUGH: "I do make action bets because it makes me more focused when I'm playing. Naturally, they're for less money— but I find that when you have money on something your focus and study is better."

PAUL BRASETH: "I'd like to say that I don't make action bets, but I have been known to just say, 'Okay, I'll make some kind of action bet.' It's the old [Steve] Davidowitz idea: He makes prime bets and action bets, and the action bet is maybe a $20 bet on a horse that's 18-1. I do that, but I do it rarely. That's going to be a pretty small percentage of what I bet when I'm serious about something."

PAUL CORNMAN: "I make action bets. If I think it's an open race, I'll take a little chance. Normally an action bet is a sixth of what I would normally do. I might make a dozen normal bets in a day. If I really like something, I might bet 20 times my action-bet amount."

DAVE GUTFREUND: "Over the last few years I've gone back and forth on whether I should make action bets. There have been times where I've tried to just cut down and make only the 'strong plays.' Ninety percent of my plays are what most people would consider action plays and there are only 10 percent that are strong, strong bets. There aren't that many strong bets anymore to my mind—once or twice a week. I don't have the patience for that."

JAMES QUINN: "I make action bets all the time in the exotics. I link horses I feel strongly about in the straight pools to leverage them in combo and serial bets. I don't make action bets in straight pools. I do make them in the exotics pools."

JIM MAZUR: "I make action bets all the time. I might even play two horses to win if the odds are right. I might go for a home run. Take a 20-1 shot and tie him up with a couple of horses in exactas or trifectas and if you hit it, it can make a nice week or a month for you."

ERNIE DAHLMAN: "Unfortunately, I sometimes force things. If I don't have any opinion, I won't bet. But sometimes I'll notice something, like a guy who's won his last three races off a claim or something from this guy and he's 4-1 and I think he's got a better shot than that, so I'll go in and make a bet where I'm undecided.

"If I'm having a bad day and I love something say two races from now, I might sit out two races to get to the one with the horse that I love, rather than get myself farther into the frying pan."

■ No to Action Bets

Two of our pros—Dave Cuscuna and Cary Fotias—questioned the entire notion of an action bet, and each with good reason. Barry Meadow was resolute in his stance against making any kind of bet just for the sake of having action.

DAVE CUSCUNA: "I tend not to sit out too many races but I might sit out a bunch of races in a row and not make a serious bet if I don't see a great opportunity. Generally, I can find some sort of perceived value in a race but is it a great opportunity, a good opportunity, a fair opportunity? What is it that I'm chasing? Am I playing a favorite that I love on top of a 35-1 that I think should be 10-1 in an exacta? I don't see that as a great opportunity but it's worth something so maybe I bet 10 percent of my big bet size on that race. Is my top choice a best bet of the day at 9-2? Then I'll bet 100 percent of my big bet size on that one. It's rare that I sit a race out completely but I will scale down my bet based on what I see as an opportunity.

"'Action bet' wouldn't be a good term for it because that implies I'm betting for the sake of betting and I don't think I do that. Sometimes somebody invites you out to Gramercy Tavern or Lutece and other nights you get pizza from a good pizzeria, like Patsy's around the corner. Both of them are good meals but hopefully Lutece is a little better than Patsy's. But there's nothing wrong with Patsy's every once in a while too. That's what I'm getting at. But I try to stay away from Burger King. That's an action bet!"

CARY FOTIAS: "Those aren't action bets, they're compulsive bets. In a way, the worst thing that can happen is to win those kinds of bets; it's negative reinforcement. I do make action bets now and again but I'm very careful to control them."

BARRY MEADOW: "I never make an action bet. I've made bad bets where the horse was marginal and I shouldn't have bet. I've certainly made mistakes but I don't bet just to have something going. There are other things you can be doing. You can watch the race for example. You learn something from watching the race. You don't have to make a bet on every race.

"It's just as important to watch a race you're *not* betting on as one you are betting on. In fact, when I bet a race, I'm watching my horse like everybody else. Then I have to watch the replay to see what actually happened. If I don't have a bet, then I'm watching much more objectively the first time around. But when I bet, I don't care about the other horses the first time I watch the race, I'm looking at my beautiful horse."

THE IMPORTANCE OF RECORD KEEPING

If you're going to be honest with yourself—if you're going to make the commitment to bolster your strengths and work on your weaknesses—you have to understand where you stand. And that means keeping records. If you have a written ledger of your wins and losses, the types of bets you make, and the types of races you typically win, you'll be able to fully understand the way you play. You'll also see which areas need improvement. While keeping good records sounds tedious and boring, it's the last and most crucial step in being honest with yourself. And if you're going to be a winning player, you need to be honest with yourself and keep records.

BRAD FREE: "When I talk about having a plan, it has to be highly personal. So you need to find out what you are good at. And the only way to do that is record keeping. There are things that I do well and there are things that I do poorly, and the only way that I would ever know that is by my own record keeping—because your mind plays tricks on you. I remember hitting a $6,000 trifecta back when trifectas were first introduced, and I spent the next five years trying to hit another one until I finally realized that, hey, trifectas just don't pay $6,000 every day. Darn! So I lowered my aim a little bit.

"Keeping records is so boring and I'm sure that less than 1 percent of all horseplayers keep wagering records. You never hear anybody talk about it. Who wants to sit down and record something every day where most of the time you lose? But if you keep records, it's the best thing you can do. I know what I'm good at and I know what I'm bad at, so I don't have an excuse anymore. I can't just say, 'Well, maybe I shouldn't have made that exacta box.' I know that I'm no good at those. But other people might be. And other people might be good at the pick six. I know that I'm not."

DAVE GUTFREUND: "Keep records! I bet mostly on a phone account and they keep unbelievable records for me: how I do at one track versus another and on the different types of bets. Self-analysis is key to success.

"You can go back and study and see that in maiden grass races you show a very nice profitable ROI. In filly-and-mare sprint races, you can't get out of your own way. So you try and increase your wagers on what you're good at and weed out the crap."

BARRY MEADOW: "I put every bet I make on the computer. I know how I'm doing with every kind of bet at every different track and I try to be totally objective. I do summaries every day, of how much I bet on each type of bet and on how much I collected and also how many races I won and lost for each type of bet. If I made three show bets, did I win two of them, did I win zero? I can check that going back years.

"When I was doing harness races, I used to use a computer then, I used to record every race with race conditions so I could immediately see what types of races I was better at, so I could see if any type of cash drain was going on. Of course, even if you know how you've done in every type of bet, if there's not enough of a type of race—say there are only 80 grass routes I bet for the year—the standard deviation is so high that you can't really draw any conclusions from that."

ROXY ROXBOROUGH: "The key here is to keep records. People fool themselves by not keeping good records. Pros keep comprehensive records for tax reasons, and you have to know if you're winning or losing. And you have to know where the money's going. If you're blowing trifectas, maybe you're betting too many combos or your parameters aren't that good. Keeping records is key."

PAUL BRASETH: "I keep records, of course, of all the bets and the

223

amounts, and what I've won or lost. And because I'm a trainer analyst, I always put down who the trainers were that I bet on, which I've found to be productive for me. I've found that there are some trainers on each of these circuits that I seem to be in step with. In other words, when they make the right move, I seem to be able to recognize it. And others I don't. I do factor that in at times. I had the best meet I've ever had a couple of years ago at Santa Anita. I've always been in step with Darrell Vienna. He goes through his ups and downs. A couple of years ago at Santa Anita he went through a real hot streak and so did I because I recognized all the stuff he was doing.

"In the mid-eighties I did a seminar in New York. I was doing Longacres at the time and I did a study of two trainers and I liked both of these trainers a lot. One was named Ron Glatt; his son trains in Southern California, Mark Glatt. I'd been trying to figure Ron Glatt out since the seventies. And there's another trainer up there named Kay Vaughn. So I did a study of these two trainers and the bets I had made on them. With Kay Vaughn I was clicking along at maybe 50 percent winners and with Ron I was down around 10 percent because I would anticipate his moves and be wrong. If you're into the trainer aspect of the game, that's something to think about. I found it to be valuable."

And racing isn't the only game where record keeping is important:

CLONIE GOWEN: "Record keeping is pretty important. I'm not the most organized person in the world but it's still important. I don't play a lot of limit, and that's because I've found out that my numbers in limit overall just aren't that good. But there are also certain places where I play that I've found I show a bigger profit. So I tend to go back to those places. So that's what my record keeping does, it tells me what games and what limits I do best in, what I do against certain players who I play regularly against.

"My records also tell me whether certain players I play against are improving or not. Mediocre players aren't going to stay mediocre for long. They're usually either going to go broke and quit the game or they're going to advance in the game, maybe without even realizing it. Just because a guy was a mediocre player a year ago doesn't mean he's going to be a mediocre player today. You really need to evaluate."

6

IT'S ONE LONG GAME

SECRET

They know how to handle their emotions
as well as their money.

Focus on decisions, *not* outcomes. If there's one statement that sums up the life of a successful gambler, then that's it. All a good gambler can do is make the best possible decisions day in and day out. If you continue to make good decisions, you are going to win in the long run. The problem is, not every one of your good decisions is going to lead to a favorable outcome. There are times when you're going to lose regardless of how good your decision is. As we said when we talked about standard deviation in Chapter 3, you can do everything right and still lose.

Why? Because there will always be external factors outside your control. Your horse can jump a shadow and get beat by a nose. A jockey can make a thrilling late charge that's just one-hundredth of a second too late. Your horse might savage another horse and get disqualified. This is all part of the game. The only thing in your control is the decision you make.

And that is why you need to focus on your decision and not on the outcome. Because if you start focusing on the outcome, your mental state is going to be adversely affected. There are just too many things that can go wrong in horse racing, and if you let them affect you, you're going to lose.

In the short term, many factors will go into whether you cash a ticket. Thus, it's important to understand the concept that "it's one long game." You need to account for that or else your money will be affected by your emotions. Richard Munchkin, author of *Gambling Wizards*, said, "You need to have the ability to not get emotionally involved in the wins and losses."

And Cary Fotias said, "Focus on making money in the long run—always keep that in focus."

If you let short-term losses affect your play, you're a guaranteed loser.

Andrew Beyer understands that keeping one's emotions in check is of paramount importance to a gambler because no matter what you do, you're still bound to lose your fair share of races.

ANDREW BEYER: "I would say that at the top of the list of requirements is the ability to handle your emotions as well as your money. There are so many emotional highs and lows in horse racing that gamblers who let themselves get unhinged by those emotionally stressful events are the ones who can't succeed. There are a lot of good handicappers around who don't win because they are their own worst enemies. If you lose a pick six in the last leg by a nose that would have been worth $25K or $50K, you've got to have the ability to come back to the track the next day with that having no effect on your thinking or your mental attitude. Obviously, at the time we all get pissed off and we scream but once it's done, it's done and you just have to wipe the slate clean.

"If someone asked me, 'What's your great strength as a gambler,' that's it. I start each day at the track with pretty much the same attitude, with the slate wiped clean from the previous day. Nobody has this ability instinctively. It's human nature to get rattled, to start pressing or getting impulsive because you want to recoup a loss or something you should have had. But you learn.

"If you miss a $10K photo and you get upset, that's the least of your problems if you go and blow another $10K just because you've become unhinged by that experience. Contrarily, when you're going well, you may want to increase your bets a little because you're on a roll. But you don't want to get carried away, get careless, to think that you're just fated to win all the time. You don't want either wins or losses to change the way you approach the game."

WHAT TYPE OF PERSON WINS AT THE TRACK? 22

What is it on the mental side that separates these players from everyone else at the track? What mind-set do they bring to the game that gives them an edge? For one thing, no matter how bad the losses might be, they don't throw good money after bad. They also don't let a bad beat affect the rest of their day, nor do they allow short-term fluctuations to impact their overall strategy. By maintaining an even keel, these players limit their emotions—when both losing and winning—and realize that one day is just part of many days in their chosen profession.

Cary Fotias and Steven Crist stressed the importance of having confidence and bringing a winning attitude every day.

CARY FOTIAS: "You need to have a winning attitude. If you don't feel you'll be able to beat the game then you won't be able to.

"I think one needs both superior information and an open, creative mind to really prosper at this game, too. But most important, one must believe he can win. There are many paths to the truth, but without a firm conviction in one's ability to win, the handicapper has little chance of financial survival."

STEVEN CRIST: "Keeping your confidence high and your stress and self-flagellation low are crucial to maintaining a winning mind-set. You can't be afraid to be wrong, very wrong, or allow yourself to be intimidated by other people's opinions, or the tote board, or the possibility of what some people would consider public humiliation. I've made speeches at seminars about how some big favorite is really vulnerable and I'm going to bet against him and the horse goes out and wins by 10. Big deal. I'm going to be right often enough to come out ahead. I thought Smarty Jones at 1-5 in the Belmont was one of the biggest underlays in the history of horse racing. That doesn't mean he couldn't have won or won by a pole. I wasn't going to feel even a little bit stupid if he won by 32 lengths. My opinion that he was a ridiculous price was the correct one either way."

Clonie Gowen told us a great story about confidence:

CLONIE GOWEN: "One of the best pieces of advice I ever received was given to me by a good friend of mine here in Dallas, Texas, named Brook Stevens. I was headed out to my first major tournament that I ever played in, which was in Costa Rica. We had played regularly in a game for five or six years so I asked him, 'Brook, what kind of advice can you give me when I go out there?' He said to me, 'You've been beating these games in Dallas for years, there's not a game in the world you can't play.' And that gave me the confidence I needed to go out and play the game. Instead of giving me some specific piece of advice telling me to do this or that, he just patted me on the back and gave me some great confidence. Confidence and positive thinking are just so much a part of anything you do in life."

Paul Braseth spoke about toughness and emotions.

PAUL BRASETH: "You have to develop what's called 'mental toughness' because you're going to be under stress at the track. I started reading a lot of books about investing in the stock market, just to see how they evaluate their stocks. I used to read these pop-psychology books, *The Psychology of Winning* and such. They were helpful in the ability to develop mental toughness and deal with situations and seeing the real problems involved and not getting caught up in the emotion of the moment.

"One book I remember was by a guy called Denis Whitely and the whole thing centered around the idea of winning. One little trick he used was the idea of positive self-talk at the racetrack. You have to keep a positive attitude and tell yourself, 'Well, you're a good player, so move on.' But the most important thing I learned was knowing how to lose and doing it in such a way where you don't disrupt your decision-making processes in the future. If you can't do that, you're sunk."

The same idea holds true in poker:

CLONIE GOWEN: "I've tried meditation. Before I went to my first major tournament, I really focused on seeing myself in first place, I focused on winning, on seeing myself advance. It really helped to see that process happening for me."

Dave Gutfreund stressed the importance of staying positive. No matter what happens—and bad things are bound to happen—you need have a positive attitude to win at the races.

DAVE GUTFREUND: "Being smart, that's obviously a trait all players must have. Emotional stability, too. It's not easy being a horseplayer. You're going to go through lots of ups and downs, especially if you're a pick-four or pick-six player, there's going to be a lot of droughts and it's difficult, it's very draining on the mind, especially when things are going poorly. It's easy to think, 'Ah, I can't beat this game, it's too tough, there's a 20 percent takeout,' etc. Having a good mental attitude is really what I mean.

"Try and stay positive whenever possible. Don't get down on yourself. It's hard to deal with when you're on a losing streak—that's human nature."

That you need to have confidence and a winning attitude in order to beat the races shouldn't come as a surprise, but one thing that was surprising to us was that none of these players had egos. In fact, they stressed the fact that you need to check your ego at the door if you're going to be successful betting the races.

RANDY GALLO: "You shouldn't have an ego. I've been playing carryover pools since 1977 and all the successful people that I know—I'm talking about really successful—none of them have egos, believe it or not. They're interested in making money. Get rid of the egos and it's just amazing. The people that just show up and do the work and don't beat their chest when their horse wins, and they treat it as a business. These guys are successful. Take my word for it."

LAS VEGAS PLAYER: "You could red-board, I guess, but having confidence in yourself and being willing to learn go hand in hand. To really get carried away with yourself because you won a race isn't a good idea. Sure, it's fun to talk about, it's part of the thrill of winning when you solve the puzzle, but you don't want to get carried away with it.

"I don't know why you would want to tell everybody how smart you are. In life, people who immediately want to spend all their time talking about themselves, do you really want to be around somebody like that? You want to be around understated people who you feel comfortable with. I don't want to be around somebody bragging about himself. That's hopeless."

DAVE GUTFREUND: "Yes, I have the capacity to learn from my mistakes. I will remain humble. I will remain driven. And those are the two things. What happens sometimes is you start thinking you're too good and you slack off on the work just a little bit and you make a few more action bets and the train of bad things starts happening."

THE IMPORTANCE OF DISCIPLINE

One of the keys to success at the track is picking and choosing your spots after you've established your edge and isolated value. Thus, having discipline is an important part of a winning player's makeup. With a vast wagering menu and a multitude of tracks to play, it's easy to lose sight of the task at hand: establishing edge and isolating value. As Brad Free noted, "You have to be disciplined. It depends on what you want to do. If you just want to go out there and fire at all nine races on a card, there's nothing wrong with that. I don't think it's the way to win. But if you want to win, you need the ability to recognize those situations where you've done well in the past and then maybe you can do so again. I don't know if you can teach discipline. It's still tough for me. I handicap every single race so I'm paid to have an opinion on every single race. The temptation is always there—every single race— to make a wager. But you need to control that."

The opposite of showing discipline is what poker players call going on tilt, which is throwing good money after bad—playing when you have no discernible edge because you've let your mental state (and the psychological burden of losing) affect the way you play. To be a winning player, you have to take your losing days in stride—turn a negative into a positive—and learn from your mistakes. You also need to get over bad beats and weather short-term losses. Not going on tilt and maintaining discipline is crucial to a process that can easily get away from you, and it's not uncommon for less disciplined horseplayers to go from losing a couple of hundred bucks to thousands just because they start pressing or double up to try to get even. It's a recipe for disaster and it's something all of our pros would shake their heads at. There's no place for emotion in successful gambling, and if you can't be disciplined in your approach to the game, you're a guaranteed loser.

It's also important to curb your compulsive tendencies, as Steve Davidowitz, our Kentucky Player, Jim Mazur, and Ernie Dahlman noted.

STEVE DAVIDOWITZ: "You need to be able to appreciate the fine line between being somewhat successful and potentially ill. Making money at the racetrack is seductive; it's more interesting than working in the Holland Tunnel or being a lawyer—it's an interesting place to be and you're not going to always live up to your own standards; you're going to make mistakes, violate your principles, bet too much money. You have to have a developing, well-balanced, positive psyche. You need to appreciate the negative pulls that winning can have, and be honest with yourself.

"Horse racing was my military service. If I was going to win, I needed to have discipline and be honest with myself."

KENTUCKY PLAYER: "To be an addicted gambler and to lose sight and not be able to control that . . . I've seen a lot of cases of that along the way—of people that were interested in racing, loved racing, loved gambling, loved playing the horses, but weren't able to handle it in the end."

JIM MAZUR: "You have to have a lot of discipline. That's by far the biggest thing for me. A successful professional handicapper, not a gambler—I think of a gambler as someone who is plunging—is going to weigh all the different angles and the odds and make the best call, the best percentage play that he can make and do it day in and day out. You should sit out races where you don't have an opinion. If you're not sure, you shouldn't be wagering your money."

ERNIE DAHLMAN: "I don't think having a big head for gambling or being a compulsive gambler is going to help you too much. You've got to be able to control yourself, to be objective, to have a certain sense of what you're watching.

"If I feel I have no clue, like if it's all 2-year-old races with first-time starters or all grass races with horses who've never been on the grass before, I could sit out a whole card. Of course, that doesn't usually happen. But that's why I like the winter more. Just about every race I'll have an opinion because they're hard-hitting horses that I've seen run quite a bit on every kind of surface. I'll sit out when I don't have any edge whatsoever. That happens more in the spring and early summer than in the winter."

Dave Cuscuna also talked about showing the discipline to not play unless you have a distinct edge—or, if you don't have a distinct edge, to be smart enough to realize that and scale down your wagers accordingly.

DAVE CUSCUNA: "Part of discipline is knowing not to bet if you haven't done enough work or knowing that your level of confidence in a given situation is low so your edge needs to be very, very high. I mentioned before about doing a job 100 percent or 98 percent. Well, sometimes in the real world, there are also jobs that can be done at 60 percent and 30 percent, and when you do one of those, you're going to need more of an edge. In other words, if you like a horse at 8-1 and he's 11-1 on the board, that's not enough of an edge if you've only done a 30 percent job handicapping. You might need 25-1. You may have overlooked 27 pieces of information.

"You may not know anything about the ticket market for Broadway shows but two years ago you'd have known to buy two tickets to *The Producers* for a Saturday night at face value if they were offered to you. You'd know that just from what you heard around. There's no way you'd take a loss on those tickets. If you couldn't use them you could sell them on eBay for $400 or whatever it was.

"But you better be careful about buying two tickets at face value for *Man of La Mancha* right now because you might not be able to get rid of them. But if somebody was going to give you $100 tickets for $5, even if you know nothing about the market for those tickets, you have to think to yourself, 'Well, they're worth a shot at $5.'

"I think discipline can have a lot of different facets to it. Knowing your strengths and weaknesses, knowing how much to bet certain strengths and knowing how to acknowledge your weaknesses, that's important too."

Several of our players talked about the discipline of sitting out races—sometimes whole cards—while waiting for the right opportunities to make a bet.

STEVE DAVIDOWITZ: "I sit out a lot of races. I once didn't make a bet for two weeks. Andy Beyer wrote a column about it. We were in Saratoga and something just didn't feel right, but that feeling went away and I cashed the first bet I made after things felt right again."

PAUL BRASETH: "I sit out races all the time. You have to because very few races these days offer much value.

"I've waited two or three days for the right opportunity to make a serious bet. In California right now, in racing during the week especially, it's very hard to find value because of the short fields. It's a difficult process. You have to have patience, obviously, and you have to know, well, something's going to come up here. And when something does come up you've got to take advantage of it.

"Right now I'm doing just Northern and Southern California. And during the week that's 16 races a day and I may be able to find value in three or four of those. I might play a pick three if I have a logical winner in a race and something around it that offers some value. Maybe it's because I'm older now but I've become much more disciplined than I used to be. There's a difference at the racetrack between winning races and winning money. Yeah, you can win races but your objective is to *make money.* I think that's a trap people fall into when they're not doing well. They say, 'Oh, I need a winner so I'm going to bet this horse even though it doesn't offer any value,' and then they lose.

"I've spent some time writing in my newsletter and such about the psychology of winning and what it takes to be a winner at the racetrack because I became perplexed at how many good handicappers there are around who don't make any money because they don't think too much about betting and what it takes to be a winner. My feeling has always been that people who get into racing, it's easy for them to learn a lot about handicapping, that's natural for them, like they are going to school. They amass all this information and they understand it. But putting it into practice—taking it beyond the classroom—is another matter and that's where your emotional makeup comes into play."

RANDY GALLO: "I was at Gulfstream today and I sat out eight of the nine races. It's a job—you're going to be doing the same thing the next day and the next day and the next day and the next day, so you don't have to play. And why would you play if it's not there? I've gone to meets when they first started, say at Saratoga, and gone two or three days without making a bet."

BARRY MEADOW: "Some days I don't have any bets. Generally speaking I'll play two or three races a day. Some days I'll play six; some days I'll play zero. Everything depends on what my opinions are of those horses and then what numbers the crowd is putting up. Sometimes there'll be three races on the schedule that I believe I might play and the crowd winds up betting all the horses I like when I didn't think they would. Then I don't play. I never had any problems sitting out races because I'm not going to play unless I believe I have an advantage. You cannot bet unless you feel you have an advantage. If you have no advantage, you can't bet. So that's the most important thing."

DAVE GUTFREUND: "You've got to sit out races. You can't play every race, are you crazy?

"I will pass entire days. I can and have been able to do that. Most days, though, I'm looking from a simulcast point of view, looking at four or five tracks. I may play six, eight, ten races a day from those four or five tracks."

Our Kentucky Player had an interesting story to illustrate discipline and what it means to focus your action on value plays where you know you have a distinct advantage. To do it right, though, takes a lot of discipline. But the reward is worth the wait.

KENTUCKY PLAYER: "My dad spends his winters in Florida—the other half of the year he's in Kentucky—and we play the horses together sometimes. This is the best analogy I can think of when it comes to discipline: I pick out specific prime plays, the kind of plays I would be making if I were betting on a very limited budget—the kind of races I would be focusing on because I feel like they're my very best opportunities and I want to bring my dad into those opportunities. And he and I will have a little fund that we set aside and specifically target just prime races. We call them prime betting spots. And we demand that everything be right in those spots. We have to have a good jockey, a good trainer, a good price—a lot of favorable things before we bet from that fund.

"And that fund, it's incredible. I don't know the specific return on it but we usually put a couple of hundred dollars apiece in it when he first comes back from Florida and we'll run thousands of dollars out of that thing. It opens my eyes a lot of times. If you could just focus on your very best, how good could you be?"

James Quinn also has the discipline to sit out races he doesn't have a strong opinion on, but he does make the interesting point that with the advance-wagering menu, you can often find value by linking these contentious races to more predictable races in parlay wagers. The point being: If you can find value, you can make a good bet.

JAMES QUINN: "When I was playing for income, it was important to me to sit out races—especially unpredictable and overly contentious races—early in my career. I still pass the unpredictable races.

"When I was playing for a living, I can remember not playing for two days. I would pass on underlays for two days and wouldn't play. When the exotic menu became more comprehensive you had other ways to deal with unpredictable races or contentious races, so you could link them to more predictable races."

Steven Crist says that taking up Texas Hold 'em in recent years has given him a helpful new perspective on passing races.

STEVEN CRIST: "When I first started playing poker seriously against real players, I was losing and quickly learned I was simply playing too many marginal hands. You learn to throw away your starting hand four times out of five because you just don't want to start out from a position of weakness. Why do I want to get involved with a race if I feel like my insight amounts to holding a three and an eight? Just turn the page and wait for a better hand."

■ Not Going on Tilt

Sitting out races is just one facet of having discipline. Another facet lies in the realm of not letting your emotions get the best of you—and that means having the discipline to not go on tilt, to not let your emotional state affect your play no matter how tough things might be.

Gerry Okuneff talked about these two aspects of discipline—sitting out races and watching people unravel. If you have the patience and discipline to sit out races, you should also have the strength to avoid letting your emotions take over the way you play. All of our players are unflappable in the face of losing streaks and adversity. And to succeed in this game, you can't have it any other way.

GERRY OKUNEFF: "I think sitting out races is imperative, especially now with the unbelievable amount of exotics and the possibilities that they create. Discipline, first and foremost, is an important trait.

"I will sit out races; I don't sit out as many as I should. Marty Ritt and I spent years at the track and he taught me some things, and if he were here he might not admit that I taught him a few things, too. Ritt was a great gambler and could sit out race after race. He'd do a fair amount of work and watch race after race. As a student of people, I think he got some pleasure out of watching people unravel.

"So one day I asked, 'Marty, how can you not make a bet in so long?'

"He pounded his fist on the table and said, 'I refuse to be a fool!'

"Well, I don't like to be a fool, either, but I'll be damned if I work seven hours handicapping the races and then sit at the track and watch people make mistakes. So I should sit out more than I do, but I don't—and that's the price I pay for fun.

"I could sit out maybe five or six races. But I don't go two or three days without making a bet."

Our Maryland Player spoke more specifically about going on tilt and how it's very easy to lose one's perspective when there's money involved, especially in the short term. The important thing to remember is that it's all one long game, and while your play on any given day will affect your short-term success, you need to show the resilience to weather losing streaks.

MARYLAND PLAYER: "A lot of people seem to go on tilt, to lose their perspective. There's a tendency in this business to forget that there are a lot of bets that happen in the course of a year. What happened in the last one really doesn't make a heck of a lot of difference.

"Yeah, you got a bad ride and you lost, and yeah, we remember those because we're human. But you tend not to remember when you won because of the bad ride on the horse that ran second. It happens. I really believe that having no emotions at all is the ideal and the closer you get to that, the better. Whatever happened in the last race, you have to be able to go on to the next race because it's over. And if you can't do that, I don't care how well you handicap, you're dead. You don't have to be calm but you have to be mentally calm."

Paul Cornman talked about the ability to recognize when your mental state is affecting your play, and then showing the discipline to put on the brakes and scale back your action.

PAUL CORNMAN: "I get worn out sometimes. I'm a guy who doesn't win a lot of photos that people can't call. I just expect to lose those. Sometimes they wear me out and psychologically I know I'm down. And one of the ways I know I'm down is if I think I'm handicapping open races and I end up with the favorite, race in and race out. Then I know I'm not doing my job correctly and then I'll take a deep breath and pull back. That might mean not betting or that might mean betting less."

Howard Lederer, our poker/sports-betting expert, talked about how easy it is to go on tilt while playing poker because the money is real and it's all right there in front of you—and one hand is dealt right after the next. It's similar to horse racing in that there's one race after the next and it's very easy to go on tilt and start betting every race without having a good opinion.

> **HOWARD LEDERER:** "With betting sports, you're a bit more removed. You're placing bets, you're calling up your bookie or going into the sports book, and you've done all your analysis and you've made all your selections beforehand if you're doing it right, in the exact opposite of the heat of the moment. You're in your house, analyzing statistics, reading injury reports, making decisions. You walk into the sports book, you make your bet and then you watch it. It's a very removed process, whereas with poker you're right there and you're making snap decisions at the moment. You're reacting to what happened to you two minutes ago. And you are literally playing with your money in your hands. It's a very different thing.
>
> "I think the connection between what you're doing and the fact that it's for money is just so much more there in poker that it's part of what makes poker a great game. And it's why I think that many of the personality issues that I brought up—about going on tilt—are connected to the fact that it is the money in your hands and you could literally throw it away. You can just start betting hand over fist on bad hand after bad hand, throwing your money into the pot with very little chance of winning."

Interestingly, though, it's a fine line. If you're too compulsive, you get into trouble. But at the same time, being compulsive can be what drives you to be successful. You just have to control it.

> **HOWARD LEDERER:** "We all have compulsive tendencies. You see, you need those. That's the balance. You need those to get really good at something. I'm probably a borderline-compulsive poker player/ gambler. I love to gamble. I love what I do. You're pushing that envelope, okay, so to keep that in control you need those other personality traits. Like an intense desire to succeed and be good to yourself. If you lack any of that and you throw in the compulsive aspect of it, it's just lights out. You just can't be successful."

Kevin Blackwood, our blackjack expert, and our Baseball Bettor stressed the importance of discipline and sticking to your game plan as an effective measure against going on tilt. By not getting caught up in the emotion of the moment, you can resist the temptation of chasing after bad bets.

23

KEVIN BLACKWOOD: "Being down doesn't really affect the level of my play. If you have confidence in card counting, it could keep you from going on tilt. You know that you need to be disciplined and keep betting the correct amount regardless of whether you're winning or losing that particular day."

BASEBALL BETTOR: "I have a partner who bets huge amounts of money. He's the most stoic person and immune person to all this stuff you could possibly imagine. He just does the same regardless of the fluctuation. We kind of aspire to that and don't want to admit that we're slaves to the emotion. But sometimes you go on tilt. You play non-optimally, lower your chances of winning; it becomes an addiction and you can't help it."

Because you're walking a tightrope—and this is true more with poker than it is with horse racing but it's still relevant—you do run the risk of going broke if you either go on tilt or a hit a losing streak. For Howard Lederer, that was just part of the learning process.

HOWARD LEDERER: "I've been broke maybe more than any of them. Although I was very young. First of all, there are lots of different reasons you go broke. And I'm not going to tell you that every time I went broke was strictly because I wasn't that good. But certainly a lot of the early going-broke stuff is just that you don't know your craft and you don't know your business well enough. You're young, you've got a bit of the compulsive tendencies, you may even have some personality issues. Because you're young, you're working things out, you're making difficult decisions in your life that maybe not everyone approves of, like your parents.

"You're doing something all the time, you don't have a lot of money, because you haven't been doing this long enough to have a big bankroll. And you may not really truly understand the concept of variance and money swings either. You're 18 and you just crushed your friends playing poker. Or now you've started playing in some very low-limit games with very bad players and if you have the talent to really become successful, you're probably just winning every week against really bad players.

"So now all of a sudden you're playing against people who eventually you're going to beat and you're probably better than now but you're a bit short on the money and you've never had a losing week so you can't imagine that ever happening to you. But now all of a sudden the competition gets just good enough that you're going to have a losing week or a losing month and when that hits, you go broke. And it's like, what happened? Well, you learn from that. You either drop down or you borrow money from a friend and you get back in action and then you step it up a little bit more and now maybe you plan for being able to lose one week or two weeks in a row, or maybe one month or two months in a row. Because your edge has gotten a little bit smaller. But you compensate for the smaller edge because you're playing bigger.

"As you're moving up the ladder, it's still a more profitable endeavor to take the smaller advantage. But you need a larger and larger bankroll to take the swings when your advantage goes down. The interval of confidence—and that's a statistical concept of how long you need to do something with an edge before let's say you have a 99 percent chance of winning—that interval gets bigger as your edge goes down and it gets drastically bigger."

■ Mental Fatigue

Still another facet of discipline is the ability to recognize mental fatigue and having the wherewithal to take a freshening so that your tired mental state doesn't affect your play. The curious thing about this, though, is that most of our players don't view this as a specific pitfall because they are so systematic in what they do—they prepare, they work hard, they treat it like a job, and they know what to expect each day, and that includes experiencing bad beats, dealing with the fluctuations of luck, and weathering severe losing streaks. There are no surprises to our seasoned pros.

Dave Gutfreund made the point that if you're doing your work and following specific meets day in and day out, you don't have to work as hard when it comes to the actual nuts and bolts of handicapping. Instead of having to start over each day, the work you've done in the past sets you up for the future and prevents you from suffering from overwork and mental fatigue.

24

DAVE GUTFREUND: "Mental fatigue is not an issue for me because I'm not spending as much time on each track. The five hours a day when I'm just watching races, that is the investment I make that takes the place of handicapping each card for two hours at a time. The time I'm putting in is the time I spend watching it, living it, experiencing it versus sitting down and studying. Having a good knowledge of what days the track was extremely biased, for example."

Paul Cornman had a similar take, saying that if he's done the work, then mental fatigue isn't an issue for him because come race day he's as prepared as he needs to be.

PAUL CORNMAN: "Here on the West Coast my races start at 9:30 in the morning. I will prepare the day before so I'm pretty much ready to roll and have some spots picked out, sort of have some betting strategies that might be correct. If I'm feeling well, I'm not going to wear down."

Kevin Blackwood stressed the importance of sticking to your game plan and playing systematically as a way to cut down on mental fatigue. He also mentioned the importance of "one long game"—to go home after a long day, get some rest, and come back tomorrow. As William Murray once wrote, "There's always fresh."

KEVIN BLACKWOOD: "Mental fatigue—that's never been a problem for me. I think that's a misconception of card counting. It really isn't draining or fatiguing once you learn how to do it. You don't have to have 'Rain Man'-type ability.

"I have parameters for each day—how many hours and how many casinos I want to visit. I do it and call it a day. If I'm out 12 hours a day, that's a lot. I'd set my sessions and come back—the casinos would still be open the next day."

CONFIDENCE AND THE ABILITY TO TAKE A RISK

The curious thing about gambling is that it is a world of dichotomies. You need discipline to sit out races and curb your emotions, but at the same time you need supreme confidence in your ability and the fortitude to take a calculated risk. The psychological makeup of a gambler is complicated, and without confidence you're playing with scared money. And a scared gambler is a losing gambler.

All of our pros walk up to the windows with confidence, knowing that they're betting with an advantage over everyone else. Part of that confidence is having the ability to risk a lot of money when you feel like you're getting the best of it.

BRAD FREE: "I love risk. That's what playing the horses is all about to me. You're not betting on a horse as much as you're buying a risk. When you bet a horse, you're buying the chance that he's going to win. I love risk."

CLONIE GOWEN: "I take risks but they're educated risks. I always try to have just a bit more information than somebody else has. I guess I've always been a risk taker. I'm very much a risk taker. Just not every risk."

PAUL CORNMAN: "You have to have nerve. A lot of people who don't gamble, they flip out when they hear how much I'm playing [$1 million a year]. It's a very psychological game, this gambling game."

ROXY ROXBOROUGH: "For lack of a better phrase, you need balls. Let's say you do everything right—handicap, find value—and if you don't pull the trigger, you'll never do anything. Great spots don't come up that often. You can't sit on your bankroll—you have to pull the trigger."

DAVE GUTFREUND: "Confidence is huge—it is for any endeavor in life. If you believe you can do something, you're a lot more likely to do it than if you don't."

AMARILLO SLIM: "I've got all the confidence in the world. I've got a lot of scalps on the wall and they didn't get there by accident. I'm not risk-averse at all. If you're accustomed to winning, then you know you're going to have some losses. But in the long run, you come out way ahead."

JAMES QUINN: "I was a winner right away and that convinced me I could play well enough to win. Confidence has never been a problem for me."

BASEBALL BETTOR: "I think I'm pretty risk-averse for a gambler, but nongamblers think of me as being a big risk taker. Among professional gamblers, I am probably somewhere in the middle. A lot of that has to do with slowly acclimating yourself to different levels of risk. Some gamblers who are very good might be stuck at lower limits because they're risk-averse to raise the stakes. They don't realize to slowly raise the temperature. Paying taxes is also an issue. Some don't want to get into higher brackets and pay more taxes. If you step up your tax liability, it's difficult. But once you do it, you get used to it.

"There are different classes of successful gamblers, and each one would have a unique set of characteristics that would help them be successful in their endeavor. For me, it's a keen analytical ability, which is the same for someone like a blackjack player. Blackjack qualities are different for successful poker players, though. I don't consider myself a big risk taker, but people say I am. To some extent they're right, because to some extent you need to be a risk taker to be a professional gambler. You also need to have an ability to separate fiction from fact. To do that oneself or to find someone that can is extremely important. I'm a calculated risk taker, not reckless."

LEN FRIEDMAN: "With some things I guess I am risk-averse, some I'm not. It's a very hard question for me to answer. I like going down rapids in rubber rafts and people think I'm crazy for doing that. But on the other hand, with a machine gun, you couldn't get me on a roller coaster. Some things yes, some things no. And I think that's also true in betting. I'm often willing to take a shot on a very speculative longshot, but I have a tendency to play them sort of conservatively. That is, if I'm playing a horse that's a long price I'm almost always playing it down to the third position in the trifecta.

"I think I bet conservatively, although every once in a while I'll take a very strong position and toss out the two favorites in a race and just say, 'If they come in, I lose.' It's hard to make generalizations about it. I think I bet a little bit too conservatively and I probably handicap a little too aggressively."

KEVIN BLACKWOOD: "I tend to be a skeptic at heart. The concept of card counting made sense to me because I could see where memory does have a factor at blackjack more than any other game. I believed I could make money. The mental aspect of gambling is underaddressed in many books. I know a lot of math geniuses, but it takes a lot more than that to be a good gambler. A lot of people have a great difficulty risking money even though they have the edge. I was always very detached from the money because I knew when I had an edge. I didn't have to sweat over hands the way I've seen some people do."

THE IMPORTANCE OF RESILIENCE, OR, LEARNING HOW TO LOSE

Resilience is a key trait of every successful gambler. We wrote earlier about the emotional state and how it's important to not let short-term losses affect your long-term play. One way to do that is to "learn how to lose." It's one of the most important skills a gambler can acquire—because no matter how much you do everything right, at times, you're going to lose. You're always at the mercy of outside factors—the horses, the cards, the pitchers on the mound. External factors play a role in whether you win or lose.

By learning how to lose, successful gamblers develop a resilience that allows them to bounce back from losses—they analyze their play, they make adjustments, they work even harder.

ROXY ROXBOROUGH: "Losing is psychological—not cashing tickets and losing money affects your personality. I never met anyone who is the same person when he's losing. It affects your mental health and other facets of your life, including your relationships.

"If losing doesn't bother you then you're not betting enough. You need to bet more."

CARY FOTIAS: "If you don't know how to lose, you don't have a prayer in this game. It's nothing to lose 20 in a row as long as when you win a few, you're paying for the others.

"You need to recognize that streaks are a part of the game. There's a point during the year where I'll lose 20 to 30 bets in a row. That's okay. I make a lot of bets that I expect to lose 90 percent of the time.

"During a losing streak, I might go back and review my play. If I can look at each bet and recognize that they were good bets then that's fine. I get more upset losing on an 8-5 action bet that runs second than a good bet that happens to not win.

"If I have a tough beat, I'll say to myself, 'Just when you think you've lost every possible way there is to lose, you find a new one.' When those things happen, take a day off or spend a few days betting light until you get your head back. When you bet without confidence, you're dead before you start. You just have to move on.

"Learn how to lose—it is very difficult to win at this game until you can get comfortable with some serious losing streaks."

STEVE DAVIDOWITZ: "You need to have the ability to lose and handle defeat—to understand how tough the game is. It's not easy! And you need to be able to deal psychologically with losing streaks. Can you recover and look yourself in the mirror and have the ego strength to deal with defeat? A good ballplayer makes out 70 percent of the time; with a horseplayer it's similar. Should I take a few days off and go back over my fundamentals? There are many things you can do to get your ship right."

ERNIE DAHLMAN: "You need to have the ability to take a punch. You've got to be able to take losing. You know 'the Wizard,' Michael Kipness? He sat in the next room from me and he thought that that was the thing I did better than everybody. And I said, 'Michael, you're wrong. That's not why I win.'

"He said, 'You're unbelievable, you can be having the worst day and you keep on trying and all at once you turn it around.'

"'Yeah, well,' I said, 'the reason that I keep on trying is because invariably I *can* turn it around. It's not like that's the reason I win.'

"You can't be an idiot. Confidence comes from success. If I stayed there and kept losing then the next time I was having a bad day, I wouldn't be so liable to keep playing and losing.

"You have to be able to keep your wits about you. You have to keep making good plays. You have to stay cool when things are going bad. Like I said, if I'm having a bad day and I look at the rest of the card and see something I really like later on, I'll take it easy until then and try and make a big hit there. Today is not the end of the world. If I lose today, I come back tomorrow. And I often tell people I'm like a ferret.

"A ferret, if you let him out of a cage and he goes into a sock, he completely panics and throws himself around until he gets out of the sock. And if you put him back in the cage and let him out 10 minutes later, he'll run to the same sock and the same thing will happen. That's what I'm like. I'll go home and say, 'I never want to bet on another horse as long as I live. This is the hardest game ever. I have no clue.'

"But I wake up the next morning and I say, 'Ooh, what looks good in the double?' I don't know why that happens but it happens time and time again. When I wake up the next day, I'm ready to go again."

JAMES QUINN: "The ability to come back whole from losing runs is very important. I admire Andy Beyer for coming back whole—he could lose a lot of money and it doesn't affect the way he plays, the way he makes decisions and solves problems, and the way he bets. It's important to play your game after long losing runs."

ANDREW BEYER: "You're not born with equanimity. You develop it through the school of hard knocks—by letting yourself get unhinged by a tough loss and having it trigger a vicious losing streak because you're trying to recoup that money. The point comes where you say to yourself, 'This is a counterproductive form of behavior.' When I lose photo finishes, I will scream and curse the jockeys as vociferously as anybody else, it's not like you need to be stoic, but with maturity you say, 'This is not going to affect my judgment.'"

KEVIN BLACKWOOD: "Keeping a log really helps a great deal in overcoming short-term losses. Look at the long run and if you're a consistent winner, then it diminishes the sting of a daily loss or a session when you lose, or those kinds of things.

"It's in the back of your mind, but if you're experienced, it's something you have to come to terms with and live with. You're going to expect a few dips in the roller coaster at some point.

"Keep a log—being able to see the long term helps a great deal to overcome that."

BASEBALL BETTOR: "You have to have the constitution to endure tremendous fluctuations without either having a nervous breakdown or without having it severely affect what it is you need to do to be successful. Many potentially successful gamblers would let those emotional swings and repercussions that almost every person would have—because they're human beings—affect what they're doing and prevent them from being successful anymore. That's an allure. Do something differently in the face of adversity even though there's no cause and effect there. You need to have some kind of ability to weather those tremendous fluctuations—emotionally so you don't go nuts and so you can continue to do what you need to do analytically to be successful."

JIM MAZUR: "I've had plenty of bad streaks also. That's a time where I should lay low and sit back and try to see if there are some trends you're missing and then get back in.

"I get the most aggravated when I miss things that come out of my book. There was a day—Whitney Day a few years ago—when there must have been five plays in the book in bold print that I missed. One was Bill Mott and Pat Day at 10-1, something I almost always play that I missed because I was on a different horse for some reason. You can start muttering to yourself after that. Basically, I stop playing for a day or two. I'll also sometimes stop playing for a day after I have a big hit because I don't think I can replicate, but not always.

"When I'm going poorly I get aggravated with myself and then I'll stop playing for a little while, give myself a breather. Sometimes you're too into it, too close, and you can't pull back from the trees. So you stop and start looking at the forest again and you get your perspective back."

DAVE CUSCUNA: "There's a psychological ramification. Why does a .212 hitter go 6 for 11 at some point during the year? It's not because he finally figured it out. I used to laugh when every year in a row there'd be one month when Rey Ordonez would hit .300, and you'd read in the paper, now that Rey Ordonez is more disciplined at the plate and has stopped swinging at those balls over his head, he's going to be a great shortstop if he can just hit .280.

"Well, guess what? The guy's a .230 hitter. Sooner or later he'll have a stretch where he hits .300 but he's also going to have more stretches where he hits .160. He's still going to swing at that pitch over his head. Part of discipline is being willing to strike out look-ing—even when you're going through a slump—at that pitch that looks like it's going over your head. Take Alfonso Soriano in the 2003 World Series. He kept swinging at that ball that was a foot and a half outside. Yankees fans were yelling at the TV, 'Why don't you take those pitches?'

"Same thing in gambling: We all go through stretches where we're swinging at those balls that are a foot and a half outside. Something isn't clicking. We're doing something wrong that we usually do right. Is it because we just broke up with our girlfriend? Or because we just met a new girlfriend? Or because the World Series is on and our atten-tion is divided? Or we've worked 10-hour days, 11 straight days and we're burned out? We get to a point where it's obvious that whatever we're doing, we're not doing it as well as we have in the past and we need to step back and take a little bit of a break. And that's hard."

MARYLAND PLAYER: "You can scream and shout and yell all you want but when it's out of your system there's another race going on and you have to be ready to bet it. And that's why I think betting is important. People mean different things by 'betting is important.' But what I think is more important than anything is the ability to see the big picture, to see that bets are coin flips and you weren't a genius when it came up heads and you weren't an imbecile when it came up tails; they just flipped the coin once. People tend to think that they're geniuses when they're winning—they're not. The best line on gambling was Earl Weaver's line about baseball: 'You're never as smart as you think you are when you're winning and you're never as stupid as you think you are when you're losing.'

"The other Weaver quote that applies is, 'This ain't a football game; we do this every day.' Again, that's like horse racing. You don't get bent out of shape by a loss when you play 162 times a year. The best teams are going to lose 60 or 70 games. In horse racing, it's the same thing. I love baseball and I see a lot of analogies between horse racing and baseball. Slugging percentage is more important than batting average, and in both games you're going to fail a lot. If you can't accept failure, horse racing is the wrong game for you. Even if you're very good, you're going to fail most of the time as an individual player. So just as a batter has to understand that two out of every three times, if he's great, he's going to be retired. One out of three can get you to the Hall of Fame. Horse racing is very similar. You can have a low batting average and still be in the game."

PAUL BRASETH: "You need to have a tolerance for pain. You do have a lot of pain in playing the horses. I think that's important. You have to figure out a way to accept that you're not going to win every race and that you're going to lose much more than you win, however you do that. I say that by just saying to myself, 'I made a bad decision and I lost.' For whatever reason I didn't win and then I move on to the next one.

"And you have to learn how to accept losing. If you're around the racetrack a lot, you hear people, even good handicappers, they lose a race and they'll say to themselves, 'How could you be so stupid? Blah blah blah,' and they carry on. I have a phrase I use—I used to use this when I was teaching as well—'I'm not a failure as a person because I made a losing bet.' My decision was wrong but that doesn't mean I'm a hopeless cause and I'm going to end up on the street, like some of these people with the way they carry on. You have to accept that you made a bad decision and that's it, it doesn't mean you're a bad handicapper or a bad person or anything else, it just means you made a bad decision and you move on."

DAVE GUTFREUND: "Andy Beyer wrote about this 25 years ago and I'm still trying to figure out why this is true: The worst losing streaks come after the good runs. That's exactly what happened to me. I had a great run, mid-July to late-July, and then the first week of August the shit hit the fan. Saratoga crushed me; Del Mar crushed me; there weren't any good grass plays at Arlington to bail me out. And that was pretty much it.

250

"Whenever I've done something good, it's always been followed by something bad. Not *if*, but *when* I win the DRF national handicapping tournament—whether it be this year, next year, in the next five or 10 years—I'm more concerned about what I'll do *after* that than I am about actually winning it, as frightening as that might sound.

"When you've just had a winning streak it's easy to say, 'Hey, I just won \$10K last week; I'm going to make back this \$5K that I lost today this afternoon!'

"It's a whole different mind-set, and what I'm going to have to do is remind myself of what to do. It's a constant struggle and it's always going to be. Even the best players go on mind-blowing losing streaks, even guys like Andy Beyer. It's a tough game and don't ever—*ever*—let anybody else tell you otherwise."

■ Luck

Over the short term, luck is going to play a role in your success. There's nothing you can do about it. If you're in it for the long haul, then you can't let short-term fluctuations affect your emotional state or your play.

Our players had some interesting things to say about luck.

JAMES QUINN: "You need to give up control—recognize that other than managing your money, you really have no control on what happens in the sport or the game: troubled trips, jockey errors, etc. Understand the 'error factor.' If you're a control freak, you can't survive this game. You need to be able to surrender to the error factor and continue to play your game."

BASEBALL BETTOR: "To an analytical gambler, they don't like to talk about luck at all.

"Good luck/bad luck can make or break a gambler at the beginning of their careers; all successful gamblers had good luck at the beginning of their careers. Not that they were better or anything else, but when you first start out, you don't realize what edge you have. Then you realize what you need to do to be successful. But luck allowed you to start your careers. If you're unlucky when you first start, you're going to quit.

"Luck and fluctuation: It has a heavy influence on the emotional stuff. Other than that you get into the philosophical realm of luck. It's theoretically possible for any professional gambler who plays with a significant edge to lose for any length of time.

"Your emotions become a slave to the luck. The best way to handle emotion is you don't try to fight it, you just accept it. If you had a bad beat or a bad month, you just accept it. Don't deny the emotion because all emotions diminish and pass eventually."

KEVIN BLACKWOOD: "Luck: It has a lot to do with winning in the short term. Over a given day, in a sense, luck would be determining if I won or lost—hot cards or cold dealer. Over time, though, I don't believe in anything as luck. I just think it's a short-term fluctuation one way or the other.

"One reason I have been successful is I was fortunate to hit a lucky fluctuation when I first started playing—otherwise I would have tapped out and lost my bankroll. So in that sense, I was lucky when I first started out."

GERRY OKUNEFF: "Luck evens out."

DAVE CUSCUNA: "On any one given race, luck has a lot to do with winning and losing. Over the course of time I've been in the business, it has nothing to do with it whatsoever. You can be as prepared as possible and you just have no way of knowing that some guy started his van in the stable area at 2:00 A.M. and startled your horse and it had nervous energy that it used up for four and a half hours that's going to cause it to run badly today. Or you don't know that maybe you made what should have been a losing pick and bet maybe the second-best horse in today's race and you won because the best horse in the race was nervous from the guy starting his van the night before. In any one event, luck has a fairly big role, but through hard work and preparation, all that stuff works itself out in the long run.

"What you won't get a lot of guys on the phone to admit to, but you'll get a lot of stories from gamblers about bad beats: how unlucky they got when some horse they had with a six-length lead saw a shadow and jumped over the rail and ended up in the infield lake. Is that bad luck to have the right horse? Yeah, I guess it's bad luck and you had the right horse. But somewhere in there, you had the wrong horse and you won when the right horse ran into the lake too. You told people you were smart because you made money. In the long run, all that stuff washes itself out."

AMARILLO SLIM: "I don't believe in luck. I think you make your own luck in life, no matter what your endeavor is. If you own a farm, you'll be a lot luckier if you're sitting on a tractor instead of teeing off at a golf course. Over the years, luck evens out. But I do believe that some people are blessed."

ERNIE DAHLMAN: "Over the course of time, luck has zero impact. On any given day, sure it can have an effect. Luck is no factor unless I bet a wrong ticket and collect on a $2 million pick six."

ROXY ROXBOROUGH: "There's luck in all gambling. It evens out, though, in the long run. People only believe in the bad luck, and they believe that good luck is their God-given right. But it all evens out."

JAMES QUINN: "The luck factor at the races is far more important for a recreational player or a losing player. There's a larger error factor and it doesn't balance out. I also think that there's a far greater degree of bad luck than good luck if you're a winning player, and that interferes. I don't feel it balances out. The occasional good luck is so occasional that you tend to remember it. There are a lot of ways to lose that might be considered unfair or unlucky."

DAVE CUSCUNA: "The reason why Vegas sets limits on the fixed-odds games, like roulette, is to protect themselves. If it's 35-1 on a number and there are 38 slots on the wheel, why won't Caesars Palace take an unlimited bet? They're getting the best of it; they're giving 35-1 on a 38-1 shot. Well, they do it because if everybody's betting small amounts and the casino is grinding out their 2 percent, they don't want somebody coming in and betting $10 million on a number and giving up $350 million on one spin. Even though the odds are in their favor, if it doesn't go right, they'll lose the year's roulette winnings. Same theory goes from the gambler's perspective. If you have a winning system, it only is a winning system if the long run gets to happen."

BARRY MEADOW: "I play exactly the same. If you flip a coin, and you hit five heads in a row, are you suddenly the greatest coin-tosser in history? And if you hit tails five in a row are you suddenly an idiot? The only time I start worrying is when my horses don't do what I think they are going to do, if it looks like I have no feel, if I see something happen and I say, 'That makes no sense.' When that happens I hope it's a short-term thing—that it's just for a day. I don't take time off because there's always something new to learn. Even if I'm on vacation, I'm still going to tape the races and look at all of them. I'm not going to say, 'I'm in a bad streak right now, what's wrong with me?' Sometimes a bad streak is just the mathematical fluctuations of the game, just like coin tossing. It doesn't mean I don't understand things. Sometimes you're wrong about a race, then you're wrong three straight races, it doesn't mean you've forgotten how to handicap."

■ Bad Beats

Card Player columnist Greg Dinkin has a policy: Before he listens to your bad-beat story, you have to pay him a dollar. It's a policy that has served him well, because you can't go five minutes into a conversation with a losing poker player before he breaks into a bad-beat story.

But what purpose does this serve? Is the brutal retelling a spiritual cleansing, some gambler's purging of the soul? Or is it the old adage, "Misery loves company"? Regardless of how you feel about a bad beat, the important thing is to get it out of your system—deal with it, turn the page, and move on.

Our players have suffered bad beats in their careers, but the reason they are still around is that they've learned how to get over these losses.

They realize that it's all part of one long game, and that there are dozens more opportunities tomorrow. We're all going to lose photos—but we're all going to win a few photos, too. It's how you deal with the losing photos that makes you a winning or losing player.

ERNIE DAHLMAN: "Usually a bad beat, any beat, takes me 30 seconds to a minute to get over. You'd be better off in that time not to talk to me; I might snap at you or something. But then I get over it and look at the next race. There's just a certain amount of time that I need after I lose to collect myself and say, 'Okay, next race.' I don't dwell on bad beats.

"My father used to go with me to the trotters and after a bad beat, he'd want to go and tell everybody, and I'd say, 'Don't go telling people, it makes their day that you had bad beats. What do you want to go making somebody's day for? We lost a race.' I tried to get him not to talk about bad beats. I knew one guy at the trotters, after he had a bad beat he'd be walking around for an hour all around the track telling everybody about it. It's your problem, you get over it. Your bad beat isn't going to ruin somebody else's day; it's just going to ruin your own day if you let it. I kind of get over it pretty quick. It bothers me and then I get over it."

BARRY MEADOW: "It depends how bad the beat is. Let's say I decide not to play a pick six for various reasons and the thing comes in and pays $100K that I would have won. Yeah, I'm going to be upset for a day or two. I'm not going to be upset for a week. On the other hand, let's say I bet $1,000 to win on a 6-1 shot and he gets beat a nose. I'll be mad for that race but by the next one I'll be ready to move on.

"You bet so many races over the years that no particular race is going to make much of a difference anyway so you just have to let it go. Because there's another race that you have to learn something from and that race is coming up and if you're thinking about how unfortunate you were in race four you're not going to be able to concentrate on race five. And race five might offer you some value that you hadn't expected so you better pay attention.

"You have to have some long-term look at what you're doing. You can't worry about every single race. First of all, you're going to have some bad luck. Second of all, you're going to make some bad bets, you're going to make errors. You have to be able to forget the previous race and go on to the next one. If I'm really upset because I lost a photo on race number four, how am I going to be able to make a decision on what to do in race number five? I think you've got to have a certain equanimity. I think it's fine to scream at the television but once that race is over that's that. Move on to the next one."

JAMES QUINN: "The thing about bad beats is that there are a lot of them. They're not isolated or infrequent. Obviously some are a lot worse than others. The worst kind of beat is the play you don't make—and then it scores and you're responsible for not having made the play. At some point, bad beats are part of the game. It doesn't affect me. I've never taken it home with me. I don't live with them. I'm good along those lines. The worst beats are the plays you didn't make but should have.

"In the parlays, if a race is a spread, a good handicapper covers all the decent horses to win. If you have to say 'I should have covered the horse,' then you misplayed the race because you had control over it. Those are the worst beats and those stay with me a little longer. Photos, I get over them. They don't affect my play.

"Advice: If you have a really bad beat that cost you a lot of money, just remember the time you had a stroke of fortune and won a lot of money. That counterbalances the bad beat."

GERRY OKUNEFF: "Now bad beats don't affect me at all. I have the philosophy that over time it evens out just as a close photo will even out win/lose. If there's cheating going on, you may be hurt, you may be helped. Racing luck could hurt and help. It evens out.

"It takes you much longer to forget a bad beat that cost you a big day than it does the close photo you've won. You don't remember the close photo that made you a lot of money. I remember the three games we lost at UCLA over the many that we won."

RANDY GALLO: "You just turn the page; you get up the next morning."

PAUL BRASETH: "If something happened beyond your control, you have to accept it. The fact is that many people have a difficult time with that. I go and get a beer. I just tell myself, 'Okay, that's the way this game is.' I don't sit around and mope about it. I always try and keep an even keel at the racetrack. Emotionally, I should be pretty much the same whether I'm winning or losing.

"When I win, I don't run around saying, 'I got a winning ticket!' And when I lose I think I've developed a way of saying, 'Okay, that's over, let's move on.' I don't dwell on it, let's put it that way. I'll say, 'I know when I made this decision, I made the best decision I could.' It gets back to the old clichés my mother used to tell me: You don't cry over spilt milk."

BASEBALL BETTOR: "You don't want to get into the mind-fuck where you replay it over and over—that will just drive you absolutely nuts. I try not to do that at all.

"Good ways of dealing with bad beats: think of the good beats! For every bad beat there's a good beat somewhere. But the mind has a selective memory. Good beats help. For me, the best thing is just distracting myself and not obsessing over the details. Baseball has its fair share, if nothing else, because of the amount of games you bet.

"In football, you're spared the number of bad beats per unit time that we have in baseball. Sometimes we have 15 bets in a day, so it's almost guaranteed that you'll have what some people consider a bad beat.

"I make sure I don't dwell on it; distracting myself; reminding myself and identifying the good beats.

"I can remember 10 bad beats for every one good beat.

"A bad beat shouldn't affect your play, though. If you can keep it in check, you'll be more successful in the long run."

ROXY ROXBOROUGH: "I'll complain to anyone who will listen! And that doesn't make me any different than anyone else. That's therapeutic for me. But, a really bad beat is when Dayjur skips a shadow and loses. Getting edged out in a three-horse photo happens four times a day, so that's not a real bad beat. You should be accustomed to that kind of thing. The best way to get over a bad beat is by getting back in action; make the next bet you normally make. If you've had a series of bad beats, though, back off. Winning and losing affects the way you play."

CARY FOTIAS: "My biggest score using The Xtras (a big pick six at Santa Anita) came just a week after one of my toughest beats. I had put together a play for the 2001 Breeders' Cup pick six at Belmont. Had Xtra Heat won the sprint, we would have had three winning pick-six tickets. Mr. Frankel couldn't break his o-for-whatever streak with Aptitude or You? No, it had to be Squirtle Squirt! Considering the pick six paid $260K with the 9-1 Squirtle Squirt, I estimated roughly a $400K payout had Xtra Heat won at 17-1, for a total payout of about $1.2 million. We got most of our investment back via five-of-six consolation tickets, but if there's one thing I know about horseplayers, it is that they are some of the most resilient people on the planet."

DAVE CUSCUNA: "I was at the track on a Wednesday and I made a mistake that cost me a large amount of money, more money than I had ever made in a year. I went home at the end of the day's races and had an ice-cream sundae and I made a decision that I had to focus on tomorrow rather than on what happened earlier that day—that was water under the bridge already. So I went home, focused on the next day's races, did a really thorough, good job and had my best winning day ever the next day.

"After that day with the huge error, the lesson that comes from it is: No matter what failures or what successes you have for that day, once you walk out of that track or that simulcast outlet, it's yesterday's news. And it's only really meaningful if you can learn from it for future races. To sit there and think you're a genius because you won so much, or a dope because you made a mistake, is wrong. There's no sense in beating yourself up. Because I had the ability to stop focusing on a huge error, I enabled myself to have a really good day the next day."

Clonie Gowen gave us the poker player's perspective on the importance of moving on to the next hand, win or lose:

CLONIE GOWEN: "I just try to forget about the hand I just played, period. And the times that I have the hardest time doing that is when I make a mistake, when I do something I shouldn't have. When someone else makes a mistake that I benefit from, like a call they shouldn't have made, I forget about those hands almost immediately.

But when I make a move and it turns out that I was completely off and wrong, I just take a deep breath and try to forget about that as much as possible."

There's an important difference between racing and poker, though. In poker, a bad beat occurs when you're getting the best of it and your opponent gets lucky and catches a card to beat you. This changes the dynamic a bit.

CLONIE GOWEN: "I'm mainly a cash player [as opposed to a tournament player]. In cash games, whenever I see someone make a critical mistake, even if it's just cost me a big pot, it makes me happy inside. Because I know that money is coming back to me. That player is not going to be capable of keeping that money if they're making those kinds of mistakes. It excites me to see a player make a critical error like that."

As a famous trainer once infamously said, "This is not a game for people in short pants." If you don't have the mental makeup to curb your emotions, deal with tough losses, and trust your convictions, then you're not going to be in this game for long. If you can't internalize the fact that good decisions, over the long run, will count more than outcomes, you're a guaranteed loser.

7

THE ROAD AHEAD

Issues Facing the Game

While conducting our interviews for this book, we had a unique chance to speak with some of the game's biggest and best players about several of the issues—political and otherwise—that face every player today.

ANDREW BEYER: "In this age of rebates, guys like Ernie Dahlman and most of the big bettors are playing a game that is totally different from what the readers of this book are going to be playing. To bet a massive amount of money and lose only a few percent is really the game."

REBATES

Beyer is alluding to the single biggest issue in racing today: rebates. Not surprisingly, some of the biggest proponents of rebates in the world are guys we interviewed. Their pro-rebate opinions make a lot of sense, but do come with a certain bias. If you don't know what a rebate is, here's a brief explanation.

The track sells its simulcast signal for a small percentage to simulcast outlets, some of which include "rebate shops." The overall takeout is high enough that the rebate shops are able to return money, sometimes as much 10 percent, back to the biggest bettors and still keep a few percentage points of every dollar bet for themselves. Because the big bettors are getting more money back in their pockets, this enables them to bet tremendous amounts of money.

But are they really good for the game?

ERNIE DAHLMAN: "I think rebates are good for racing. When I was in New York and betting at the OTB place I was betting like $10 million a year, and when I went to Vegas the next year, they said that the OTB fired 32 people because one bettor went to Las Vegas—that bettor was me. They put a big story in *Newsday* about it, about me. I thought, 'Wow, 32 people were getting paid off my betting and all they needed was one person to punch my tickets and 32 people were getting paid!' Those 32 people, I doubt if any of them were horseplayers. Is racing better that 32 people have jobs and get money off of my betting or are they better off that I get money off of my betting and am able to stay in the game, make a living, and keep betting?

"I put my money back in the game. I use it to buy horses, and breed horses, and a lot of the money I make goes into the game. So to me, a rebate is giving back to people who are in the game and it allows them to stay in the game or to become a bigger player in the game. It's money that instead of going to the government or to certain people that have no-show jobs, it's staying in races."

BARRY MEADOW: "Rebates are extremely important because rebates will turn a player who is close to breaking even into a winner, a player who is slightly losing into a winner, and they'll make a player who is winning into a bigger winner. It's very difficult to get takeout rates to change because you have to go through legislatures and it's a very big political problem. Rebates have proven a very quick and effective way to not only keep players in the game but to expand the amount of money bet . . . If you're getting money back, you can bet a lot more. It changes everything. It's good for the game to have rebates because players are going to bet a lot more money than they would ordinarily."

Of course, that example ignores the little player who isn't betting enough to get a rebate. We hate the idea that because of the rebate, there are situations all the time where there's value on a certain number for a player getting a rebate but there's no value for us.

ANDREW BEYER: "You're not on a level playing field. I know a lot of good players who keep saying, 'It's getting tougher and tougher to win.' Let's say there's an exacta whose correct value is $20. In the old days, when the crowd wasn't too sophisticated, maybe you were getting $28 on that exacta. And there was a lot of value out there. Over the years, the public got more and more sophisticated and the edge that you got on that particular combination, your potential margin would be narrower. But now you've got the players out there who will hammer that down to $19 or $18. So it's a losing bet for you while it's a winning bet for them over the long run. They're creating an underlay with which they can still win but you can't. That makes it a pretty tough game."

One theme that came up again and again (and that we agree with wholeheartedly) is that it would be to the betterment of every single horseplayer if the takeout could simply be lowered to a point where it would be competitive with other gambling games. Then the rebate wouldn't be necessary.

DAVE CUSCUNA: "If you listen to some people in the industry, you'd think that anyone paying or getting a rebate should be lined up and shot. Wouldn't you think, if you were a track owner, that you'd rather see money in your customers' pockets than in the pockets of a service provider? It's pretty basic. I don't get it. You can sum up rebates in two words: 'lower takeout.'

"If takeouts were lower, there'd be less of a margin to pay rebates and there'd be more money in all the bettors' pockets and it would be a healthier industry. Every economic study in the last 20 years has told the industry, 'Lower takeouts.' Horse racing is one of the few businesses whose solution to diminishing revenue is to raise prices. If you own a steak house and business is starting to suffer, you're not going to start charging $70 a steak. But in racing, every time they feel that business is going down, they add a percentage to the takeout."

■ Is There Looser Money Out There?

One idea that came up in a few interviews was that the rebate might actually cause a big player to play in a looser, more inefficient way since he's getting money back. Perhaps in a weird way, opportunities for a tighter, more contrarian player could be created by the size of these bets. This idea was echoed by a couple of our players.

> **KENTUCKY PLAYER:** "With the rebates, there's some looser money out there. These guys are sharp and they're serious and they have to know something or they can't bet at those levels very long, but I think that rebates encourage some less-than-brilliant money to be put in the pools in pretty significant chunks. I'm an example of that. I talked about how smart the first million that I bet is; well, the last three million I bet is probably not smart at all. That's my goal every year. It's not to bet more, it's to bet smarter, whatever that level comes out to be. But I have a very hard time doing it. It's just human nature; you're constantly fighting that. As you have success the tendency is to get looser and to push the envelope and to feel invincible and to keep betting until the racetrack brings you back to reality. And I think a lot of people who get rebates fall into that mentality. It's easy to say, 'I'm getting X percent back on every dollar I bet, let me throw some money into this race.'"

> **DAVE CUSCUNA:** "It does put the non-rebate receiver at a disadvantage because the people who are making those big spread plays with their rebates are taking a good amount of the value out of the pool. On the other hand, they're not always right. And so, when you have some of these big groups using computers, there are things that they miss and when they miss those things—maybe a speed horse ran a good second on a day when you couldn't win on the lead and today he runs back on a speed-favoring track—the big players won't necessarily catch an angle like that, and then you gain an advantage."

We asked a couple of the players if the idea of being more tight and aggressive than ever might be a strategy for the small player to survive.

> **MARYLAND PLAYER:** "Put it this way, that's what I knew in the pre-rebate world. That's the only way I knew to survive. The other thing I

suppose you could try to do is be better at something, some particular aspect of betting, than anybody else. In a game with as high a takeout as racing has, it's doubtful that you're going to find that sort of an advantage. You just have to be very selective and be very careful about when you fire the rifle.

"For the Saturday bettor who wants to bet every race, if that's what you want to do, the rational thing to do is say, 'This is entertainment and I'm willing to pay for entertainment.' That's fine and there's nothing wrong with that. But you just have to understand that that's what you're doing and at some level, what's the difference between that and a round of golf or a football game or whatever? But you should look at it as something that you're willing to do for entertainment. If you want to play every race on a Saturday, chances are you're going to be paying for it. I think horse racing does a relatively poor job of saying that: 'This is entertainment. You can have fun doing this.' And the game would be better served if they did do that more."

■ Betting High

We asked Howard Lederer for an outsider's perspective on how rebates change the game.

HOWARD LEDERER: "Right, well, the rebate makes all the difference for these guys. But in a strange way that rebate thing hasn't had the effect that a lot of people assumed it would have. A lot of people thought, 'My God, look at all these people who are betting small and breaking even, now they're going to get the rebate and it's all over, it's lights out, being a horseplayer is the greatest thing that ever happened to anybody.' But what happened was, it allowed the smart guys to be much less selective. All they're doing is they're betting more and on more horses at the same small edge. So for the marginally talented horseplayer, even for the ones getting the rebate, there's so much smart money now because of the rebate, that the prices are getting squashed down to the right spot again."

Historically, in gambling, when you bet high you have to be better than you ever were before because you're going to be hurting your price; the amount of money you're putting down will alter the odds.

HOWARD LEDERER: "It's definitely a problem that they're always trying to overcome. I was always trying to overcome it when I was betting high as best I could. It's just like anyone, I mean a big stock trader, he's trying to get his two million shares of Microsoft at the best price he can but he's going to have to pay more. If he's looking to buy two million shares he's not going to average the same price as a person looking to buy 10 shares. Everyone's trying to minimize transaction costs, I guess you could call them. And horseplayers certainly have a problem and it's a glass ceiling for them too.

"And the treadmill they can get themselves on, if you're looking to bet $10 to win on a horse and you've made your great selection, you're going to win X amount, but if you want to bet $10K you're going to get a worse price. The amount you bet affects the price. So I'm sure there are plenty of horseplayers out there who can win when they bet a certain amount of money—these are the very good but not the most talented guys—and I'm sure they go on good plus upticks when they're betting small and they start playing a little bigger and they still win but then they get to a certain amount where the amount they're betting is affecting the price and they need to make cold calculations, cold, objective decisions about how much they're going to bet. And they need to be very objective about their opinion about a horse; they can't fall in love with a horse. They pick a horse, they decide he's a great bet and then they're willing to bet it beyond the point where it's value. I'm sure you've heard that from your horseplayers."

The rebates do change this dynamic, but not entirely, according to one of our players.

KENTUCKY PLAYER: "Imagine yourself trying to bet like I do. Last year I averaged $50K a day. Over $50K a day. Imagine walking into the track every day and you have to bet that much in a day. You walk in and there's Aqueduct on the inner track, and Fair Grounds and Gulfstream and maybe Beulah Park, maybe Turfway that night or one of the West Coast tracks, and you've got to look around and find spots.

"That's one point I really want to make. It's easy to sit on the other end of it and say, if I was getting 5 percent back or whatever and still bet the same amount and stay within your comfort zone then obviously, everyone could do a lot better. But a big part of playing on a rebate is just being able to have that piano on your back and being able to drag it around all year and not let it crush you."

TAKEOUT

So it seems obvious that takeout reduction is the path that the game should be on. Could that be something on the horizon?

KENTUCKY PLAYER: "There's no chance of anything like that happening, I don't think. The biggest impediment is that each state has their own laws and good luck trying to go to Maryland or somewhere and getting them to change their laws."

What might be realistic?

KENTUCKY PLAYER: "I think what is maybe doable down the road is that maybe the blended take around the country is somewhere around 20 percent and if you got that moved down to where the blended take was maybe 16, win bets were 12, and the highest gimmick bet was 20—if you got all that moved down I think the tracks would make more money than they do now. I think what's going to happen is that it's an awareness, learning, comfort-level change that has to happen with the tracks. It's a big move for them to go from where we were 10 years ago to lowering their takeout dramatically. It's going to take some time. I think in a horseplayer's mind, we've been knowing about rebates and talking about them for a few years. I think in track management that this is just an issue that in the last two years probably that they've talked about that much."

Rebates seem to us like an acceptable real-world solution to a complicated political problem. And today, where even players at our level can do a Google search and in five seconds find a place willing to rebate us a few points on our action, it doesn't seem worth getting overly upset about. Len Friedman's thoughts sum up our feelings pretty well.

LEN FRIEDMAN: "I have a mixed feeling about rebates. The way the game is structured now the rebates make a lot of sense because the takeout is ridiculous. Just ridiculous. You've set up a gambling game where the takeout is six or seven times what it is at all the other gambling games. You've made it into an impossible situation, and except for in New York all the racetracks do is keep on edging the takeouts up. The way to end the rebates is to cut the takeout. And that'll end it, and believe me, I will feel much more comfortable. I would much rather have a situation where everybody was betting into a 10 percent takeout than one where some of us are betting into a 20 percent takeout and getting 10 percent back. I can't believe that almost every serious player—including all the ones currently getting rebates—wouldn't prefer that situation. I'd rather have a level playing field.

"I don't mean to suggest for a second that the current system is fair, it isn't. It's the wrong way to organize the game, but the people who run the game have set it up in such a way that there's no way they can stop it. I don't care what they make legal or illegal, I guarantee you that as long as the take is 20 percent, there will be rebates. The cat's out of the bag and there's no way for them to end it other than to cut the takeout down. It might even lead to a rebirth of horse racing."

COMPUTER GROUPS AND
CONSPICUOUS ODDS DROPS

ANONYMOUS PLAYER: "As big as Ernie Dahlman is, he's a mosquito compared to these computer guys."

ANDREW BEYER: "It's not my direction but I think some of the people who are having the more spectacular success in the modern game and leaving Neanderthals like me in the dust are people who are doing it with sophisticated computer models that analyze handicapping factors and assign probabilities to horses and then mathematically calculate the betting strategy. A lot of the last-second drops in odds in this country are evidently being influenced by people with these programs. When I was in Hong Kong a few years ago I met one of the guys there who was doing that, having spectacular success and using no human judgment at all.

"In the old days, we'd sit in the grandstand with four minutes to post time and say, 'Well, I like this horse and at 5-1 he's an overlay.' Now with all this money coming into the pool in the last two minutes, looking for overlays by the seat of your pants is a thing of the past."

The biggest bettors in the country today are using a sophisticated computer model to calculate what the correct odds should be on each horse in a race. They then use those odds to figure out what they think the correct prices are for the exotics. Using what is called "batch betting" with a computer linked directly into the tote system (known as computer-to-computer wagering), they can then make dozens of bets just before the gates open—if any of the crowd's exacta prices are higher than the ones on their computer's grid.

Is it possible for the small player to win, going up against these guys? We asked Andrew Beyer if the existence of the groups makes it necessary to be more contrarian than ever.

ANDREW BEYER: "Yeah, but you have to be realistic. We're all up against it because the guys who are going to be playing this way are going to have an enormous impact on the pool. I've never sat beside these guys to see how they operate, but if that is the game, my guess is that they don't bet normally, that the idea of going out and looking for a live 8-1 shot to bet to win, that concept is probably not on their radar screen. If you're looking to bet the most money you can bet to break even or lose a little, typical kinds of bets may not be appealing. I don't know but for the purposes of this book, understanding how these people operate is very important."

So we asked around.

ANONYMOUS PLAYER: "You have the monitors so you know what the exactas are paying. You can handicap all night and determine prices that you think the tickets are worth. You might come up with three races and exactas. And let's say you get on the third race and you mark down that a certain exacta should be $60. And you look up at the board and it's $80 or whatever so you're apt to make a bigger bet. If you think it should pay $60 and you look up and it's paying $42 then naturally you're not going to play it. But with the computer groups now, there's such a drastic change in the last minute of racing, you can have an exacta you like that's going to pay $70 on the board, and you have it at $50. You could go up and play it for $200 or $300 or whatever, that exacta may be $36 by the time they get done with it.

"The computer-to-computer technology that they have now is amazing. I'm kind of envious, it's pretty ingenious, they're excellent, it's far superior to almost anything that's out, it's almost unbelievable."

Are there any strategies for dealing with the computer players?

ANONYMOUS PLAYER: "There's a lot of racing out there, smaller pools, different racetracks. I don't think they're really doing too much right now at a place like the Fair Grounds, until they get slots in there. I don't think they're doing too much at a Bay Meadows or a Golden Gate or a Turfway, something like that.

"Limit your plays if you're going to play with them, I don't know what else to tell you. They're not always on your horse. It works both ways. If they're on your horse, you're going to get half the price you should get, and if they're not on your horse, you're going to get an overlay.

Have they changed the way our experts play?

MARYLAND PLAYER: "If you're betting serious money it makes no sense to bet it late. You want your money in so when the computer group is looking at the price of the horse you're betting, it's not as good. You don't want to land on the combinations after them. You'd rather they have the information that your money is already in the pool. For a guy betting a $5 exacta box, who cares? But let's say you're betting serious money, you want your money in the pools before the computer group makes its decision. You're going to have incomplete information no matter what.

"One of the reasons people bet late is that they want to have as complete information as possible. With two-thirds of the pool in the last two flashes, you're not going to have complete information anyway so you might as well bet before they do so at least you can discourage them from your numbers. That's just common sense. It's not game theory so much as it is thinking the process through. For 99.9 percent of the people buying this book, this doesn't matter. But if you're looking to grab $20K or $30K out of a pool of $200K, you certainly want that information in there so that at the very least the computer group will bet less."

Are there any other specific strategies he'd advise for the average player?

MARYLAND PLAYER: "I kind of view what I do as at least it still has possibilities. The film stuff that I do is probably at least somewhat outside of their purview. That's why I say that the physical stuff [looking at horses in the paddock] is fantastic because you know that's 100 percent outside of their purview. That's one skill they can never take away—they can't take away your edge on that. Old-fashioned handicapping? They're going to grab a very significant portion of the equity in that market. So you have to find a neighborhood where they're not and looking at horses is probably the single best place to go, your best probability of long-term survival.

"Yes, I can still get an edge watching tape. I'm not foolish enough to think that they're not going to stumble on many of my horses, because of course they are. But I've got to believe that I'm still looking at some stuff that's going to get around where they are. But the old-fashioned stuff, I think you're really up against it if you think you're just going to be an old-fashioned handicapper."

Almost all of the players we interviewed for this book believe that computer-to-computer wagering is responsible for all those maddening late odds drops that it seems you see every day now. Your horse is 4-1 when you bet, 3-1 going into the first turn, and when he crosses the wire in front he's 5-2.

MARYLAND PLAYER: "That, as I understand it, was going on in Hong Kong forever. The U.S. was the last area where that happened. It was also going on in Australia for a long time. When it came to the U.S.— I guess it was how it came in that was the problem. It came in kind of surreptitiously.

"I think the racetracks really owe it to their customer base to make it available to anyone who wants to do it. And the model that's evolved is not a particularly good model because of that. It's not available to everybody and anyone who doesn't understand that it's an advantage, just doesn't understand gambling. I think the racetracks have erred. My own view is that they should have it in a language that is easily accessible so that anybody with a laptop who wants to take advantage of it can go into a racetrack and do so. You basically just plug in the numbers and it will tell you how much you bet."

CARY FOTIAS: "Another way to put the little guy on the same footing is technology. You give the little guy the same ability to put in 20 bets at once, even if they're two-dollar bets. The little guy can't afford to invest in systems like the big guy can so the way you equal the playing field is you provide it free to the little guy. What these big bettors have done for themselves, the industry should do for the little bettor.

"You spend a couple of hundred thousand in programming. Hey, you want to scan the exacta pools and bet 30 bets at once? If the odds cycle went to 15 seconds and all of a sudden they can scan the grid and see what prices are out of order, now you're playing on the same playing field; it's just a difference of magnitude, which is fair."

ANDY SERLING: "I think that guys who have computer programs who are using batch bets and putting them in at the last second, that's unfair. I'm not criticizing the guys who are doing it but if it isn't available to everyone it shouldn't be allowed."

With the odds dropping so late, what does that do to the traditional definition of value?

MARYLAND PLAYER: "The old-fashioned definition is gone because you don't know the price you're going to get. Value implies that you know the price that you're going to get but you don't anymore, not close to it. The board does cartwheels. You can anticipate what they're going to do; you can't be 100 percent right. If you were, you'd be doing the same thing they're doing. But you at least owe it to yourself to try to figure out what's going to happen, and if you're betting a speed horse, you better figure out if you like him at a few points less than what you're looking at on the board.

"Favorites get crushed late. It is astounding how much the groups will take these horses down. But if you've got a model and it says the horse is 3-5 and he's even money, you're going to bet."

STEVEN CRIST: "I think some of the complaining that players are doing about the computer and rebate guys is sour grapes, the perpetual fear of horseplayers that someone's getting a better deal than they are and is somehow to blame for their not having a mansion. The most important thing to remember is that these computer guys are not winning outright. They've found a way to get something like 90 to 95 percent of their money back, and then they're getting over 100 because of the rebate. I understand that mathematically they're depressing prices, but they're still losing and still adding to the amount of money in the pool available for the taking.

"The software they have is good because they're beating at least half the takeout, but it's still losing. There's no magic machine to win at the races. And I see many more horrendous, vulnerable odds-on favorites now than I did five or 10 years ago. For me, that's just more opportunity."

BETTING EXCHANGES

One last development in the industry we'd like to mention briefly is the emergence of betting exchanges. Very popular in the United Kingdom, the exchanges allow you to play the role of the house. Instead of betting a horse to win, you can back a horse to lose. What you're essentially doing is playing head-to-head with another customer and the exchange takes a commission. If you did a quick Internet search you could find several betting-exchange websites. Again, it's a complicated issue. On one hand, we like the idea of being able to have another wagering menu choice and of possibly gaining an edge by finding a situation where there's a smaller takeout. On the other hand, the very idea of being able to back a horse to lose, for large amounts of money, seems like an invitation to larceny.

At the time we conducted these interviews, not too many of our players were currently very active in exchanges, though they certainly seem like a frontier that would be appealing to them. Barry Meadow talked about them.

BARRY MEADOW: "Now I'm spending the time I was doing my newsletter on these betting exchanges. They have them in England and now there's one in Costa Rica. I play those every day. I'm always looking for discrepancies between my opinion and what's out there. You're buying and selling horses and my commission rate is only 3 percent. You start at 5 percent.

"The odds you have to offer are higher than what the track odds are. If a horse is 4-1 at the track, you might have to offer 5- or 6-1 so you better not be wrong a lot. I mostly play against horses. I identify horses I don't like and also try and identify horses who are going to be overbet.

"There was a race last week at Golden Gate with a favored entry and I didn't care for either half and there were other horses I thought could win. I made one bet, I boxed the horses I did like and then I booked as much as I could against the entry. As it happened, my horses ran two-three but the entry ran out of the money. I wound up making a bunch of money and I was wrong—my horses didn't win but the entry ran out. That's the kind of race I'm looking for, where the crowd is betting a horse heavily that I don't care for. Or if they're betting something on a horse I give no shot to. Say I have a horse at 100-1 on my line and the crowd has him at 25-1 or 40-1 on the exchange. Well, to me, that's still a giant underlay on that horse."

THE END OF THE ROAD

The difficult thing about writing a book like this about horse racing is that you're really trying to hit a moving target. Changes are happening all the time. Despite that, we're still amazed at how, despite all of those changes, there really are certain traits that remain the same for winning players, from long before Pittsburgh Phil right up to the present: You've got to have an entrepreneurial spirit; you've got to learn to process the available information in an elegant way; you can't bet unless you have an edge; you need to know how to manage your money; you need to be able to handicap yourself; and you must remember that it's all one long game.

Writing this book has been like earning a Ph.D. in handicapping. As difficult as the game is today, we believe that if you live by the ideas in this book, you can still win at the racetrack. Andrew Beyer echoed our sentiments and talked about the great challenge of betting on Thoroughbred racing.

ANDREW BEYER: "It remains the most intellectually engaging of all gambling games. There are people who have great success. People who are studying the game are clearly not going up a blind alley. It's tough but it's doable. The process of trying to beat the game, there are few things more fun and challenging. That's the reason that people like me are hooked for life."